The
Chopra Centre
Cookbook

The
Chopra Centre
Cookbook

NOURISHING
BODY AND SOUL

DEEPAK CHOPRA
with **David Simon** and **Leanne Backer**

HAY HOUSE

Australia • Canada • Hong Kong • India
South Africa • United Kingdom • United States

First published and distributed in the United Kingdom by:
Hay House UK Ltd, 292B Kensal Rd, London W10 5BE. Tel.: (44) 20 8962 1230;
Fax: (44) 20 8962 1239. www.hayhouse.co.uk

Published and distributed in Australia by:
Hay House Australia Ltd, 18/36 Ralph St, Alexandria NSW 2015. Tel.: (61) 2 9669 4299;
Fax: (61) 2 9669 4144. www.hayhouse.com.au

Published and distributed in the Republic of South Africa by:
Hay House SA (Pty), Ltd, PO Box 990, Witkoppen 2068. Tel./Fax: (27) 11 467 8904.
www.hayhouse.co.za

Published and distributed in India by:
Hay House Publishers India, Muskaan Complex, Plot No.3, B-2, Vasant Kunj, New Delhi – 110 070.
Tel.: (91) 11 4176 1620; Fax: (91) 11 4176 1630. www.hayhouse.co.in

A catalogue record for this book is available from the British Library.

Previously published by John Wiley & Sons, Inc., 2002,
ISBN 978-0-471-45404-5

ISBN 978-1-84850-330-4

Printed and bound in Great Britain by TJ International, Padstow, Cornwall.

MIX
Paper from
responsible sources
FSC® C013056

CONTENTS

PREFACE

The world's most ancient and profound wisdom tradition proclaims that a single undifferentiated reality – Spirit – differentiates itself into all forms and phenomena. Observer and observed, knower and known, seer and scenery are different expressions of the same underlying spirit. The science of Ayurveda takes this insight to a very deep level, in which body, mind and soul are understood as interwoven domains along the continuum of consciousness. These differentiated aspects of consciousness, which is in its essence, pure existence, pure knowledge and unbounded love, express themselves as our physical body of matter, our subtle body of energy and transformation, and our causal body of information and intelligence.

Wherever there is energy, there is information, intelligence and transformation. Life evolves by regularly consuming and recreating itself. On our sun-drenched planet, the energy of our nearest star nurtures the lavish and extravagant growth of the ecosystem that supports the great chain of Being. Ultimately, we are all beings of light, the dust of stars circulating in the cosmos. Quantum physics tells us that at its essence all matter is trapped light. The same field of electromagnetic energy that creates thunder and lightning in the sky also generates the ideas that emanate from the synaptic networks of our brains. Human language, emotions and thoughts are as much an expression of the pattern of swirling energy of the universe as a rock, a tree or a human body. In other words, even our thoughts are photons of light originally trapped by the plants that grow from the earth. All life nourishes itself through this light.

Ayurveda holds that food is more than just protein, carbohydrate and fat. It is concentrated intelligent energy of the universe. In fact, an ancient Vedic hymn boldly declares, 'Food is Brahman,' i.e., 'Food is Consciousness.' When we nourish ourselves with food that is derived from the blissful marriage of Father Sun and Mother Earth, this food nurtures not only our bodies, but our minds and souls as well. The same intelligence that differentiates into seer and scenery, biological organisms and their environments, and messenger molecules and their receptors, differentiates into six types of taste receptor and the six codes of intelligence that are expressed as the flavours in food. No other biological science has this deep and profound understanding that our taste receptors are designed to access the intelligence of the universe so that we can nourish ourselves in body and soul.

Subconsciously, we recognize the relationship between food and spirit, because our language uses taste metaphors to denote emotions. We are all familiar with expressions such as sweet love, sour grapes, salt of the earth, pungent remarks, bitter resentment, and astringent humour. Ayurveda suggests that a little sweetness adds delight to life, whereas too much can be cloying. A touch of sour adds interest, but too much makes us grimace. A little salt provides endurance but too much raises our blood pressure. Bitterness, pungency and astringency add spice and complexity to life, but too much may cause us to feel irritable, resentful and withdrawn. The flavours of life in the right proportion add richness to both our food and our experience.

All this might be interesting philosophy were it not for the fascinating recent scientific discoveries that the most healing foods are those that contain potent concentrations of plant chemicals that are responsible for their flavour and colour. The six tastes present in food are clues to these healing phyto-chemicals (phyto is Greek for plant), which demonstrate that good food is good medicine. Although a popular myth suggests that food that is good for you cannot be pleasing to the senses, the fact is that healthy food was designed by nature over millions of years of evolutionary time to be pleasurable. With our modern emphasis on nutritionally empty, highly processed, and additive-rich foods, it is no wonder that we have epidemics of heart disease, cancer and degenerative disorders. It is time for us to remember that nature provides us with the nutrients we need to create meals that are delicious and nutritious.

Over the years, thousands of people have come to The Chopra Center to heal themselves, to learn more about themselves, to improve their relationships, and to accelerate their spiritual evolution. Repeatedly they have told us that the meals they enjoy with us are among the most gratifying components of their experience. The food at The Chopra Center is designed to delight the senses, enliven vitality, and create joy at just being alive and having the opportunity to eat. As a result of the frequent requests of our guests we offer you the recipes of The Chopra Center for Wellbeing. We trust that you will experience for yourself how food can nurture not only your body, but also your soul.

ACKNOWLEDGEMENTS

This book was nurtured with the love and support of many people. Our deep appreciation goes to our dedicated Chopra Center Family, including Vicki Abrams, Brent Becvar, Fran Benedict, Corrine Champigny, Janice Crawford, Nancy Ede, Jenny Ephrom, Ana Paula Fernandez, Roger Gabriel, Kristin Hutchins, Gary John, Sara Kelly, Joe Lancaster, Carolyn Rangel, Felicia Rangel, Jill Romnes, Geeta Singh, Dennis Sugioka, Maureen Sutton and Lizzie Upitis, along with the many beloved guests and friends that have passed through our doors and shared their lives with us. Our special thanks go to Chefs Teresa Robles, Nicolas Ruiz and Gene Gales for their dedication to the fine culinary craft of recipe testing.

To the members of our personal families, Rita, Mallika, Sumant, Tara, Gotham, Candice, Pam, Max, Sara, Isabel, Travis, Kelley, Tom, Bea, Rick, David and Karen; our love and appreciation flow to you for nourishing our bodies, minds and souls.

Finally, we offer our gratitude to Annapurna, the Divine Mother, who inspires the nurturing, creative being within us all.

Deepak, David and Leanne
The Chopra Center at La Costa Resort and Spa
Carlsbad, California

INTRODUCTION

'We owe much to the fruitful meditation of our sages, but a sane view of life is, after all, elaborated mainly in the kitchen'
– JOSEPH CONRAD

'You become what you eat'. This basic principle proclaims the straightforward yet profound fact that almost every molecule that currently resides in your body was derived from food you put into your mouth. From the chemical-rich blood that flows through your circulation to the jelly-like mass of neurons that comprises your brain to the rigid calcium-reinforced girders that make up your skeleton, your body is, in essence, food woven round your DNA.

Did you have a piece of cantaloupe for breakfast this morning? Within hours, carbohydrate molecules of the melon will be in your liver, waiting to supply you with energy when it is time to shop for more fruit. The vitamin C in your cantaloupe will be a component of your antioxidant shield, protecting your lungs from carcinogens you inhale on the way to the shops. Some of the beta-carotene contained in your breakfast fruit will be converted into Vitamin A, shoring up the pigment cells in your retina so you can distinguish a ripe melon from one that has passed its prime.

At its most fundamental level, food is energy and information. The energy component of food is quantified by the number of calories it carries. The informational component of food is characterized by its composition of vital nutrients. The proportion of protein, carbohydrates and fats, vitamins and minerals and the specific natural chemicals that a food source provides all describe the informational aspect of food. Digestion is the process of metabolizing the energy and information of food into the energy and information of your body. When your diet provides the right constituents and your body is capable of extracting the energy and information you need, you create a healthy, vital body.

Healthy Nutrition Should Be Easy

Next to breathing, eating is the most natural process in the world, and we believe that it should be easy and enjoyable to follow a healthy diet. Nevertheless, we see people every day who are confused about what to eat. Why has nutrition become so complicated? Partly it is due to the amazing choices that are currently available. Never before have so many people had so many food options. We enjoy choosing from dozens of different kinds of pasta, cereals, grains and nuts. We appreciate the opportunity to sample fruits and vegetables from distant countries and exotic places around the world. We welcome the access to unprecedented varieties of milk and dairy products, as well as other protein sources. And yet, with these expanded choices arise greater uncertainty. Is there a difference between frozen, canned and fresh vegetables? Are wholegrain products really better for you than refined and enriched pastas and breads? Should you be drinking skimmed, semi-skimmed or whole milk? Are organic foods worth the additional cost? These are some of the questions we hear each day at The Chopra Center that reflect the sometimes overwhelming options available today.

Our access to diverse sources of information has also generated confusion. On a regular basis, new experts in nutrition offer their convincing arguments for an innovative dietary plan. One exhorts you to eat more protein and fewer carbohydrates, while another proclaims the opposite is best. One tells you to eat more animal products, another encourages you to become vegan. One author has even suggested that your blood type has a role to play in your nutritional choices. For every diet or nutritional plan that is aggressively promoted you can find a contradictory approach that is as vigorously advocated. It is not surprising that people are confused.

Re-establish the Mind–Body Connection

We believe that part of the problem underlying this confusion is a loss of connection between mind and body. People are so busy thinking about what to eat that they have lost the ability to hear what their body is asking for. This breakdown in communication probably began in childhood when orders to 'finish everything on your plate' were obeyed even when you may not have been hungry. Most of us were taught to eat when it was time to eat and eat as much as was on our plate. Considering how many children were encouraged to disregard the signals of their body, it does not surprise us here at The Chopra Center that overeating and obesity are at epidemic levels.

One consequence of the disconnection between body and mind is that many people view their appetites as the enemy. They fear that if left unchecked their hunger for food will compel them to eat vast quantities. This shows the extent to which we've lost mind–body integration, for a strong appetite is one of the most important signs of good health. When consciously listened to it can tell you when and what to eat in order for you to remain vital and free from illness.

People have as much emotional attachment to their diet as they do to their politics and religion. We define ourselves by what we eat, and this is not entirely inappropriate, for our body is made of food. We just don't believe that healthy nutrition has to be so complicated. If you are straining to follow a diet that is supposed to be good for you, the stress probably outweighs the benefits. Eating is biological alchemy that transforms vegetables and grains into muscles and bones. Celebrate the Magic!

Eat food that is good for you and you will enliven renewal in your body and mind. The question that everyone is asking is, what food is good for you? That is what this cookbook is about – teaching you how to eat in healthy ways so your need for nutrition and your need for enjoyment are both satisfied. The recipes are simple and delicious. They are nutritionally balanced and consistent with both modern nutritional science and the most ancient healing system on the planet. We have seen the benefits of this programme both personally and professionally. Enjoy and share the information contained within these pages. Together we can live long and healthy lives.

THE WISDOM OF FOOD

'In cooking, as in all arts, simplicity is the sign of perfection'
– CURNONSKY

This book is a practical guide to help you prepare delicious, healthy meals that nourish your body and soul. The principles of our programme have their roots in both modern nutritional science and the world's most ancient health system known as Ayurveda (ah-yur-vay'-duh). Ayurveda is a Sanskrit word that can be translated as the 'wisdom of life' or 'the science of longevity'. It offers a holistic approach to living that is based upon a fundamental principle: your choices are metabolized into your body.

Make healthy choices and you will have a healthy body. To the extent that you can choose, select the option that is most likely to nourish you, and avoid choices that are toxic or depleting. One of the most direct choices you make on a daily basis is what to put into your mouth. We encourage you to choose to eat healthy, delicious foods so you can create a healthy, vital body. Pay attention to these seven simple precepts and your diet will help you create greater mental and physical wellbeing.

1. Eat a wide variety of foods during the day.
2. Listen to your body's signals of hunger and satiety.
3. Use food to fill the emptiness in your stomach, not your heart.
4. If the meal isn't delicious, it isn't nourishing you.
5. Favour foods that are natural and vital.
6. Use herbs and spices liberally as both flavour and health enhancers.
7. Eat with awareness.

Let's explore each point in more detail.

1. Eat a wide variety of foods during the day.

Most anthropologists date the origin of modern human beings to about 150,000–200,000 years ago. Up until about 10,000 years ago we spent most of our days hunting and gathering food. During the course of a day we sampled dozens if not hundreds of food sources. In addition to any animal protein we could snare, we ate a diverse range of roots, leaves, fruit, nuts, berries, beans, mushrooms and seeds. Some primates in the wild today have been observed to nibble on more than 200 different kinds of plants each day.

The average Western diet is much more limited in variety, and as a result we miss out on the extensive natural pharmacy that is available. Unfortunately, burgers, fries and a diet drink do not allow us to take advantage of the health-promoting, reversing properties that a delicious, widely varied diet offers. Each day nutritional scientists are discovering new health-promoting chemicals that are available to us through food. Think variety when it comes to your diet, and be sure to include the six tastes described later in this chapter.

2. Listen to your body's signals of hunger and satiety.

Jonathan Swift once said, 'My stomach serves me instead of a clock'. Your appetite is your ally. Listen to it. You probably don't go to the petrol station when you petrol tank is half full. So don't sit down at the meal table if your stomach is half full. Consider your appetite as a fuel gauge from 0 (empty) to 10 (full). Do not eat before you are at a level 2 (very hungry) or 3 (definitely hungry). Eat until you reach a level 7 (satisfied). Do not go beyond this to a level 8 (rather full), 9 (uncomfortably full) or 10 (completely stuffed). Once you have reached your satisfaction level of 7, wait until you are back down to a level 2 or 3 before you eat again.

Appetite Gauge

10 (stuffed)
9 (uncomfortably full)
8 (rather full)
7 (satisfied)

6   (almost satisfied)
5   (no hunger awareness)
4   (could eat)
3   (definitely hungry)
2   (very hungry)
1   (hunger pains)
0   (completely empty)

Eat at level 2 or 3.
Stop at level 7.

3. Use food to fill the emptiness in your stomach, not your heart.
We learn to associate comfort with food at an early age. When you were
upset as an infant, the chances are your mother offered you a bottle or
her breast to calm you. As adults we sometimes seek food for its soothing,
rather than nutritional properties. If you do this on a regular basis, you are
almost certainly not listening to your appetite. This often results in poor
digestion, disturbed sleep and weight gain. Use food to feed your body.
Develop conscious communication skills to fill your heart.

4. If a meal isn't delicious, it isn't nourishing you.
Enjoy your meals. Delicious food is nourishing to your body, mind and
soul. If you are struggling with a diet that you believe is good for you, but
do not find at all appetizing, it will not ultimately be nourishing and you
will not be able to stay with it for long. In this book we will convince you
that you do not have to sacrifice delicious meals for good health.

5. Favour foods that are natural and vital.
According to most traditional health systems, food carries a vital force in
addition to carbohydrates, proteins, fats, fibre, vitamins and minerals. This
life force is known as *prana* in Ayurveda and *chi* in traditional Chinese
medicine. Freshly picked green beans from your garden are abundant in
prana; beans that have been sitting in your cupboard for six months are
lacking in *prana*. To the extent possible, favour fruit and vegetables that
are locally grown, freshly harvested and prepared as soon as possible after
picking. Not only are they more delicious, but you are sending your body

the message that it is receiving the highest-quality, health-promoting nutrients.

The longer that a food has been sitting on a shelf after its harvesting, the more likely it is to be affected by oxidation. Free radicals initiate the decomposition of a fruit or vegetable immediately after it is disconnected from its source. A sliced apple or banana that has been sitting around for an hour begins turning brown because free radical molecules floating in the air deplete it of its natural antioxidants. Rancid food is this process taken to the extreme. We therefore encourage you to favour fresh foods as often as possible and to the extent that is practical reduce your intake of frozen foods, leftovers, highly processed, microwaved and canned foods. Remember the acronym 'FLUNC' when considering the best sources of nutrition:

	Reduce	Favour
F	Frozen	Recently harvested, when possible
L	Leftover	Freshly prepared
U	Unnatural (highly processed)	All natural ingredients
N	Nuked (microwavable)	Conventionally prepared
C	Canned	Fresh, when possible

As more information becomes available on the harmful effects pesticides have on our personal and environmental health we encourage you to favour organic fruit, vegetables and dairy products as much as you can. Reduce your consumption of processed and highly refined foods. Favour fresh as opposed to canned or frozen, but recognize that there are some foods, such as chickpeas, tomato sauce, diced tomatoes, salsas and condiments, that are just too difficult to regularly prepare fresh. Whenever you can, avoid leftovers or reheated foods. We are not encouraging you to become overly zealous about this point. Simply have the intention to eat as freshly prepared foods as possible.

6. Use herbs and spices liberally as both flavour and health enhancers.

We encourage you to take advantage of nature's edible gifts to make your meals delicious and nutritious. Become familiar with the culinary and health-promoting effects of herbs and spices and use them generously. Even the simplest, quickly prepared meal can be transformed into a culinary delight through the appropriate use of seasonings. We will share with you what we consider to be the essential ingredients to create the nutritional alchemy that will bring pleasure to your senses and wellbeing to your body.

7) Eat with awareness.

A principle of Ayurveda is: how you eat is as important as what you eat. If you are gobbling down your meal while driving or watching television, it will not be as nourishing or life supporting as when you are eating it with awareness. Savour your food through all five senses. Try to minimize the chaos in your environment while you are eating. Even if you only have fifteen minutes for lunch, hold the phone calls and allow yourself to appreciate the miracle of food.

Occasionally eat a meal alone and notice the sounds, sensations, sights, tastes and smells that are available to you. If you are following the previous principles, your meal will not only be sumptuous to the taste, but will also look and smell delicious. A healthy meal nourishes all the senses, and when you pay attention to all five senses, your food will be more nourishing.

The Six Tastes

A simple and practical approach to ensure you have healthy nutritional variety is to pay attention to the tastes of your food. According to Ayurveda everything edible can be classified according to one or more six basic tastes: sweet, sour, salty, pungent, bitter and astringent. If you sample foods that correspond to each of these tastes throughout the day, your meals will provide a wide assortment of health-promoting nutrients. Let's look at these six tastes one by one.

Sweet. Sweet is the taste of carbohydrates, proteins and fats. Foods that carry the sweet taste increase your body bulk. Breads, grains, nuts, pasta, most fruit, starchy vegetables, dairy, oils and all animal products are considered sweet. Sweet foods supply the majority of what we consume in a day. In every category of taste, there are foods that are highly nutritious and others that should be eaten more sparingly.

Favour fresh fruit and vegetables, whole grains, cereals, breads and nuts. In addition to supplying your energy needs, they are good sources of dietary fibre. If you are not ready to go vegetarian, reduce your intake of red meats, favouring cold-water fish and egg whites. Minimize your intake of highly refined sugar and wheat products. Favour low-fat or light dairy and polyunsaturated and monounsaturated oils, while minimizing cholesterol-rich products and foods with partially hydrogenated oils.

Sour. Any food that is mildly acidic is experienced as sour. Citric acid, lactic acid, ascorbic acid and butyric acid are just a few of the acidic chemicals you may have heard of that contribute to the sour taste of foods. As with the sweet taste, there are sour foods that are more nutritious than others.

Favour oranges, grapefruits, strawberries, blueberries, raspberries and tomatoes, while reducing your intake of pickled foods, green olives, alcohol and vinegar. Small helpings of low-fat yogurt and buttermilk can aid digestion. Although aged sour cheeses can be delicious, use them judiciously as they are usually high in cholesterol and difficult to digest.

Salty. Salt is the flavour of ion-producing minerals on the tongue. The principal salt of our diet is sodium chloride, which comes from mines or naturally salty bodies of water. The salty taste is also carried in soy sauce, many sauces, seaweed, fish and salted meats. In the right dose, salt adds flavour and stimulates digestion. Too much salt can contribute to high blood pressure and fluid retention.

Pungent. We often use the term 'hot' to describe the pungent flavour. The spiciness of pepper, ginger and other pungent sources comes from essential oils that interact with chemical receptors on our tongue. Most pungent foods contain natural antioxidants and infection-fighting chemicals. Due in part to their anti-spoiling properties, pungent spices have been highly prized for millennia. A shortcut to the land of spices was a major incentive for the fifteenth-century explorers. Pungent flavours stimulate digestion and help mobilize stagnant secretions. Recent studies have suggested components of garlic and onions may help lower cholesterol levels and high blood pressure.

Commonly available pungent foods include: chilli peppers, cayenne, black pepper, fresh and powdered ginger, horseradish, onions, garlic, leeks, mustard, cloves, cinnamon, peppermint, thyme, cumin, cardamom, basil, oregano and rosemary. Adding spice to your life will serve both your palate and your health.

Bitter. Bitter is the taste of most green and yellow vegetables. Some green leafy vegetables such as endive and kale are particularly bitter. The bitterness is due to natural plant chemicals known as phyto-chemicals (phyto means 'plant' in Latin). These phyto-chemicals have detoxifying, disease-preventing and healing chemicals that improve our chances of living long, healthy lives. Broccoli and cauliflower, for example, are rich in the phyto-chemicals known as isothiocyanates, which have been shown to help fight cancer and heart disease. Asparagus, green peppers and cabbage are rich in flavonoids, which help resist genetic injury, fight infections and may even reduce your risk of memory loss. The bottom line: eat your vegetables – they are good for you.

Astringent. The last of the six tastes is more of an effect than any actual flavour. Astringent foods have a drying, compacting and puckering influence on your body. Beans, pulses and peas are considered to fall within the astringent category, and provide excellent sources of vegetable protein, complex carbohydrates and fibre to your diet. Several fruits are astringent, such as tart apples, cranberries, persimmons and tart pomegranates. Green tea is also astringent and has been found to be a rich source of natural cancer-preventing chemicals. Astringent foods are an essential component of diets that promote renewal.

Weight Loss and Wellness

Many people struggling to shed unwanted weight seek quick and effortless solutions, often bouncing from one weight-loss diet to another. Unfortunately, quick-fix diets seldom produce lasting benefits and may not be nutritionally balanced. At The Chopra Center for Wellbeing, we believe that attaining and maintaining an ideal weight is most easily achieved by following a consciousness-based approach. The principles outlined previously in this chapter, combined with a regular fitness programme, will enable you to lose about 450g per week until you reach your optimal weight.

Honouring your appetite and eating with awareness will reawaken a healthy connection between your mind and body. When listened to, your body will tell you when it is hungry and when it is satisfied. Pay attention to the messages it is sending – it is trying to tell you what it needs to be healthy and fit. Ensure that all six tastes are available at every meal and you will satisfy the cravings that can sabotage your efforts to lose weight.

Please avoid crash diets. Although you may see quick results, study after study has demonstrated that the benefits cannot be sustained. Start a nutritional and lifestyle programme today that will serve you throughout your entire life. Do not try to lose weight through diet alone. Exercise your body to enhance your cardiovascular system and convert fat into muscle. You will feel better about your body and about yourself. We encourage you to shift you goal from achieving a specific number on your bathroom scale to attaining an optimal level of physical and emotional wellbeing. The Chopra Center 30-Day Nutritional Plan will support you in achieving this goal.

Wine and Wellbeing: A Word on Alcohol

The fermentation of fruit and grains into alcoholic beverages dates to antiquity. Egyptian references to an intoxicating beverage derived from fruit stored in warm places can be identified more than 4000 years ago. Around 1500 BC, Middle Easterners created the first malt beverage from fermented grains. Wine, beer and distilled alcoholic drinks have long played a role in cultures around the world, offering the potential for both pleasure and suffering to humanity. Although over-indulgence in alcohol-containing beverages can contribute to emotional and physical distress, an occasional offering to Dionysus, the god of grapes and ecstasy, can be part of a healthy lifestyle.

Studies have shown that there are natural health-promoting chemicals in wine that may have a protective effect against heart disease and cancer. These natural disease-fighting substances, which have been shown to have potent antioxidant properties, go by such names as polyphenols, flavonoids and resveratrol. These compounds are most concentrated in the skins of grapes. Because the production of red (but not white) wine involves prolonged contact of the juice with the grape skins, red wine has the highest concentration of these health-enhancing chemicals.

If you are so inclined, enjoy an occasional glass of wine as part of a delicious meal in the company of friends and loved ones. From a taste perspective, wine contains predominantly sour and astringent flavours, with traces of bitter and sweet; therefore, it can complement and contribute to a balanced meal. This is not the case for distilled alcohol.

With many families affected by a family member with alcoholism, it is important to remember that alcohol has potentially adverse effects on almost every system and cell in the body and can contribute to serious illnesses affecting the nervous system, liver and digestive tract. It is also a source of essentially empty calories with each gram of alcohol yielding about 7 calories – almost as much as a gram of fat. A pint of beer or 225ml of wine carries about 200 calories, while a shot of distilled spirits yields about 80 calories; therefore, alcohol is not a useful component of a weight-losing programme. Our bottom line is to consider an occasional glass of wine as another source of flavours and phyto-chemicals that can be part of a healthy nutritional programme.

THE ART OF COOKING, THE ART OF EATING

'One cannot think well, love well, sleep well, if one has not dined well'
— VIRGINIA WOOLF

'The true cook is the perfect blend, the only perfect blend of artist and philosopher.
He knows his worth: he holds in his palm the happiness of mankind'
— NORMAN DOUGLAS

Nutritious food is a celebration of life, capable of enlivening your vitality and engaging all your senses. Unfortunately, due to the hectic pace of modern life, eating is more often an exercise in refuelling than a celebration. Like many, your typical dinner may consist of microwaving a frozen ready-meal, heating up a can of soup or stopping off for fast food on the way home from work. Your dining time may be spent in front of the television, catching up on your mail or in a heated discussion with your teenage children. It is no surprise that more than one-third of adults are regularly troubled by indigestion and heartburn and a growing proportion is overweight. The environment in which you eat can be an important component of the nourishment you receive from your meal. We encourage you to consider that the sounds, sights, sensations and smells you ingest while eating are as important as the flavours you put in your mouth. If you are watching the evening news while eating dinner, you are consuming those turbulent sounds and images along with your salad. If you are arguing with your family, you are metabolizing anger and frustration together with your pasta. When you fall into habits that don't support the celebration of life, you lose the opportunity to enhance your wellbeing and enliven renewal.

Ask yourself, 'Am I being nourished by all my senses when I sit down to eat?' If you are eating while watching television, on the run, in your car or in front of your computer, the chances are you can improve your sensory nourishment. Make a commitment to get back in touch with the delights of dining, and you will see benefits in your health, your vitality and your relationships.

Preparing and eating delicious food can be an art form. It provides a daily opportunity to express your creativity. Have the intention to be more conscious as you plan your meals, shop for ingredients, cook your dishes and, finally, enjoy the delicious product of your efforts. Your body, mind and soul will relish the experience.

Create a Nurturing Environment

Your kitchen and dining area are great places to create living space that reflects your personal tastes, integrates the healing energy of nature and brings beauty and richness into your life. Pay attention to colours, sounds and textures that enliven your senses. Consider eating in your formal dining room on a regular basis, rather than saving it only for those rare holiday meals. Use your special dishes occasionally for a family meal, savouring the sumptuousness of food served on beautiful plates. Light candles and play beautiful music during your meals. Make a pact with your family to engage only in light-hearted conversations while eating, saving the heavy discussions for later. Even when you are eating alone, make your dining experience special. You can be your own delightful dining companion.

Become an artist in the kitchen. Begin by renewing your relationship with Mother Earth. Take a walk outside and connect with the energy around you. Appreciate the beauty of the plants, flowers, land and natural bodies of water that comprise your environment. The energy of the earth becomes the energy of your body through your intake of fresh fruits, vegetables and whole grains. Favour foods that are in season and, to the extent possible, locally grown.

Artists thrive on inspiration. Develop a collection of inspiring cookery books. Arrange your kitchen so it is beautiful, alive and inviting. Plant an herb garden in your home or flat – you can create an amazing botanical bounty in pots. Take a walk through your local food shop and pay attention to the vibrant colours, fragrances and textures of the fruit and vegetables available to you. Appreciate the luscious red peppers, yellow squashes and white mushrooms. Savour the aroma of ripe strawberries and fresh asparagus. Enjoy the cobbled texture of sweetcorn on the cob, the smoothness of tomatoes, the velvety softness of peaches. Listen to the sounds of the people moving about you. Feel their energy and excitement.

If you feel intimated by the food market because you have not previously considered yourself an inspired cook or chef, try this simple experiment: go into your grocery store and select one item from the produce department. We suggest you begin with broccoli, cauliflower or courgette. During the week, try cooking your chosen vegetable in every conceivable way. Stir-fry it, steam it, blanch it, marinate it for a salad, make it into a soup or casserole, cut it into bite-sized pieces for a dip. In a very short time, you will begin to build your confidence and ability to cook creatively. Envision yourself as a culinary artist. Tap into your creative ability to produce beautiful and delicious food.

Involve your family. Children have the wonderful ability to make a routine task fun. The kitchen may end up a mess, but the time spent together will be well worth it. Be passionate about food and encourage your family to share in your enthusiasm. Celebrate the planning process, the cooking process and the eating experience. The food you eat carries the wisdom of the earth, the intelligence of the farmer and the love of the cook. Every nurturing meal is a celebration of the seasons, cycles and rhythms of nature. Delicious, lovingly prepared food renews, revitalizes and nurtures your body, your mind and your spirit.

The Basics of Nourishment

*'I like a cook who smiles out loud when he tastes his own work.
Let God worry about your modesty, I want to see your enthusiasm'*
– ROBERT FARRAR CAPON

Every delicious meal is created from wholesome ingredients. When your storecupboard is stocked with high-quality staples, you have the foundation for delectable, nutritious meals. The longer something has been sitting on your shelf, the less likely it is to contribute to an appetizing and healthy meal. Begin the process of cooking and eating with awareness by detoxifying your kitchen. Clean out those supplies you will never use – rid your cupboards of old cake mixes, ancient spices, dented tins, stale grains and anything else that may be rancid. Keep the highest-quality ingredients in stock and you will create delicious, nutritious meals. Make the commitment to bring only the purest, most natural and wholesome foods into your home. Stock your cupboards with quality ingredients to ensure that your meals are delicious and provide optimal nourishment for your body. Your body is made from the food you eat. Purchase and consume the highest-quality food to create the highest-quality body.

Storecupboard List

The following items can be found in natural foods stores and most regular grocery stores. Mainstream food markets are also beginning to carry more natural and organic foods. As increasing numbers of people purchase natural and organic items, the market for these products will grow and they will become more widely available. If you live in an area where a natural food store is not available, encourage your local food shop manager to stock food products that are healthy and organic. Give the manager a list of a few items that you will buy, and then buy them.

Stock up on essential items for your storecupboard, but also plan on purchasing food on a regular basis to have the freshest possible foods available. If you live in an area where a particular food staple is not readily accessible, you'll need to plan ahead. Try not to keep food items too long. The Ayurvedic approach to health values freshness and encourages limiting canned, packaged or frozen foods. If you are eating meat, poultry or fish, use fresh, not frozen, products whenever possible. Remember – fresh is best!

Herbs and Spices

Purchase your spices and dried herbs in small quantities. Buy only what you will use. If available, buy spices from the bulk bin, as they are usually less expensive. Check with your source to ensure that they are as fresh as possible. Always keep the following spices on hand:

Indian spices	Herbs, dried	Sweet spices	Odds and ends
asafoetida (hing) *	basil	allspice	black pepper
cardamom seeds	dried mixed herbs	cinnamon	curry powder
coriander	oregano	cloves	Chinese five spice
cumin	sage	fennel seeds	chilli powder
fenugreek seeds	tarragon	garam masala*	red chilli flakes
mustard seeds	thyme	nutmeg	ginger
turmeric			sea salt

* Found in health food shops and Indian, Asian and Middle Eastern markets

Grains, Nuts and Seeds

Buy organic whole grains, nuts and seeds whenever possible in quantities of 500g–1kg at a time. Because of their high oil content nuts and seeds can go rancid rapidly, so it is best to buy these in smaller quantities. When possible, buy them from the bulk bin and check for freshness. If you don't use your nuts and seeds right away, store them in glass jars or plastic resealable bags in the refrigerator. Store your grains in recycled glass jars with tight-fitting lids as well. Label all jars and bags and include any cooking instructions printed on the original packaging. Maintain a stock of the following grains, nuts and seeds:

- porridge oats
- basmati rice
- quinoa
- millet
- six-grain cereal
- dried pasta – spaghetti, penne, lasagne
- couscous – white for pilaf and wholemeal for breakfast cereal
- pearl barley
- wholemeal flour
- wholemeal pastry flour
- flax seeds
- sesame seeds
- sunflower seeds
- pine nuts
- walnuts
- pecan nuts
- almonds, whole and sliced

Beans and Other Pulses

Buy beans and pulses in quantities of 500g–1kg at a time. Also keep on hand some canned or jarred cooked beans for speedy meal preparation. You will find dried fresh beans and lentils in bulk bins at whole food shops, or packaged in plastic bags at supermarkets. You may be able to find organic beans, both dried and canned in health food shops. Store the beans and pulses in recycled glass jars with tight-fitting lids. Label them and include any cooking instructions that were printed on the packaging. We consider the following to be staple beans and pulses:

- red lentils
- brown lentils
- mung beans
- chickpeas

- split peas – green and yellow
- white beans – cannellini and haricot
- black beans
- pinto beans

Condiments and Baking Supplies

Look for condiments that have pure ingredients. There are a vast variety of curry sauces, pasta sauces, salsas, salad dressings and marinades available. Favour items with vinegar or lemon juice, which are natural preservatives. Many salsas, sauces and salad dressings can be made from scratch, however it is convenient to have quality prepared condiments available at home when you are short of time.

Keep on hand small quantities of basic baking supplies. Packages of flour, baking powder and thickeners often end up sitting on shelves for years, so buy these in quantities that you will use over weeks or months to ensure the highest-quality breads and baked goods.

Keep these basic condiments and storecupboard items on hand:

- raw organic honey
- maple syrup
- Bragg Liquid Aminos (a non-fermented soy sauce found in health food shops; use like soy sauce.)
- tamari soy sauce (this is the substitute we suggest for Bragg Liquid Aminos if you can't find it.)
- apple cider vinegar
- balsamic vinegar
- rice vinegar
- ghee, home-made or purchased (see the recipe for making on page 39)
- Olive oil and/or vegetable oil spray for greasing tins and baking sheets
- extra virgin olive oil
- sesame oil
- Dijon mustard
- salsa
- vinaigrette salad dressing

- lemon juice
- apple juice
- kombu seaweed
- tomato paste
- light coconut milk
- plain and vanilla soya milk or rice milk, especially the light versions if you can find them
- firm or extra-firm tofu, especially the low-fat version if you can find it

We also recommend the following basic supplies:

- turbinado sugar
- raw sugar
- sultanas
- dried cranberries
- currants
- baking powder
- bicarbonate of soda
- cold-pressed rapeseed oil
- arrowroot and cornstarch
- vanilla extract

Organic Foods

Whenever possible, use organic fruit and vegetables, freshly harvested from a local source. In many areas, you will find wonderful farmers' markets where you can purchase fresh vegetables and fruits. If you can't find organic, choose the freshest produce you can. By using freshly harvested and naturally ripened fruits and vegetables, you will be ensuring the intake of valuable vitamins, nutrients and life-supporting energy in your diet. As part the 30-Day Nutritional Plan diet, we recommend five to nine servings of fresh fruit and vegetables each day. This is easily accomplished by favouring a mostly vegetarian diet (see the following page).

There are many different varieties of organic grain products. Reduce refined flours and bleached grains whenever possible, favouring products such as basmati rice, quinoa, millet, kashi, rolled oats and brown rice.

Purchase quality wholemeal flour products, including bread flour, pastry flour and unbleached plain flour. Spelt, an ancient grain similar to wheat, is a good alternative to wheat products. Try turbinado sugar, an unbleached cane sugar, and maple syrup as sweeteners.

To Be or Not to Be Vegetarian

The choice to avoid or eat animal products is a highly individual one. Culture, upbringing, personal health issues and environmental concerns, as well as religious and spiritual beliefs, all contribute to a person's dietary preferences. Our basic recommendation is to eat with awareness and follow your heart. While the Ayurvedic approach to diet does not require strict adherence to a vegetarian diet, we encourage vegetarianism as the optimal nutritional plan for health and vitality. There is abundant scientific evidence that a vegetarian or mostly vegetarian diet plays an important role in reducing your risks for heart disease and cancer. For health, environmental and ethical reasons, reducing your intake of animal products makes sense.

We recognize that if you are accustomed to eating meat on a daily basis, you will not be inclined to stop abruptly. We suggest you initially try substituting one or two vegetarian meals a week and see how you feel. If you consume animal products, choose those that are raised as humanely as possible and are free from hormones and antibiotics. Also, consider changing the way you consume meat. Rather than devouring a large piece of meat along with a few vegetables, try eating a smaller helping of meat with a larger quantity of vegetables. Favour fish and free-ranging fowl while reducing your intake of red meat.

Although most of the recipes in this book are vegetarian, if you choose, you can add small portions of chicken or fish to many of the dishes. Most importantly, eat with awareness, gratitude, respect and delight. These are the most important qualities to awaken renewal of the body and mind.

THE CHOPRA CENTER 30-DAY NUTRITIONAL PLAN FOR RENEWAL

A health-promoting nutritional plan is both balanced and delicious. It should be rich in essential nutrients and have the appropriate proportions of carbohydrates, proteins and fats. It should provide a variety of flavours and textures and be easy to prepare and follow. The 30-day programme we offer meets all these criteria. If you follow this programme as outlined, you will attain your desired weight whilst consuming a diet that reduces your risks for heart disease and cancer. Over the course of a month, The Chopra Center 30-Day Nutritional Plan will provide the following nutritional components:

Total fat	less than 22% of total calories
Saturated fat	less than 7% of total calories
Protein	between 15 and 20% of total calories

Although some proponents of a heart-healthy diet have suggested lower intakes of total fat, The Chopra Center 30-Day Nutritional Plan is low in saturated fat and cholesterol, which makes it much more palatable than more restrictive diets. It is also high in protein and dietary fibre.

This nutritional plan provides a guideline for planning your weekly meals. We have included information on total calories, fat and protein per meal and per day to help you choose more consciously the quality and quantity of the foods you eat. Depending on your needs – building muscle, losing weight or maintaining your current body size – you will be able to mix and match each menu to create a nutritious and well-balanced diet. Most of the recipes are for four servings. If you are cooking for one or two people, simply cut the recipe in half, and don't forget to decrease the amount of black pepper and red chilli flakes when dividing a recipe. You can always add more spice to a dish but it's difficult to cover up too much spicing.

As you balance your eating habits and daily routine, you will likely find your food cravings will decrease. Use your eating awareness techniques to help gauge the amount of food you prepare for a meal. Ask yourself, 'How hungry am I?' Prepare the quantity of food that reflects the hunger you are feeling.

Healthy desserts bring joy and delight. Get into the habit of eating small portions of dessert to satisfy your cravings for sweets without over-indulging. The Ayurvedic approach to eating is about nurturing and honouring the signals your body sends to you. Depriving yourself of the basic foods you love may cause more harm than the few extra calories you may consume. Be moderate and balanced in your eating habits.

Thinking up to a few days ahead can be helpful. If you want to make Rosemary White Bean Soup (page 158), for example, soak the beans overnight the night before and cook them slowly in a slow-cooker while you are at work, finishing the soup when you get home.

Look for the asterisk (*) in the 30-Day Nutritional Plan. The asterisk indicates a Staple Recipe. Review the general instructions and recipes in that chapter, beginning on page 35. All other recipes included in our programme are found later in the book beginning with the chapter 'Breakfast and Baked Goodies' and ending with the chapter 'Desserts'. All of the daily menu choices include the six tastes in each meal. Remember the six tastes — sweet, salty, sour, pungent, bitter and astringent — should be present in each meal to create balance and harmony in the body. We also feel more satisfied after we eat a meal where the six tastes are all present. As you become more aware of the six tastes in your daily meals, you will find that you can easily round out a meal by, for example, adding a squeeze of lemon to enhance the sour taste or by adding some quickly stir-fried spinach to a meal to complete the bitter taste.

Learning to make the Staple Recipes will increase the variety of food choices and enable you to add additional 'tastes' in your daily meals. In so doing, you will be able to incorporate the recommended five to nine servings of fruit and vegetables and the six tastes into your diet.

The basic principles and recipes presented in this book will serve you well as you prepare meals that are sumptuous, health promoting and delicious. Enjoy!

The nutritional analysis for the 30-Day Nutritional Plan is detailed in the Appendix of this book, beginning on page 296.

DAY 1	DAY 2
Breakfast	*Breakfast*
Morning Bliss Shake	Vegetable Tofu Scramble
Breakfast Bar	Coriander Mint Sauce
	Apple Raisin Muffin
Main Meal	*Main Meal*
Tomato Florentine Soup	Tofu or Tempeh Fajitas
Rainbow Risotto	Mango Tomato Salsa
Nutty Spinach Greens	Spanish Pilaf
Almond Tart	Stir-fried Carrots and Cauliflower ★
	Apple Custard Pie
Light Meal	*Light Meal*
Vegetable Hummus Wrap	Italian White Bean Stew
Ginger Cookies	Oatmeal Power Cookie

★ Staple Recipes

DAY 3

Breakfast
Rolled Oats Hot Cereal
Blueberry Syrup
Sautéed Peaches ★

Main Meal
Spinach Soup
Vegetable Paella
Aubergine Tapenade
Dilled Asparagus
Sautéed Strawberries ★

Light Meal
Vegetable and White Bean Chilli
Great Bread ★
Peanut Butter Cookie

★ Staple Recipes

DAY 4

Breakfast
Coffee Bliss Shake
Nutty French Toast
Sautéed Apples ★

Main Meal
Summertime Tomato Basil Soup
Spinach Polenta
Ratatouille
Savoury Swiss Chard ★
Walnut Chocolate Chip Cookie

Light Meal
Egg-less Tofu Salad or Sandwich
Lemon Poppy Seed Cake

DAY 5

Breakfast
Chai Bliss Shake
Chopra Granola
Fresh Berries and Banana ★

Main Meal
Vegetable Hot-and-Sour Soup
Buddha's Delight
Steamed Rice ★
Kim Chi Chutney
Unbelievable Double Chocolate Cake

Light Meal
Roasted Tofu and Yams
Garden Salad
Coriander Pecan Dressing
Sautéed Apricots★

★ Staple Recipes

DAY 6

Breakfast
Broccoli Tofu Scramble
Mango Tomato Salsa
Great Bread with Almond Butter

Main Meal
Potato Leek Soup
French Vegetable Stew
Toasted Millet ★
Steamed Broccoli ★
Linzertorte Cookies

Light Meal
Split Pea Dahl
Indian Rice
Apple Leek Chutney
Cardamom Butter Cookies

DAY 7

Breakfast
Almond Bliss Shake
Apples and Rice Hot Cereal

Main Meal
Italian Vegetable Soup
Curry Filo Tarts
Walnut Yogurt Sauce
Roasted Sweet Potatoes *
Berry Tofu Sorbet

Light Meal
Tofu Thai Wrap
Cranberry Bliss Balls

* Staple Recipes

DAY 8

Breakfast
Mango Yogurt
Tempeh and Potato Hash
Orange Pear Chutney

Main Meal
Butternut Squash Soup
Aubergine and Yam Curry
Curried Potatoes
Cucumber Raita
Sautéed Apples and Blackberries *

Light Meal
Asian Clear Broth
Thai Tofu Vegetable Stew
Coconut Cookie

DAY 9

Breakfast
Chopra Granola
Very Berry Yogurt

Main Meal
Italian Vegetable Soup
Fresh Spinach Pasta *
Tofu Balls with Roasted Tomato Sauce
Stir-fried Rocket and Roasted
    Aubergine *
Lemon Birthday Cake

Light Meal
Potato Leek Soup
Poached Peaches and Blueberries *

* Staple Recipes

DAY 10

Breakfast
Mango Bliss Shake
Vegetable Tofu Scramble
Russian Borscht Chutney
Cinnamon Roll

Main Meal
Vegetable Barley Soup
Tofu Burger with Leek Sauce
Steamed Carrots and Green Beans *
Berry Tofu Sorbet

Light Meal
Roasted Tofu and Yams
Steamed Asparagus
Blueberry Lemon Cake

DAY 11

Breakfast
Tofu and Potato Italiano
Home-made Chilli Sauce
Courgette Pecan Bread

Main Meal
Red Lentil Dahl
Aubergine Cauliflower Curry
Steamed Green Beans ★
Apricot Salsa
Sautéed Pears with Cardamom

Light Meal
Black Bean and Yam Stew
Oat Groat Pilaf with Spinach
Apricot Pecan Cookie

★ Staple Recipes

DAY 12

Breakfast
Chai Bliss Shake
Breakfast Burrito
Whole Apple ★

Main Meal
Tortilla Soup with Avocado and
Coriander
Braised Tofu with Mango Tomato
  Salsa
Roasted Carrots and Yams ★
Stir-fried Greens ★
Banana–Cocoa–Tofu Mousse

Light Meal
Black Bean and Rice Wrap
Simple Carrot Soup ★
Traditional Awesome Brownies

DAY 13

Breakfast
Traditional French Toast
Sautéed Banana and Blueberries ★

Main Meal
Vegetable Barley Soup
Moroccan Vegetables
Dill Lemon Courgettes
Sautéed Apples and Blackberries ★

Light Meal
Roasted Winter Vegetable Stew
Organic Field Greens with Dressing
Kabocha Pumpkin Pie

★ Staple Recipes

DAY 14

Breakfast
Masala Potatoes
Apple Leek Chutney
Mango Yogurt

Main Meal
Tomato Florentine Soup
Mediterranean Pasta
Savoury Swiss Chard
Steamed Asparagus ★
Ginger Cookie

Light Meal
Tofu, Aubergine and Potato Stew
Greek Goddess Salad on Greens
Blueberry Orange Cake

DAY 15

Breakfast
Broccoli Tofu Scramble
Russian Borscht Chutney
Blueberry Muffin

Main Meal
Rosemary White Bean Soup
Vegetable Paella
Stir-fried Green Beans and Almonds ★
Raspberry Lemon Cake ★★

Light Meal
Curried Chickpea Stew
Steamed Rice ★
Ginger Cookie

DAY 16

Breakfast
Wholemeal Crêpes with
    Strawberries
Blueberry Syrup
Country Potatoes

Main Meal
Sweet Potato Ginger Soup
Broccoli Almond Stir-Fry and
Basic Asian Cookery Sauce
Szechuan Baked Egg Rolls
Spicy Lime and Red Pepper Sauce
Chinese Five-Spice Garden Pilaf
Sautéed Peaches with Nutmeg ★

Light Meal
Mexican Tofu Stew
Garden Salad with Coriander Dressing
Peanut Butter Cookie

★ Staple Recipes ★★ Variation of Blueberry Orange Cake

DAY 17

Breakfast
Coffee Bliss Shake
Pumpkin Muffin

Main Meal
Italian White Bean Soup
Pizza with Basil Pesto and Courgettes
Baked Spaghetti Squash ★
Savoury Swiss Chard ★
Almond Apple Tart

Light Meal
Curried Chickpea Stew
Steamed Rice ★
Chocolate Mousse with Walnut Praline

DAY 18

Breakfast
Quinoa Hot Cereal
Apple Breakfast Syrup
Strawberry Banana Yogurt

Main Meal
Vegetable Hot-and-Sour Soup
Thai-style Noodles with Tofu
Nutty Spinach Greens
Kim Chi Chutney
Double Almond Cookie

Light Meal
Tofu, Aubergine and Potato Stew
Green Quinoa Pilaf
Cardamom Butter Cookie

★ Staple Recipes

DAY 19

Breakfast
Great Toast with Almond Butter
Sautéed Peaches and Currants ★
Very Berry Yogurt

Main Meal
Courgette Tofu Bisque
Curried Filo Tarts
Cauliflower and Braised Tomato Sauce
Sweet Mixed Fruit Chutney
Mother Earth's Apple Pie

Light Meal
French Lentil Dahl
Steamed Rice ★
Steamed Carrots, Broccoli and
    Courgettes
Cranberry Bliss Ball

★ Staple Recipes

DAY 20

Breakfast
Toasted Millet Hot Cereal
Pear Breakfast Syrup

Main Meal
Spinach Lentil Soup
Winter Vegetable and Couscous
Courgettes, Tomatoes, Feta and
    Fresh Dill ★
Walnut Chocolate Chip Cookie

Light Meal
Curried Potatoes
Cucumber Raita
Organic Field Greens with
    Dressing
Berry Tofu Mousse

DAY 21

Breakfast
Tempeh and Potato Hash
Tomato Salsa
Courgette Pecan Bread

Main Meal
Courgette Tofu Bisque
Tuscany Bulgur Pilaf Stuffed Courgette
Leek Sauce
Braised Carrots and Fennel ★
Almond Apricot Tart

Light Meal
Aubergine and Yam Curry
Oat Grouts Pilaf with Spinach
Oatmeal Powder Cookie

★ Staple Recipes

DAY 22

Breakfast
Chai Bliss Shake
Seasonal Fruit Salad
Strawberry Banana Yogurt

Main Meal
Very Simple Pumpkin Soup
Rainbow Risotto
Stir-fried Spinach ★
Steamed Asparagus with Lemon ★
Unbelievable Double Chocolate
    Cake

Light Meal
Asian Clear Broth Soup
Lettuce Wraps with Two Sauces
Peanut Butter Cookie

DAY 23

Breakfast
Wholemeal Crêpes
Sweet Fruit Chutney
Strawberry Breakfast Syrup

Main Meal
Italian Vegetable Soup
Spinach Polenta
Roasted Tomato Sauce
Garden Salad with olive oil
Linzertorte Cookie

Light Meal
Cajun Beans and Tempeh Stew
Steamed Rice ★
Steamed Broccoli ★
Apple Cinnamon Cake

★ Staple Recipes

DAY 24

Breakfast
Seasonal Fruit Salad
Apple Maple Yogurt

Main Meal
Tortilla Soup with Avocado and
    Coriander
Mexican Tofu Stew
Spicy Mexican Rice
Steamed Yellow and Green
    Courgettes ★
Apricot Pecan Cookie

Light Meal
Vegetable Hummus Wrap
Apple Cobbler

DAY 25

Breakfast
Cream of Couscous Hot Cereal
Sautéed Apples and Blackberries ★

Main Meal
Spinach Soup
Ratatouille
Oat Groat Pilaf with Spinach
Steamed Carrots, Asparagus, Broccoli ★
Chocolate Tofu Mousse with Praline

Light Meal
Spinach Lentil Soup
Greek Goddess Salad
Coconut Cookies

★ Staple Recipes

DAY 26

Breakfast
Coffee Bliss Shake
Cardamom Wholemeal Pancakes
Fresh Blueberries and Sliced
    Banana ★

Main Meal
Nutty Broccoli Soup
Tuscany Bulgur Pilaf
Roasted Sweet Potatoes ★
Steamed Yellow and Green
    Courgettes ★
Traditional Awesome Brownies

Light Meal
Vegetable and White Bean Chilli
Stir-fried Spinach ★
Traditional Chocolate Chip Cookie

DAY 27

Breakfast
Country Potatoes
Krazy Ketchup
Traditional French Toast
Strawberry Syrup

Main Meal
Vegetable Barley Soup
Pizza with Roasted Tomato and
    Spinach
Steamed Carrots and Green Beans ★
Mother Earth's Apple Pie

Light Meal
Butternut Squash Soup
Egg-less Tofu Salad on Greens
Oatmeal Power Cookie

★ Staple Recipes

DAY 28

Breakfast
Morning Bliss Shake
Pumpkin Muffin

Main Meal
Yellow Split Pea Dahl
Tofu Burger with Leek Sauce
Steamed Rice ★
Steamed Broccoli, Carrots and
    Courgettes ★
Sautéed Strawberries with
    Cinnamon ★

Light Meal
Thai Tofu Vegetables Stew
Kabocha Pumpkin Pie

DAY 29

Breakfast
Nutty French Toast
Nectarine and Blueberry Breakfast
    Syrup

Main Meal
Sweet Potato Ginger Soup
Buddha's Delight with Tofu Cubes
Chinese Five-Spice Garden Pilaf
Lemon Birthday Cake

Light Meal
Roasted Aubergine and Spinach Pasta
Organic Field Greens with Dressing
Sautéed Mango and Blueberries★

★ Staple Recipes

DAY 30

Breakfast
Polenta Hot Cereal
Apple Breakfast Syrup
Cinnamon Roll

Main Meal
Summertime Tomato Basil Soup
Mediterranean Pasta
Roasted Butternut Squash Rings ★
Braised Fennel, Green Beans and
    Almonds ★
Poached Peaches with Blackberry
    Sauce ★

Light Meal
Very Simple Pumpkin Soup
Tofu Thai Wrap
Double Delight Cookie

STAPLE RECIPES

'Pray for peace and grace and spiritual food,
for wisdom and guidance, for all these are good,
but, don't forget the potatoes'
– JOHN TYLER PETTEE

In a perfect world, you would have freshly baked bread and steaming, wholesome soup waiting for you as you walked through the door each night. Unfortunately, this scenario is not available to most of us. With a little planning, however, you will be able to create delicious, healthy meals easily and quickly. Our goal is to make your life easier. We encourage you to learn the following basic staple recipes for soups, sauces and stir-fries described in this chapter. Once you have mastered these staple recipes, you will have a foundation for creating wholesome, healthy meals.

Look for the * on the 30-Day Nutritional Plan. This asterisk indicates recipes that are found in this chapter. These are recipes ripe for personal adaptation. Become familiar with each of the Staple Recipes so you can increase your personal repertoire and create simple basic meals using whatever ingredients you have on hand.

STAPLE RECIPES INDEX

Basic Dahl
Ghee: the Golden Oil
Ginger Elixir
Ginger Tea
Simple Basic Soup
Vegetable Stock

Sautéed Fruit and Syrups
Simple Frozen Fruit Syrup
Simple Fruit Sauté
Simple Great Wholegrain Bread
Simple Marinade for Tofu and Tempeh
Simple White Sauce: Basic Roux
Soya: the Perfect Food
Very Best Dairy-free Muffins
Wholegrain Baked Goodies

Greens
Basic Mixed-vegetable Stir-fry
Basic Roasted Vegetables
Simply Vegetables
Stir-fried Greens

Cooked Grains

BASIC DAHL

~ SERVES 4 ~

We consider dahl to be a staple in a well-balanced diet. Dahl is a very nutritious soup made of pulses and a simple masala curry paste, and we include recipes for both here. Dahl is easy to digest and low in fat. Eaten with rice it provides a complete protein. It also includes all six tastes and is made with many prized healing spices. Pulse choices include green lentils, brown lentils, Puy lentils, red lentils, yellow and green split peas and whole or split mung beans.

> 200g dried lentils (see list above), picked over and rinsed
> Vegetable stock or water
> ½ tsp ground cumin
> 1 pinch of ground asafoetida (hing)
> 1 pinch of turmeric
> 5–7.5cm kombu seaweed (found in Asian markets and health food shops)
> 1 recipe quantity Curry Paste (recipe follows)
> Steamed basmati rice, to serve
> Selection of steamed vegetables, to serve

Put the lentils and enough stock to cover them by 7.5cm into a heavy-based stockpot or large saucepan. Bring the lentils to the boil and skim as the foam rises to the surface. To help reduce gas and aid digestion, add the cumin, asafoetida, turmeric and kombu to the lentils as they cook.

Reduce the heat to low and simmer the lentils for 1 hour, stirring occasionally, or until they are very tender. Add the curry paste to the cooked lentils and simmer for a further 5–10 minutes, stirring occasionally, until blended and hot.

Serve the dahl with steamed basmati rice and steamed vegetables for simple, delicious and healthy meal.

CURRY PASTE

1 tsp ghee or olive oil
½ tsp brown or yellow mustard seeds
½ tsp fenugreek seeds
cardamom seeds from 5 green pods and crushed in a pestle and
mortar, or ½ tsp ground cardamom
1 pinch of red chilli flakes
1 cinnamon stick, or ½ tsp ground cinnamon
45g leeks or onions, chopped
2.5cm root ginger, peeled and finely chopped, or ½ tsp ground ginger
40g sultanas, chopped coarsely
125ml vegetable stock or water
1 tsp ground cumin
½ tsp turmeric
1 pinch of ground asafoetida (hing)
½ tsp ground coriander
1 tbsp tomato paste
1 tsp Bragg Liquid Aminos or tamari soy sauce
4 tbsp chopped fresh coriander
125ml low-fat coconut milk or light soya milk
1 tbsp lemon juice

Heat the ghee in a frying pan. Add the mustard seeds and let the seeds pop briefly. (The seeds can pop out of the pan.) Add the fenugreek, cardamom, chilli flakes, cinnamon, leeks, ginger and sultanas in that order and stir-fry for 5 minutes, adding a little of the stock if the mixtures begins to dry. Stir in the cumin, turmeric, asafoetida and coriander and add a little more stock, if necessary, then add the tomato paste and the aminos. Simmer for 2–3 minutes, then stir in the coriander, coconut milk and lemon juice.

❖ ❖ ❖ ❖

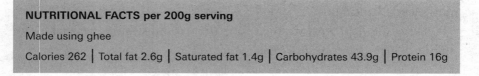

NUTRITIONAL FACTS per 200g serving
Made using ghee
Calories 262 | Total fat 2.6g | Saturated fat 1.4g | Carbohydrates 43.9g | Protein 16g

GHEE: THE GOLDEN OIL

Ghee is clarified butter. Ordinary butter contains about 80 per cent butterfat, 15 per cent water, 3 per cent salt and 1 to 2 per cent milk solids or curds. During the process of making ghee, the water is boiled off and the curds are cooked into a sediment that is easily removed. The result is a fragrant, flavourful oil that does not become rancid, even without refrigeration. In the tradition of Ayurveda, ghee is prized for its unique medicinal and balancing qualities. Even those with sensitivity to dairy products can usually enjoy ghee, as it is free of milk proteins and sugars. Ghee plays an important role in Indian and Ayurvedic cuisines, lending a subtle taste and fragrance to the food. It is heat tolerant, making it useful for quick stir-frying and browning.

You will need the following ingredients to make 350g of ghee:

> 450g organic unsalted butter
> large heavy-based, stainless-steel saucepan
> sieve
> piece of muslin for straining
> heat-resistant bowl or pan for straining the hot ghee into
> clear glass container with a tight-fitting lid

Place the butter into the saucepan. Bring the butter to the boil, then reduce the heat to produce a slow, steady rolling boil. Keep a constant eye on the butter to avoid burning it. Allow the foam that is produced to settle to the base of the pan. As the foam is reduced, it produces a crackling sound, which is due to moisture evaporating from the butter. Allow the butter to simmer for up to 30 minutes, and keep the heat on the hob as low as possible (use a heat diffuser if you have one). The ghee is complete when you see browned butterfat caramelized on the base of the pan, while the top portion of the ghee is mostly clear. Turn off the heat and leave the mixture to cool slightly, then strain it through the muslin into a heat-resistant container and allow it to cool completely before storing it in the clear glass jar. You can keep the ghee for up to one month without putting it in the fridge.

You can also make ghee in a slow-cooker on the lowest possible setting without the risk of burning it. It usually requires about 6 hours for the solids and moisture to completely separate, leaving the pure golden ghee.

Ghee is delicious drizzled on toast, porridge and rice; it adds flavour and character to any initial stir-frying for soups, sauces and stews. A teaspoon of ghee contains 5 grams of fat, 3 grams of saturated fat and 8 milligrams of cholesterol. A teaspoon of ghee each day in your cooking supplies 7.5% of your recommended daily fat, 15% of your saturated fat and 3% of your daily cholesterol intake. If your diet is otherwise low in saturated fat and cholesterol, ghee will make only a minor contribution.

If you wish to avoid completely the saturated fat and cholesterol of ghee, however, we recommend olive oil as a useful and tasty alternative. Olive oil is rich in the monounsaturated fatty acid, oleic acid. Diets rich in olive oil may help reduce cholesterol levels, lower high blood pressure and reduce the risk for colon cancer. Always use extra virgin olive oil, which meets the highest standards for purity. Most of the recipes in this book call for ghee or olive oil, which can be used interchangeably.

GINGER ELIXIR

A great way to fire up the digestive system is with a ginger elixir. Consider the ginger elixir your way to 'jump start' a sluggish digestive system. Take 30g of fresh root ginger elixir before lunch and dinner to kindle your digestive fire.

225ml fresh ginger juice (juiced from fresh root ginger; see below)
225ml lemon juice (4–6 lemons)
225ml purified water
85g raw and organic honey
¼ tsp ground black pepper

Cut a 7.5–10cm piece of unpeeled root ginger into 1cm slices. Using a powerful juicer, push the ginger through the juicer and juice enough ginger to make 225ml. Stir in the lemon juice, then whisk in the water, honey and pepper, whisking until well blended. Drink right before your meals to give your digestive tract a spark.

GINGER TEA

Ginger is known as the universal medicine and can be found in cuisines worldwide. Ginger tea has a strong cleansing effect on the body, helping to mobilize toxins and restore balance. Ginger tea benefits the digestive system and can help reduce cravings for sweet and salty items. Ginger helps soothe and cleanse the respiratory tract, making it a valuable tea during cold and flu season. We recommend that you drink two or three cups of hot ginger tea a day. Make it a habit. Try sweetening your tea with raw organic honey and chopped mint or lemon slices.

ONE LITRE OF GINGER TEA

Coarsely chop an unpeeled 5cm piece of root ginger. Place the pieces into a saucepan with 1 litre of purified water. Bring the water just to the boil, then reduce the heat to low and simmer for 15 minutes. Strain out the ginger pieces and put the tea into a thermos bottle or store in a glass jar and then reheat as needed. You can then use the ginger pieces from the tea in your vegetable stockpot (page 45).

ONE CUP OF GINGER TEA

Grate 1 heaping teaspoon of unpeeled root ginger into a cup of hot water. Allow the tea steep for 2 minutes, then strain or let the ginger settle to the bottom of the cup before drinking.

SIMPLE BASIC SOUP

This basic soup is perfect fare for a light dinner or as part of a hearty lunch. Select two or three different vegetables to create a soup, choosing from any of the following: acorn squash, asparagus, broccoli, butternut squash, carrots, cauliflower, celery, cooking greens, corn, courgettes, potato, pumpkin, spinach, sweet potato, tomatoes or yams.

~ SERVES 4 ~

1 tsp olive oil or ghee
25g leeks, onions or celery, chopped
1 pinch of ground black pepper
1 tsp dried dill
1 tsp thyme leaves
½ tsp ground nutmeg
1 tbsp Bragg liquid aminos or tamari soy sauce
450g mixed vegetables (see above), washed, prepared as necessary and cut into bite-sized pieces
900ml–1.2 litres vegetable stock, ideally home-made (see page 45)
1 recipe quantity Tofu Cream (recipe follows, optional)

Heat the oil in a stockpot or large saucepan. Add the leeks, pepper, dill, thyme, nutmeg and the aminos, and stir-fry until the leeks just begin to brown. Add the remaining vegetables and stir-fry for a further 3 or 4 minutes, making sure the vegetables are well coated with the spices. Pour on 900ml of the stock and bring to the boil. Reduce the heat and allow the soup to simmer at a gentle rolling boil for 10 minutes, or until the vegetables are tender. Take care not to over-cook them. The soup can be left chunky or puréed to a smooth consistency with an immersion blender, or in a blender or food processor. If desired, add the tofu cream (for additional protein) and continue to blend together. If the mixture is too thick, add the remaining stock. Gently reheat and serve.

NUTRITIONAL FACTS per 225ml serving

Made with olive oil, without tofu cream

Calories 72 | Total fat 1.5g | Saturated fat 0.3g | Carbohydrates 11.6g | Protein 2.9g

TOFU CREAM

125ml vegetable stock
125g firm or extra-firm tofu, ideally low-fat, cubed
1 tsp lemon juice or rice vinegar

Slowly combine all the ingredients with an immersion blender, or in a blender, until well mixed.

NUTRITIONAL FACTS

Made using low-fat tofu

Calories 79 | Total fat 2.6g | Saturated fat 0g | Carbohydrates 5.1g | Protein 8.8g

VEGETABLE STOCK

One of the most nutritious and practical kitchen projects is to make a large pot of vegetable stock. Your home-made vegetable stock will be fresh, salt-free and add valuable nutrients to your diet. The first step is to buy a large, flat plastic container that fits in your refrigerator and begin collecting the outer layers of vegetables that you would normally toss into the rubbish bin. These 'scraps' will make a delicious stock for your soups, sauces and stir-fries. Save the ends and peels from the following fruit and vegetables: apple cores, broccoli, carrots, cauliflower, leek ends, use onion skin sparingly, lemon or orange peels and any green bits and pieces, such as leaves and cores from lettuce or unappealing cooking greens. Just about any type of fruit, herb or vegetable scraps can go into a stockpot. However, avoid large amounts of green or red cabbage, beetroots, beetroot greens and banana peels, as they will all cause the soup stock to be cloudy or discoloured. Save all the discards in the plastic container for up to five days.

When you have a good supply, place all the scraps and discards into a stockpot or large saucepan and cover with water to 5cm above the scraps. Place the pan on the hob and bring to the boil, then reduce the heat and simmer for at least 1 hour. The vegetables will look very sad indeed after this cooking. Allow the stock to cool, then strain the liquid from the scraps and pour the resulting stock into glass or plastic containers. Label the top of the containers with a bold 'STOCK' sign and store in the fridge until you are ready to use. If you are an avid gardener, the vegetable scraps will be very welcomed in your compost pile.

Use the stock in place of extra oil for a low-fat cooking process. Keep it handy for use in making dahl, soups, sauces and stocks. In addition to its cooking uses, stock can be drunk as a relaxing and healing cup of nutritious broth, add a small amount of Bragg Liquid Aminos to each cup as it heats. After a few days, water your plants with the stock and make a new batch.

Equipment needed to make stock

large plastic container with tight-fitting lid that fits in the refrigerator
stockpot or large saucepan
glass or plastic containers
sieve

SAUTÉED FRUIT AND SYRUPS

Look in your fruit bowl. Towards the end of the week, you may discover overly ripe pieces of fruit that no one will eat – bananas with brown spots, softening apples, peaches with mushy spots. You might think these fruit belong in the rubbish, but actually, these are just the type of fruit that make the most flavourful fruit syrups, breakfast fruit chutneys and dessert fruit sautés.

Common fruit to sauté include apples, apricots, bananas, berries, peaches, pears and strawberries. Wash the fruit, then cut it into slices or bite-sized pieces. You may want to peel the fruit first, especially if the skin looks less than desirable. If is the skin's not too bad looking, however, leave it on as it provides important dietary fibre.

Sautéed fruit are easy to digest and make a great complement to any meal. Including fruit chutney or sautéed fruit in a meal is one way to ensure that you are incorporating the six tastes into a meal. Fruit are generally sweet or sour and when sautéed with spices and savoury ingredients, such as leeks, can balance any meal.

Keep a few bags of frozen berries in the freezer. Buy the best-quality product you can afford. Use the frozen fruit in desserts, muffins and as a wonderful complement to the hot morning cereals. Some great combinations include blueberries and bananas; raspberries and apples; mixed berries, cherries and apricots; and strawberries and mangos. Also try different sweet spices to create new tastes. Experiment with allspice, cardamom, cinnamon, cloves, ginger and nutmeg to enhance the flavour in fruit sautés.

SIMPLE FROZEN FRUIT SYRUP

~ SERVES 4 ~

300g frozen organic fruit (see choices below)
1 tsp ghee
½ tsp ground cinnamon
½ tsp ground nutmeg or cloves
1 tsp arrowroot, dissolved in 1 tbsp fruit juice (optional)
1 tbsp apple or other fruit juice (optional)
2 tbsp maple syrup

Heat the ghee in a small frying pan. Add the frozen fruit, then as the fruit thaws and the liquid begins to fill the pan, simmer over a low heat for 3–4 minutes until the liquid reduces. As the fruit simmers, add the spices. If the fruit is too juicy, add the dissolved arrowroot to the syrup as it simmers. It the mixture begins to dry out, add the extra juice. Continue simmering until the syrup is the consistency of maple syrup. Stir the maple syrup into the hot fruit just before serving. Serve spooned over pancakes, hot cereal, dessert cakes and ice cream.

Recommended frozen fruit choices: blackberries, blueberries, cherries, mango, raspberries and strawberries.

❖ ❖ ❖ ❖

NUTRITIONAL FACTS per 75g serving

Made with frozen strawberries

Calories 90 | Total fat 1.4g | Saturated fat 0.8g | Carbohydrates 18.9g | Protein 0.6g

SIMPLE FRUIT SAUTÉ

~ SERVES 4 ~

1 tsp ghee
350g fruit, prepared as necessary and sliced or cubed (see choices listed below)
2 tbsp apple or other fruit juice, plus extra if needed
2 tbsp sultanas, cranberries or currants (optional)
½ tsp ground cinnamon
½ tsp ground nutmeg
2 tbsp maple syrup

Heat the ghee in a small frying pan over a medium heat. Add the fruit and simmer for 2 minutes. Add the juice, dried fruit, if including, and spices and continue simmering for 4–5 minutes until the fruit is almost soft. Add a little bit more juice if the mixture appears to be drying out. Stir the maple syrup in just before serving. Use this simple sauté as a dessert or breakfast fruit.

Recommended fruit choices are apples, apricots, blackberries, blueberries, figs, nectarines, peaches, persimmons, plums and strawberries.

❖ ❖ ❖ ❖

NUTRITIONAL FACTS per 75g serving

Made with apples

Calories 99 | Total fat 1.4g | Saturated fat 0.8g | Carbohydrates 21.1g | Protein 0.3g

SIMPLE GREAT WHOLEGRAIN BREAD

~ MAKES 2 LOAVES; 8 SLICES PER LOAF ~

2 tbsp dried yeast
2 tbsp turbinado sugar
900ml water, very warm
660g wholemeal pastry flour
660g strong wholemeal flour, plus extra for kneading
1 tbsp salt
Seasonings (see options below)
1 tbsp olive oil (optional), plus a little for greasing the bowl and baking
sheet or loaf tins
Olive oil or vegetable spray (optional)

Dissolve the yeast and sugar in the water in a large metal, ceramic or glass bowl and set aside until the yeast becomes frothy. Meanwhile, sift together the flours, salt and your choice of seasonings, tipping in any bran left in the sieve. Make a well in the centre of the flours.

When the yeast has foamed, add it to the flour mixture. Use your hands to mix the flour and yeast mixtures together until a soft dough forms. Knead the dough on a lightly floured work surface for about 5 minutes or until it is smooth and elastic. Place the dough in a greased bowl, cover and leave to rise in a warm place for 1 hour or until doubled in size.

Meanwhile, preheat the oven to 180°C/Gas mark 4 and lightly grease a baking sheet or 2 loaf tins.

When the dough has risen, turn it out on to a floured surface and punch it down with your hand to release the air and flatten. Knead the dough for 3–4 minutes, then form the dough into 2 loaves – or rolls, cinnamon rolls, flat bread or pizza – and place on the baking sheet or in the tins. Allow the loaves to rise again for 10–15 minutes. Place the dough in the oven and bake for 30 minutes, or until the loaves are browned, crusty and hollow sounding when tapped on the bottoms. Spray water or oil on to the bread towards the end of the baking time to add a crusty texture. Transfer the loaves to wire rack to cool before cutting.

Any of the following optional ingredients can be added to the flour before adding the yeast:

225g sautéed apples with 1 tbsp ground cinnamon or sage
150g raisins mixed with 1 tbsp ground cinnamon
55g chopped cranberries, 70g chopped blanched almonds and 1 tsp ground nutmeg
75g chopped dates, 30g chopped walnut halves, 1 tbsp dried basil and 1 tsp ground allspice
2 tbsp flax seeds, sesame seeds, roasted fennel seeds or caraway seeds
4 tbsp chopped fresh basil, cilantro, marjoram, rosemary or thyme – or a combination of herbs
45g sautéed leeks or onions
4 tbsp sliced kalamata olives and 1 tbsp dried rosemary

NUTRITIONAL FACTS per slice

Made with olive oil but no optional ingredients

Calories 156 | Total fat 1.4g | Saturated fat 0.3g | Carbohydrates 30.4g | Protein 5.8g

SIMPLE MARINADE
FOR TOFU AND TEMPEH

~ SERVES 4 ~

175ml Bragg Liquid Aminos or tamari soy sauce
175ml rice vinegar
2 tbsp balsamic vinegar
2 tbsp maple syrup
1 tsp ground ginger
1 tsp ground cumin
½ tsp red chilli flakes
1 tsp sesame oil
450g firm or extra-firm tofu or tempeh, ideally low-fat, cut into 0.5cm
slices or cubed

Combine all the ingredients, except the tofu, in a shallow baking tin and mix together. Add the tofu or tempeh and refrigerate overnight.

Or, to speed up the process, preheat the oven to 180°C/Gas mark 4. Place the tin in the oven and bake for 20–30 minutes. Remove the tofu from the marinade and allow it to cool completely. Use it in a variety of dishes, such as stir-fries, sandwiches, casseroles, soups and stews.

❖ ❖ ❖ ❖

NUTRITIONAL FACTS per 12g serving.

Made using low-fat tofu

Calories 215 | Total fat 6.5g | Saturated fat 0.2g | Carbohydrates 16.5g | Protein 22.5g

SIMPLE WHITE SAUCE: BASIC ROUX

Use this sauce as a base for soups, stews and casseroles. There are many variations that can be utilized to change the character of this basic sauce. Add cheese, herbs, marinated cubed tofu and steamed vegetables. Blend the sauce with steamed vegetables to make a vegetable soup, add it to a stew to thicken it, use it as the base of your favourite Alfredo sauce, or make a cheesy sauce for macaroni and cheese.

~ SERVES 4 ~

1 tbsp ghee or olive oil
1 pinch of ground black pepper or red chilli flakes
45g leeks or onions, chopped
1 tbsp Bragg Liquid Aminos or tamari soy sauce
2 tbsp wholemeal pastry flour or unbleached plain white flour
225ml light soya milk

Heat the ghee in a saucepan. Add the leeks and stir-fry for 1 minute. Stir in the pepper and aminos and continue frying until the leeks are lightly browned. Whisk in the flour and continue whisking until it browns slightly. Slowly pour in the soya milk, whisking constantly. Use the amount of soya milk that creates the thickness you desire – less for a thick sauce, more for a thinner sauce.

◈ ◈ ◈ ◈

NUTRITIONAL FACTS per one-quarter of the recipe
Calories 79 | Total fat 4.5g | Saturated fat 2.8g | Carbohydrates 7.3g | Protein 2.5g

SOYA: THE PERFECT FOOD

Non-vegetarians and vegetarians alike will benefit from including soya-based products in their daily diet. Over the past 30 years, the taste, texture and quality of soya-based products has improved greatly. Some of the soya products available today include: soya cheese, soya burgers, tofu ice cream, tofu breakfast 'sausages', ground 'meat', soya 'cold cuts' and soya 'hot dogs'.

Soybeans are an important source of phyto-estrogens. Phyto-estrogens are naturally occurring plant-based substances that contain chemicals related to the hormones produced by mammals. One type of phyto-estrogen called isoflavones has been credited with many health-promoting benefits. Including soya products in your diet may help to reduce the risk of osteoporosis and some of the uncomfortable symptoms of the menopause. Studies have shown that the daily use of soya products may also help lower cholesterol levels and protect against certain types of cancer. Soybeans are rich in protein, iron, B-vitamins and zinc. Soya products also provide a good source of omega-3 and omega-6 fatty acids. We recommend the regular use of soya products in a well-balanced diet.

Soya Products

Tempeh is a type of fermented soybean cake originally from Indonesia. It is made from the whole soybeans and is high in protein. Like tofu (below), tempeh can be marinated to enhance its flavour. Use tempeh as a minced-meat replacement in chilli, Italian sauces, savoury casseroles and Mexican dishes.

Tofu, originally from Japan, is composed of fermented soybeans made into a concentrated cheese-like form. Tofu is astringent, sweet, cooling, heavy and mild tasting. It is very versatile and will take on the flavours of any food with which it is cooked, making it suitable to combine with flavourful, warming spices. It is high in calcium, iron and phosphorus, and is easy to digest. There are two types of tofu: fresh tofu, packaged in water, and silken tofu, which is best used in sauces. We generally recommend using firm or extra-firm tofu, and ideally the low-fat version.

Soya milk is the liquid that comes from soybeans that have been cooked and pressed, and it can be used to replace cow's milk in many recipes. Soya milk is naturally high in calcium and contains no cholesterol. You will find it flavoured with chocolate, strawberries and vanilla, or just plain. Plain soya milk is also sold in a light version, which we recommend. When a recipe calls for a reduced level of fat and a vanilla flavour we suggest you add a little vanilla extract to the light soya milk.

Textured Vegetable Protein (TVP) is made from defatted soya flakes. It is a dried, granular product, often sold in bulk at natural food shops. TVP needs to be reconstituted in liquid to become soft and flavourful, and marinades work particularly well with it. Use TVP in recipes that would normally include minced meat.

Fresh soybeans (edamame) are high in protein and phyto-estrogens, and look much like Chinese mangetouts. They are best eaten steamed, which takes about 20 minutes. They can be found in most food stores and Asian markets, either fresh or frozen.

Cooking Tofu or Tempeh

Marinating tofu or tempeh overnight allows the flavours to incorporate into these otherwise bland foods. To speed up the process, place the tofu or tempeh and the marinade into a cake tin and place in a preheated oven at 180°C/Gas mark 4 for 20–30 minutes. Keep some marinated tofu on hand in the refrigerator. Use slabs of marinated tofu in sandwiches, cubed in stir-fries or crumbled for breakfast sautés.

VERY BEST DAIRY-FREE MUFFINS

~ MAKES 12 MUFFINS ~

Vegetable oil spray for the muffin tin
290g wholemeal pastry flour or spelt flour
110g turbinado sugar
1 tsp ground cinnamon
1 tsp finely grated lemon rind
2 tsp baking powder
½ tsp bicarbonate of soda
½ tsp salt
225ml light soya milk or rice milk
A few drops of vanilla extract, to taste
2 tbsp rapeseed oil
80g maple syrup
185g mango purée, mashed banana or apple sauce
75g fresh, thawed or dried fruit

Preheat the oven to 180°C/Gas mark 4 and spray a deep, American-style muffin tin with 12 holes with oil, then set aside. Stir the flour, sugar, cinnamon, lemon rind, baking powder, bicarbonate of soda and salt together in a bowl with a wire whisk. Combine the soya milk, vanilla, oil, maple syrup, fruit purée and fruit in a separate large bowl. Add the dry ingredients to the wet ingredients and combine gently with a rubber spatula. Spoon the mixture into the muffin tin, filling each hole about two-thirds full. Put the tin in the oven and bake for 15–20 minutes until the muffins are golden brown and a wooden cocktail stick inserted in the centre of each one comes out clean. Immediately tip the muffins out of the tin on to a wire rack and leave to cool.

❖ ❖ ❖ ❖

NUTRITIONAL FACTS per muffin

Calories 178 | Total fat 2.7g | Saturated fat 0.4g | Carbohydrates 36.1g | Protein 2.5g

WHOLEGRAIN BAKED GOODIES

'Open thine eyes, and thou shalt be satisfied with bread'
PROVERBS 20:13

Bread is the staff of life, the foundation of our soul, the memory of ancient wisdom and the treasure of the ages. In every culture, tradition, religion and cuisine, bread has always captured the human heart and soul with aroma, taste, texture, romance and intrigue – always challenging our resistance to indulge in more. Why do we love home-made bread so? Someone – our mother, wife, lover or friend – has put much love and attention into the bread: carefully and gently combining the yeast and sugar with not too hot nor too cold water; mixing the stoneground wheat, then kneading with the energy that comes only from within. With every stroke of attention creating soft and flexible dough to sculpt into a vision of perfection – a loaf of bread, a batch of sweet cinnamon rolls, an abundant pizza, pitta bread for a dip, a pastry filled with savoury delight.

Baking is a gift. You don't need to be gifted to bake; baking is a gift to be shared. As part of a healthy balanced diet, freshly baked biscuits, breads, cakes, muffins, fresh pastas and freshly cooked whole grains bring sweetness into our lives, adding comfort and pleasure. Using the highest-quality organic ingredients – whole grains, fresh organic butter and milk, raw and natural sugars and spices – your baked goods will be not only delicious but also very nutritious and fulfilling.

GREAT GREENS

There are numerous benefits to incorporating greens into your diet, and there are many varieties of greens available these days. Greens are high in calcium, Vitamin A, Vitamin C, Vitamin K, Vitamin E and numerous phyto-nutrients. In a healthy, well-balanced diet, greens play an important role in reducing the risk of heart disease, cancer and other ailments. We recommend that a serving of greens be part of your daily diet.

Let's look at some of the common greens available. Purchase organic whenever possible. Green choices can also include spinach, mustard, and beetroot greens.

Chard has a slightly bitter, yet mild taste. Also called Swiss Chard, it is a member of the beetroot family. The leaves can be red, white or rainbow in colour, and it is good for improving bowel function. Chard is easy to grow in the garden.

Collards are part of the kale and cabbage family. They are mild and very popular in American Deep South cooking. Kale has a crisp and sweet taste when young, and gets bitter as it matures. It is helpful in building immune strength, easing congestion and aiding in digestion. Kale is an excellent source for calcium, iron and vitamins A and C.

Pak choy is a sweet, crisp, cooling and mild-tasting green. It comes from China and is beneficial in cooling the body and reducing mucus in the system.

Rocket has a sharp, bitter and peppery taste. It is originally from the Mediterranean region where it is considered an aphrodisiac. This tasty green is excellent for stimulating digestion. Rocket is easy to grow and mixes well with other greens.

BASIC MIXED VEGETABLE STIR-FRY

~ SERVES 4 ~

1 tsp ghee or olive oil
45g leeks or onions, chopped coarsely
½ tsp ground black pepper
1 tbsp Bragg Liquid Aminos or tamari soy sauce, plus extra to serve
(optional)
110g cauliflower, cut into small florets
125g carrots, sliced thinly
90g broccoli, cut into small florets
125g courgette, cut into 0.5cm half-moon slices
60g baby spinach leaves, rinsed
1 tsp dried dill
1 tsp ground cumin
60–125ml vegetable stock
Balsamic vinegar, to serve (optional)

Heat a large wok or frying pan over a high heat. Add the ghee, leeks, pepper and the aminos and stir-fry for 2–3 minutes until the leeks begin soften. Add the cauliflower and carrots and pour in 60ml vegetable stock to help speed up the cooking process. Continue stir-frying for 4–5 minutes until the liquid evaporates, then add the broccoli and courgette and stir-fry for a further 2 minutes. Add the spinach, dill and cumin and a small amount of additional stock, if necessary, and keep stir-frying until all the vegetables are al dente, or just tender. Remove the wok from heat. An extra teaspoon of aminos or balsamic vinegar sprinkled on top of the stir-fried vegetables will add to the character of the vegetables. Serve with a chutney or spicy sauce.

NUTRITIONAL FACTS per 150g serving

Made using ghee

Calories 54 | Total fat 1.6g | Saturated fat 0.8g | Carbohydrates 7.4g | Protein 2.7g

BASIC ROASTED VEGETABLES

~ SERVES 4 ~

Olive oil spray for the roasting tin
2 tsp ghee or olive oil
1 tbsp Bragg Liquid Aminos or tamari soy sauce
1 tbsp balsamic vinegar
1 tbsp dried basil
½ tsp ground black pepper
1 tsp dried dill
80g aubergine, peeled and cut into 1cm cubes
135g yam, peeled and cut into 1cm cubes
135g asparagus, trimmed and cut into 2.5cm pieces
125g carrots, cut into 0.5cm slices

Preheat the oven to 180°C/Gas mark 4 and spray a roasting tin with olive oil, then set aside. Combine the ghee, aminos, vinegar, basil, pepper and dill in a large bowl and whisk together with a fork. Add the prepared vegetables to the bowl. With plastic sandwich bags on your hands, combine the vegetables and the oil mixture until the vegetables are well coated. Spread the vegetables out in the tin. Place the tin in the oven and roast for 20–30 minutes until the vegetables are tender. As an alternative, you can thinly slice the vegetables, toss in the oil mixture and grill the vegetables on a barbecue – just remember to spray the rack with olive oil first.

SPICING VARIATION

Replace the basil with 1 teaspoon curry powder and 1 teaspoon garam masala.

NUTRITIONAL FACTS per 105g serving

Made using ghee

Calories 95 | Total fat 2.8g | Saturated fat 1.6g | Carbohydrates 14.8g | Protein 2.6g

SIMPLY VEGETABLES

Eat your vegetables! Vegetables play a predominant role in a healthy, well-balanced diet. If you include at least five servings of fruit and vegetables each day in your diet, you will need to eat a variety of them. How can you cook vegetables so you and your family (even the kids) will really like them and want to eat them? Be creative and mix colours and flavours that appeal to you. Our favourite combinations include: carrots and broccoli, cauliflower and greens, aubergines and sweet potatoes, and courgettes and tomatoes. There are many different ways to cook vegetables, such as roasting, stir-frying, steaming, braising and blanching. You can also include vegetables in many soups, stews, sauces and casseroles.

In the Ayurvedic approach to eating, we recommend that most vegetables and fruit be lightly cooked or steamed to aid in digestibility. This does not mean that you should avoid fresh salads made with beautiful organic cucumbers, tomatoes, shredded carrots, sprouts and organic field greens. For ease in digestion, however, we recommend that cold foods, such as a salad, always be eaten before a soup or hot main dish. People with delicate digestive systems should mostly eat slightly cooked or steamed vegetables for ease of digestion and comfort. A wonderful way to add greens to your meal is to place a handful of salad greens, such as field greens, spinach, watercress or rocket, on the plate then add hot steaming grains or vegetables on top to lightly steam the greens. It also makes the plate look beautiful.

Preparing Vegetables

Plan on 135–175g of different vegetables per person at each meal and at least 140g of greens per person. That may look like quite a large amount but they reduce in volume during the cooking process. Start with your favourite vegetables. Peeling vegetables is not necessary if you are using organic vegetables. The skins of most vegetables are abundant in vital nutrients and fibre so it is best to keep them on whenever possible. Wash all fruit and vegetables, organic or non-organic, before you use them. (Remember to keep all the washed ends and scraps for your stockpot – see page 45.) Most varieties of squash are best peeled, unless you are using the squash as a 'boat'.

Use lots of fresh and dried herbs with your vegetables. Not only will the vegetables taste better, you will benefit from the medicinal qualities found in them. As mentioned in the Condiments and Baking Supplies in The Basics of Nourishment (see page 22), we also recommend the use of a product called Bragg Liquid Aminos that can be found in most health food shops. It is a non-fermented soya-based product that provides a savoury and salty taste similar to soy sauce. Use it to flavour vegetables. If you can't find it, substitute tamari soy sauce.

Vegetables should always be cooked al dente, or almost tender, but cook them longer to make them easier to digest for anyone with a delicate digestive system. Begin your stir-fry or steaming process with the vegetables that will take the longest time to cook, such as cauliflower, asparagus, carrots, potatoes, squash and any other 'hard' vegetables. They will take 5–6 minutes to cook to a tender stage, whereas broccoli, green beans, courgettes and other 'soft' vegetables will take only 3–4 minutes. Time your vegetables accordingly.

STIR-FRIED GREENS

~ SERVES 4 ~

Very fast and easy to cook, greens provide a source of the 'bitter' taste in your meals. Use about 140g fresh greens per person. Heat 1 teaspoon ghee or olive oil and 1 tablespoon vegetable stock in a large frying pan. Add a pinch of ground pepper and 330–440g assorted cooking greens (see the list on the previous page) and stir-fry until the greens are slightly wilted but still maintain a vibrant green colour. Sprinkle with balsamic vinegar and serve.

❖ ❖ ❖ ❖

NUTRITIONAL FACTS per 35g serving

Made using olive oil

Calories 32 | Total fat 1.3g | Saturated fat 0.2g | Carbohydrates 3.7g | Protein 1.4g

COOKED GRAINS

Freshly cooked whole grains provide an excellent source of carbohydrates, nutrients and fibre. Grains also provide the sweet taste for balancing the diet. All grains can be cooked on the hob and most grains can also be cooked in a rice cooker. Most grains require two to four parts water to one part dry grain, but read the recommended ratio on the packaging or check the chart below. If you prefer using a rice cooker, try to find one with a stainless-steel insert rather than an aluminium one. Whichever method you choose, rinse the grains first and dry them in a wire strainer before cooking, and be on the lookout for small rocks or twigs.

Cooking on the Hob

Cover the pan and bring the water and grains to the boil, then reduce the heat to the lowest possible temperature (use a heat diffuser if you have one). Most grains cook best when left alone. Don't be tempted to raise the lid and look inside. If the temperature is as low as possible and the appropriate amount of water is used, the grain will cook to a perfect consistency if you resist looking inside. Try lightly stir-frying the grains in a dry pan before adding the water. The heat will release the flavour and lightly toast the grain, imparting a rich, nutty flavour. Experiment with your favourite grains.

Cooking Grains Table

Use vegetable stock or purified water for cooking grains. Add a pinch of salt, herbs or spices to enhance the flavours.

~ SERVES 4 ~

Grain (200g)	Liquid (225ml)	Cooking time (minutes)
basmati rice	2	15–20
brown rice	2	45
buckwheat/kasha	2	20–30
bulgur wheat *	1½	15
couscous *	1½	7
millet	2½	30
oat groats	3	40
pearl barley	4	45
polenta	3½	15
porridge oats	3	15
quinoa	2	15–20

* Couscous and bulgur wheat are not cooked, but absorb the added liquid. To prepare, bring the liquid to the boil, then add the grain and remove the pan from the heat. Stir and place a lid on top of the pan, then set aside and allow the grain to rest for the appropriate time. Fluff with a fork before using in your favourite recipe.

NUTRITIONAL FACTS

Per 1 cup of uncooked grain (weights given below)

Grains	Calories	Total fat	Sat. fat	Carbs	Protein
brown rice (130g)	170	1.4	0.3	35.7	3.7
bulgur (225g)	147	0.6	0.1	32.0	3.5
couscous (230g)	158	0.3	0.1	33.5	5.5
groats/kasha (170g)	152	1.1	0.2	30.7	4.8
millet (200g)	187	2.1	0.4	36.4	5.5
pearl barley (200g)	181	0.6	0.1	38.9	5.0
polenta (165g)	124	0.6	0.1	26.8	2.9
quinoa (175g)	158	2.9	0	28.0	5.0
rice (210g)	171	0.3	0.1	38.7	3.2
rolled oats (100g)	154	2.7	0.5	25.8	6.6

Remember: Delicious meals begin with wholesome basic ingredients. Approach cooking as a unique opportunity to express your creativity. Like any artistic endeavour, cooking will yield wonderful results if the ingredients are the best quality and the artist (you, the cook) has the intention to create something wonderful.

BREAKFAST AND
BAKED GOODIES

'Breakfast is a forecast of the whole day: Spoil that and all is spoiled'
— LEIGH HUNT

We provide breakfast recipes for every occasion. For a breakfast on the run try Breakfast Bars and Almond Bliss Shake. For a morning when you are hungry and crave a big healthy meal, there is Broccoli Tofu Scramble, Strawberry Banana Yogurt and Courgette Pecan Bread. For a Sunday morning brunch extravaganza try Wholemeal Crêpes with Blueberry Syrup, Country Potatoes with Mango Tomato Salsa (page 113) and Coffee Bliss Shakes. Listen to your body's signal of hunger in the morning and eat accordingly.

One of our favourite breakfasts here at The Chopra Center includes a small bowl of Hot Grain Cereal served with Sautéed Mixed Berries, topped with a sprinkle of Chopra Granola, soya milk and maple syrup. This breakfast includes all the six tastes, is balanced nutritionally and is very satisfying.

BREAKFAST INDEX

Almond Bliss Shake
Apple Maple Yogurt
Apple Raisin Muffins
Apple and Rice Hot Cereal
Apple Syrup (Variations: Apricot, Pear, Nectarine)
Blueberry Banana Syrup (Variations: Strawberry,
Raspberry, Blackberry)
Blueberry Muffins
Breakfast Bars
Breakfast Burritos
Broccoli Tofu Scramble
Cardamom Wholemeal Pancakes
Chai Bliss Shake
Chopra Granola
Cinnamon Rolls
Coffee Bliss Shake
Country Potatoes
Courgette Pecan Bread
Home-made Almond Butter
Hot Breakfast Cereal (Rolled Oats, Rice, Quinoa, Millet,
Couscous and Polenta)
Mango Bliss Shake
Mango Yogurt
Masala Potatoes
Morning Bliss Shake
Nutty French Toast
Pumpkin Muffins
Seasonal Fruit Salad
Strawberry Banana Yogurt
Tempeh and Potato Hash
Tofu and Potato Italiano
Traditional French Toast
Vegetable Tofu Scramble
Very Berry Yogurt
Wholemeal Crêpes, Sweet or Savoury

ALMOND BLISS SHAKE

~ SERVES 1 ~

1 tbsp almond butter
2 tsp raw organic honey or maple syrup
1 scoop plain or vanilla soya protein powder
1 pinch of grated nutmeg
1 pinch of ground cardamom
225ml light soya milk or rice milk
A few drops of vanilla extract, to taste
1 banana, sliced

Place all the ingredients into a blender and blend until smooth.

NUTRITIONAL FACTS per serving

Calories 487 | Total fat 12.4g | Saturated fat 3.3g | Carbohydrates 61.1g |
Protein 32.9g

APPLE MAPLE YOGURT

~ SERVES 4 ~

1 tsp ghee
1 large apple, peeled or unpeeled, and chopped into 1cm pieces
1 tsp ground cinnamon
½ tsp ground nutmeg
1 tbsp apple juice
2 tbsp maple syrup
450g low-fat vanilla yogurt

Heat the ghee in a small frying pan. Add the apple, cinnamon and nutmeg and simmer, stirring, for 3–4 minutes. Stir in the apple juice when the mixture gets dry. Remove the pan from the heat and transfer the apples into a mixing bowl. Allow the apples to cool slightly, then pour the maple syrup and the yogurt on top of the apples and stir until well combined. Serve for breakfast with fruit, granola and hot cereals, and also as a cooling side dish.

NUTRITIONAL FACTS per 175g serving
Calories 184 | Total fat 3.1g | Saturated fat 1.9g | Carbohydrates 33g | Protein 6.1g

APPLE RAISIN MUFFINS

~ MAKES 12 MUFFINS ~

Vegetable spray for the muffin tin
370g wholemeal pastry flour or spelt flour
55g turbinado sugar
2 tsp baking powder
½ tsp bicarbonate of soda
½ tsp ground nutmeg
1 tsp ground cinnamon
150g raisins or currants
60g walnut halves, chopped
225ml apple juice
60g apple sauce
1 tbsp rapeseed oil
4 tbsp maple syrup
1 vanilla extract
1 medium egg, beaten, or 2 egg whites
250g apple, unpeeled and grated or finely chopped

Preheat the oven to 180°C/Gas mark 4. Spray a 12-hole deep American-style muffin tin with oil and set aside. Combine the flour, sugar, baking powder, bicarbonate of soda, nutmeg, cinnamon, raisins and walnuts in a bowl and use a wire whisk to stir together. Combine the apple juice, apple sauce, oil, maple syrup and vanilla in a separate bowl, then stir in the egg and the grated apple. Add the dry ingredients to the wet ingredients and combine gently. Spoon the mixture into the muffin tin, filling each hole about two-thirds full. Bake for 15–20 minutes until golden brown and a cocktail stick inserted in the centre of each muffin comes out clean. Tip the muffins out of the tin and transfer to a wire rack to cool.

NUTRITIONAL FACTS per muffin

Calories 234 | Total fat 5g | Saturated fat 0.5g | Carbohydrates 42g | Protein 4.9g

APPLE AND RICE HOT CEREAL

~ SERVES 4 ~

600ml light soya milk or rice milk
200g basmati rice, rinsed
1 cinnamon stick
3 cardamom pods
3 large apples, such as Granny Smith or a pippin, unpeeled and cubed
35g currants
60–125ml apple juice
1 tbsp lemon juice
1 tsp ground cinnamon
½ tsp ground nutmeg
1 tsp vanilla extract
1 tbsp maple syrup
1 tbsp coconut flakes, toasted
60g walnut halves, toasted

Bring the soya milk and rice to the boil in a large saucepan. Add the cinnamon stick and the cardamom pods, reduce the heat to the lowest possible level, cover and simmer for 15–20 minutes until the rice is tender. Fluff the rice with a fork and set aside.

Bring the apple juice to the boil in a large frying pan. Add the apples, currants, lemon juice, cinnamon and nutmeg, then reduce the heat and simmer for 5 minutes, adding more juice if necessary. Remove the pan from the heat and stir in the vanilla and maple syrup. Place the rice into a serving bowl or individual bowls. Spoon the apple mixture over the rice and drizzle some of the juice on top. Garnish with the walnuts and toasted coconut.

❖ ❖ ❖ ❖

NUTRITIONAL FACTS per 150g serving

Calories 382 | Total fat 6.8g | Saturated fat 2g | Carbohydrates 71.9g | Protein 8.2g

APPLE SYRUP

~ SERVES 4 ~

1 tsp ghee
2 large apple, unpeeled and cut into 1cm chunks
2 tbsp currants, raisins or dried cranberries
1 tsp ground cinnamon
¼ tsp ground nutmeg
125ml apple juice
1 tbsp lemon or orange juice
2 tbsp maple syrup

Melt the ghee in a small saucepan. Add the apples, currants, cinnamon, nutmeg and apple juice and simmer, stirring, for 2 minutes. Add the lemon juice and continue simmering for a further 3–4 minutes until the apples are lightly cooked. Just before serving, stir in the maple syrup, stirring until the apples are well coated. Serve warm or chilled. The quantities for all the ingredients and spices can be adjusted according to your taste.

VARIATIONS
Use 6 apricots, 3 pears or 3 nectarines instead of the apples.

❖ ❖ ❖ ❖

NUTRITIONAL FACTS per 125g serving

Calories 124 | Total fat 1.6g | Saturated fat 0.9g | Carbohydrates 27.1g | Protein 0.3g

BLUEBERRY BANANA SYRUP

~ SERVES 4 ~

1 tsp ghee
300g blueberries, thawed if frozen
150g banana, sliced
½ tsp ground nutmeg
¼ tsp ground cloves
2 tbsp apple juice, orange juice or lemon juice
1 tsp arrowroot
2 tbsp maple syrup

Melt the ghee in a small saucepan. Add the blueberries, banana, nutmeg, cloves and apple juice and simmer, stirring, for 3–4 minutes for fresh berries and 5–8 minutes for frozen berries, until the liquid begins to evaporate. To thicken the sauce, dissolve the arrowroot in 1 tablespoon water, add to the berries and stir until a smooth consistency is achieved. Stir in the maple syrup just before serving. Pour over breakfast cereal or use as a dessert topping.

VARIATIONS
Use blackberries, nectarines, peaches, raspberries or strawberries instead of blueberries

❖ ❖ ❖ ❖

NUTRITIONAL FACTS per 50g serving
Calories 123 | Total fat 1.9g | Saturated fat 1.1g | Carbohydrates 25.9g | Protein 0.8g

BLUEBERRY MUFFINS

~ MAKES 12 MUFFINS ~

Vegetable spray for the muffin tin
290g wholemeal pastry flour or spelt flour
55g turbinado sugar
2 tsp baking powder
½ tsp bicarbonate of soda
½ tsp salt
1 tsp ground cinnamon
1 tbsp finely grated lemon rind
225ml light soya milk or rice milk
A few drops of vanilla extract, to taste
1 tbsp rapeseed oil
120g mango purée or apple sauce
4 tbsp maple syrup
300g blueberries, thawed if frozen

Preheat the oven to 180°C/Gas mark 4. Spray a 12-hole deep American-style muffin tin with oil and set aside. Combine the flour, sugar, baking powder, bicarbonate of soda, salt, cinnamon and lemon rind in a bowl and use a wire whisk to stir together. Combine the soya milk, oil, fruit purée, maple syrup and the blueberries in separate bowl. Add the dry ingredients into the wet ingredients and combine gently. Spoon the mixture into the tin, filling each hole about two-thirds full. Bake for 15–20 minutes until golden brown and a cocktail stick inserted in the centre of each one comes out clean. Tip the muffins out of the tin and transfer to a wire rack to cool.

❖ ❖ ❖ ❖

NUTRITIONAL FACTS per muffin

Calories 138 | Total fat 1.7g | Saturated fat 0.4g | Carbohydrates 27.6g | Protein 2.9g

BREAKFAST BARS

~ 12 SERVINGS ~

Vegetable oil spray for the baking tin
160g organic porridge oats
165g wholemeal pastry flour or oat flour
1 tbsp flax seeds
1 tbsp sesame seeds
1 tsp baking powder
½ tsp salt
145g currants or dried cranberries
50g hulled sunflower seeds, pecans or cashew pieces
90g coconut flakes
1 tsp ground cinnamon
1 tsp ground nutmeg
1 tsp ground ginger
55g turbinado sugar
350ml light soya milk or rice milk
A few drops of vanilla extract, to taste
4 tbsp maple syrup
4 tbsp rapeseed oil or ghee
60g mango purée or apple sauce

TOPPING

1 tbsp turbinado sugar
1 tbsp ground cinnamon

Preheat the oven to 180°C/Gas mark 4. Spray a 32.5 × 22.5cm baking tin with oil. Put the oats, flour, flax seeds, sesame seeds, baking powder, salt, cranberries, sunflower seeds, coconut flakes, cinnamon, nutmeg, ginger and sugar in a bowl and use a wire whisk to stir together. Place the soya milk, vanilla extract, maple syrup, oil, mango purée and sugar in a larger bowl and whisk together. Add the dry ingredients to the wet ingredients and use a rubber spatula to gently combine. Be as gentle as possible while mixing the two together. Transfer the mixture to the prepared pan and distribute evenly, gently patting into place with the spatula. Combine the cinnamon and the sugar for the topping and sprinkle over the mixture. Bake for about 30 minutes until the bars are golden brown and a cocktail stick inserted in the centre comes out clean. Leave to cool in the pan on a wire rack. When cool, cut into 12 bars and wrap individually. Breakfast bars are great as a breakfast-on-the-run or as a healthy, handy snack.

NUTRITIONAL FACTS per 5 x 5cm bar

Calories 339 | Total fat 11.4g | saturated fat 3g | Carbohydrates 50.9g | Protein 8.2g

BREAKFAST BURRITOS

Be creative. This is a great way to make quick, healthy meals and snacks. They are great for children's lunch boxes, too.

~ SERVES 4 ~

Vegetable oil spray for the baking sheet
4 wholemeal or plain tortillas, each 20cm or larger
8 tbsp grated Cheddar cheese (optional)
About 300g burrito filling, see suggestions on the following page
4 tbsp tomato salsa

Preheat the oven to 180°C/Gas mark 4. Lightly spray a baking sheet with vegetable oil. Arrange the tortillas on top and sprinkle with the cheese. Place the filling of your choice in the centre and add the salsa, spreading all the ingredients to the edge of the tortilla. Place the baking sheet in the oven for 5 minutes, or until the cheese has melted. Remove from the oven and gently roll the tortilla into a rectangle by folding in two of the sides and then rolling the mixture over into a box shape.

   To prepare one burrito, place the tortilla in a heated frying pan, add the ingredients and heat until the cheese has melted.

BURRITO FILLING SUGGESTIONS:

Tempeh and Potato Hash (page 100)

Tofu and Potato Italiano (page 101)

Vegetable Tofu Scramble (page 103)

Vegetable stir-fries

Refried pinto beans, rice and guacamole

Country Potatoes (page 87), topped with chopped soya 'bacon' or soya 'sausage'

Black beans, rice and tomato salsa

Sautéed apples

Rice and bananas with almond butter, drizzled with honey

NUTRITIONAL FACTS per 20cm burrito

Made with wholemeal tortillas, cheese and salsa

Calories 213 | Total fat 8.6g | Saturated fat 4.3g | Carbohydrates 25.8g | Protein 8g

BROCCOLI TOFU SCRAMBLE

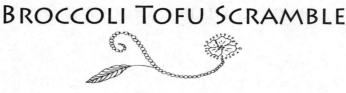

~ SERVES 4 ~

450g firm or extra firm silken tofu, ideally low fat, drained and crumbled
1 tsp ghee or olive oil
90g leeks or onions, chopped
1 tbsp Bragg Liquid Aminos or tamari soy sauce
1 pinch of ground black pepper
90g broccoli, cut into small florets
1 courgette, cut into 0.5cm slices
1 large red or green pepper, deseeded and chopped
1 tsp curry powder
1 tsp ground cumin
½ tsp garam masala
1 tsp dried dill
Vegetable stock, as needed

Place the tofu in a bowl and set aside. Heat a large frying pan. Add the ghee, leeks, Aminos and black pepper and stir-fry for 2 minutes. Add the broccoli, courgette and red or green pepper and stir-fry for a further 2–3 minutes until the broccoli begins to soften. Add the tofu, curry powder, garam masala and dill, and a small amount of vegetable stock if the mixture looks too dry. Combine well and continue stir-frying until hot. Serve with Country Potatoes (page 87) and Great Wholegrain Bread (page 50).

◆ ◆ ◆ ◆

NUTRITIONAL FACTS per 150g serving

Made using low-fat tofu and olive oil

Calories 181 | Total fat 6.9g | Saturated fat 0.2g | Carbohydrates 13.9g | Protein 15.9g

Cardamom Wholemeal Pancakes

~ Serves 4 ~

250g wholemeal pastry flour
1½ tsp baking powder
½ tsp ground cardamom
½ tsp ground nutmeg
½ tsp salt
1 egg, beaten
2 tbsp ghee or rapeseed oil, plus extra for brushing the griddle
4 tbsp maple syrup
300ml light soya milk or rice milk

Preheat the oven to 130°C/Gas mark ½. Combine the flour, baking powder, cardamom, nutmeg and salt in a bowl and use a wire whisk or fork to stir together. Combine the egg, oil, maple syrup and soya milk in a separate bowl and beat together. Add the dry ingredients to the wet ingredients and stir until smooth but take care not to over-mix. Heat a griddle or frying pan until a splash of water sizzles in the pan. Brush the pan with oil. Pour 4 tablespoons of the batter into the hot pan and cook until bubbles appear all over the surface. Turn the pancakes over and continue cooking for a further 2 minutes, or until the pancakes are golden brown. Keep the pancakes warm in the preheated oven until all the batter is used. Serve with fruit, fruit syrup or maple syrup.

❖ ❖ ❖ ❖

NUTRITIONAL FACTS per serving of three 7.5cm pancakes
Calories 333 | Total fat 10.4g | Saturated fat 5.8g | Carbohydrates 50.7g | Protein 9.1g

CHAI BLISS SHAKE

~~ SERVES 1 ~

225ml chai (traditional masala chai, yogi tea, or Chopra Center tea),
made by steeping 2 teabags in boiling water for 10 minutes
1 banana, sliced
1 pinch of grated nutmeg
1 pinch of ground cinnamon
2 tsp raw organic honey or maple syrup
1 scoop plain or vanilla soya protein powder
2 tbsp light soya milk with vanilla extract to taste

Combine all the ingredients in a blender and blend until smooth.

NUTRITIONAL FACTS per serving

Calories 289 | Total fat 1.2g | Saturated fat 0.7g | Carbohydrates 43.6g | Protein 26g

CHOPRA GRANOLA

~ SERVES 10 ~

Vegetable oil spray for the baking tray
160g organic porridge oats
4 tbsp sunflower seeds
4 tbsp pine nuts
4 tbsp flax seeds
4 tbsp sesame seeds
75g almonds or pecans, chopped or sliced
2 tbsp poppy seed
45g coconut flakes
1 tbsp ground cinnamon
1 tsp ground nutmeg
1 tsp ground allspice
2 tbsp ghee or rapeseed oil
2 tbsp apple juice
2 tsp vanilla extract
170g maple syrup
4 tbsp dried cranberries
70g currants or chopped dates

Preheat the oven to 180°C/Gas mark 4. Lightly grease a baking tray and set aside. Combine all the dry ingredients, except the cranberries and currants, in a bowl. Combine all the wet ingredients in a separate bowl and use a wire whisk or fork to beat together. Add the dry ingredients to the wet ingredients. Place plastic sandwich bags on your hands and toss together until well combined. Spread out in the baking tray and bake for 30 minutes or until golden brown, stirring often for even cooking. Add the currants and cranberries after the granola is baked. Set aside and leave to cool completely, then store in re-sealable plastic bags. Enjoy with soya milk. Chopra Granola makes a good snack any time of the day.

NUTRITIONAL FACTS per 55g serving

Calories 353 | Total fat 15.6g | Saturated fat 4.4g | Carbohydrates 43.8g | Protein 9.8g

CINNAMON ROLLS

~ MAKES 24 ROLLS ~

BASIC DOUGH

1 tbsp plus 110g turbinado sugar
1 tbsp dried yeast
225ml water, warm
370g wholemeal pastry flour or unbleached organic plain white flour
370g wholemeal bread flour
1 tsp salt
1 tbsp ground cinnamon
1 tbsp ghee, melted butter or rapeseed oil, plus extra for greasing the bowl
225ml soya milk or rice milk
1 egg (optional)

CINNAMON FILLING

2 tbsp ghee or butter, melted, plus extra for greasing the baking tray
2 tbsp apple juice
2 tbsp maple syrup
4 tbsp turbinado sugar
2 tbsp ground cinnamon
60g walnuts, chopped, raisins or both

Dissolve the yeast and 1 tablespoon sugar in the water in a large bowl and set aside until the yeast becomes frothy. Meanwhile, stir together the flours, salt, remaining 110g sugar and cinnamon. Make a well in the centre of the flour mixture. When the yeast has foamed, add it, the ghee, milk and egg, if using, to the flour mixture. Use your hands to mix the mixtures together until a soft dough forms. Knead the dough on a lightly floured work surface for about 5 minutes, or until it is smooth and elastic. Place the dough into a greased bowl, cover and leave to rise in a warm place for 45–60 minutes, until doubled in size.

Meanwhile, prepare the cinnamon filling. Combine the ghee, apple juice and maple syrup in a small bowl. In a separate small bowl, combine the sugar and cinnamon. Set aside both bowls. Preheat the oven to 180°C/Gas mark 4. Lightly grease a baking tray and set aside.

When the dough has risen, turn it out on to the floured surface and punch it down with your hand to release the air and flatten. Knead the dough for 3–4 minutes, then roll it into a rectangle 0.5cm thick. Use a pastry brush to brush the ghee mixture over the rolled-out dough. Sprinkle over the cinnamon and sugar mixture, then sprinkle over the nuts and/or raisins. Starting at a short end, gently roll up the dough, like a Swiss roll. Cut into 4cm-thick slices and place them on the baking tray about 2.5cm apart. Allow the rolls rise again for 10–15 minutes. Place the baking tray in the oven and bake for 20–25 minutes until risen and golden brown. Remove the baking tray from the oven, turn the rolls over and brush with maple syrup while they are still hot. Transfer the rolls to a wire rack to cool.

❖ ❖ ❖ ❖

NUTRITIONAL FACTS per roll
Calories 149 | Total fat 3.9g | Saturated fat 1.5g | Carbohydrates 24.8g | Protein 3.6g

COFFEE BLISS SHAKE

~ SERVES 1 ~

125ml strongly brewed coffee, or 1 shot espresso
1 pinch of ground cardamom
1 banana, sliced
2 tsp raw organic honey or maple syrup
2 tbsp light soya milk with vanilla extract to taste

Combine all the ingredients in a blender and blend until smooth.

NUTRITIONAL FACTS per serving

Calories 194 | Total fat 1g | Saturated fat 0.6g | Carbohydrates 44.2g | Protein 2.1g

COUNTRY POTATOES

~ SERVES 4 ~

4 floury potatoes, unpeeled or peeled, cubed
3 tsp ghee or olive oil, plus extra, if necessary, and for the baking sheet (optional)
135g leeks or onions, chopped
150g red or green peppers, deseeded and chopped
1 tsp salt
1 tsp ground black pepper
1 tsp ground cumin
1 tsp dried dill

Cooking on the hob: Bring a large saucepan of water to the boil. Add the potatoes and boil for 4–5 minutes until just tender, then drain and set aside. Heat 1 teaspoon of the ghee in a large frying pan over a high heat. Add the leeks, red or green peppers, salt, black pepper, cumin and dill and fry, stirring, for 3 minutes, or until the vegetables are tender. Transfer them to a bowl and set aside. Re-heat the pan with 1 teaspoon of the ghee. Add the drained potatoes and fry, stirring, until golden brown. Keep turning the potatoes and continue to drizzle the remaining teaspoon ghee into the pan to prevent sticking. Stir in the leek and potato mixture and reheat just before serving

Oven method: Preheat the oven to 180°C/Gas mark 4. Grease a baking sheet and set aside. Toss the raw, cubed potatoes and the vegetables together into a large bowl. In a small bowl, combine the oil and the spices and whisk together with a fork. Pour the oil mixture over the potatoes and toss together until well combined and coated with the oil mixture. Arrange the potatoes in a single layer on the baking sheet and bake for 20–30 minutes until the potatoes are tender, yet crispy and golden brown.

◈ ◈ ◈ ◈

NUTRITIONAL FACTS per 185g serving

Cooked on the hob using ghee

Calories 218 | Total fat 7.9g | Saturated fat 4.6g | Carbohydrates 32.5g | Protein 4g

Roasted in the oven using olive oil

Calories 180 | Total fat 3.8g | Saturated fat 0.5g | Carbohydrates 32.5g | Protein 4g

COURGETTE PECAN BREAD

~ MAKES 1 LOAF; 8 SLICES ~

Vegetable oil spray for the loaf tin
250g wholemeal pastry flour
165g turbinado sugar
1 tsp baking powder
½ tsp bicarbonate of soda
½ tsp salt
1 tsp ground cinnamon
1 tsp ground nutmeg
Finely grated rind of 1 orange
55g pecans, chopped
2 eggs, or 4 egg whites
2 tbsp rapeseed oil
60g apple sauce or mango purée
175g courgettes, grated

Preheat the oven to 180°C/Gas mark 4. Spray a 23 × 10cm loaf tin and set aside. Combine the flour, sugar, baking powder, bicarbonate of soda, salt, cinnamon, orange rind and pecans in a bowl and use a wire whisk to stir together. Combine the eggs, oil, apple sauce and courgettes in a separate bowl and stir together with a wire whisk. Add the dry ingredients to the wet ingredients and fold together to gently combine. Place the thick batter into the prepared tin and bake for 50 minutes, or until a wooden cocktail stick inserted in the centre come out clean. Leave to cool in the tin on a wire rack.

NUTRITIONAL FACTS per slice

Made using whole eggs

Calories 269 | Total fat 10.1g | Saturated fat 1.1g | Carbohydrates 39g | Protein 5.5g

HOME-MADE ALMOND BUTTER

~ MAKES 145G ~

145g raw almonds, sliced
2 tsp ghee, melted

Preheat the oven to 180°C/Gas mark 4. Put the almonds on a baking sheet and roast for 20 minutes, stirring occasionally, or until golden brown and aromatic. Place the roasted almonds in a blender and begin to process into a coarse grind. Slowly drizzle the ghee on to the almonds as they purée. Scrape the sides of the blender and then continue to purée until a smooth consistency is achieved. Allow to cool and store in a jar with a tight-fitting lid. Spread 1 or 2 teaspoons on slices of toasted bread.

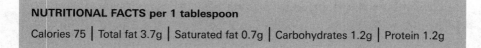

NUTRITIONAL FACTS per 1 tablespoon
Calories 75 | Total fat 3.7g | Saturated fat 0.7g | Carbohydrates 1.2g | Protein 1.2g

HOT BREAKFAST CEREAL

~ SERVES 4 ~

Porridge oats or other grains of your choice
900ml water
½ tsp salt (optional)
½ tsp ground nutmeg
1 tsp ground cinnamon
A few drops of vanilla extract, to taste
225ml light soya milk or rice milk, plus extra if needed
2 tbsp maple syrup

Using the quantity listed in the Nutritional Facts chart below, combine your choice of grain with the water and salt, if using, in a large saucepan. (Toasting the grains until golden brown first in a dry frying pan lends a nutty flavour to the cereal.) Bring to the boil, reduce heat and simmer. Stir in the nutmeg, cinnamon and vanilla, and begin to add the soya milk as the mixture starts to thicken. Be prepared to add more milk, if necessary, to create a thick and creamy cereal. Allow the cereal to simmer for 5–7 minutes for the oats, couscous and polenta; 10–15 minutes for the rice, quinoa and millet. Just before serving, add maple syrup. Serve with sautéed fruit or fruit syrup

NUTRITIONAL FACTS

4 servings per measurement of uncooked grain

Grain	Quantity	Cal.	Total fat (g)	Sat. fat (g)	Carbs (g)	Protein (g)
couscous	260g	289	1.1	0.7	60.4	9.3
millet	300g	330	3.9	1.1	64.8	9.3
polenta	260g	221	2.3	0.8	45.4	4.7
porridge oats	160g	208	3.3	1	37.3	7.5
quinoa	240g	293	4.4	0.1	54.1	9.4
rice	300g	296	1.2	0.7	65.7	5.9

MANGO BLISS SHAKE

~ SERVES 1 ~

225ml low-fat plain yogurt
1 fresh mango, cubed, or 120g mango purée or 80g frozen cubes
4 tbsp apple juice
2 tsp raw organic honey or maple syrup
¼ tsp ground cardamom

Place all the ingredients into a blender and blend until smooth.

NUTRITIONAL FACTS per serving
Calories 281 | Total fat 4.1g | Saturated fat 2.6g | Carbohydrates 47.5g | Protein 13.4g

MANGO YOGURT

~ SERVES 4~

1 mango
4 tbsp mango purée or apple sauce
2 tbsp maple syrup or raw organic honey
1 pinch of cloves
½ tsp ground cinnamon
¼ tsp ground cardamom
350ml low-fat vanilla yogurt

To prepare the mango, cut it lengthways on each side of the stone. Cut each half into cubes inside the skin, then remove the cubes with a small knife. Put the mango cubes and fruit purée in a large mixing bowl. Add the maple syrup, spices and yogurt and beat together by hand or use an electric mixer or food processor. Serve for breakfast with fruit, granola and hot cereal – or as a creamy sauce or a cooling side dish.

NUTRITIONAL FACTS per 175ml serving

Calories 178 | Total fat 1.5g | Saturated fat 0.8g | Carbohydrates 36.4g | Protein 5g

MASALA POTATOES

~ SERVES 4 ~

3 large floury potatoes, peeled, cubed and soaked in salted water to cover
1 tsp ghee or olive oil
1 tsp cumin seeds, or 2 tsp ground cumin
1 tsp brown mustard seeds (caution, the seeds will pop while cooking)
1 tsp fenugreek seeds
90g leeks or onions, chopped
2 tsp finely chopped peeled root ginger, or 1 tsp ground ginger
½ tsp turmeric
1 tbsp Bragg Liquid Aminos or tamari soy sauce
2 tsp ground coriander
1 tsp ground garam masala
75g fruit chutney or apricot jam
125ml vegetable stock
2 tsp lemon juice
175ml light coconut milk or soya milk
300g frozen peas
4 tbsp chopped fresh coriander

Bring a large saucepan of water to the boil. Drain the potatoes, then add them to the pan and boil for 4–5 minutes until just tender. Drain the potatoes well and set aside. Wash and dry the saucepan, then heat the ghee in it over a medium heat. Add the next 12 ingredients (cumin through lemon juice) in the order listed, using only half the vegetable stock. Keep the remaining stock close at hand to add as the mixture begins to dry out. Stir in the potatoes and simmer for 2 minutes. Add the coconut milk and the peas and simmer for a further 2 minutes, then add the coriander and continue simmering for 3–4 minutes until the potatoes are hot. Serve as a breakfast dish, a side dish or in a Breakfast Burrito (page 78) or calzone. Serve with Cucumber Raita (page 241).

NUTRITIONAL FACTS per 150g serving

Calories 372 | Total fat 6.2g | Saturated fat 2.5g | Carbohydrates 67.7g | Protein 11.2g

MORNING BLISS SHAKE

~ SERVES 1 ~

5 almonds, unblanched and soaked overnight in 125ml water
2 tsp raw organic honey or maple syrup
2 tbsp plain or vanilla soya protein powder
1 pinch of ground cinnamon
225ml light soya milk with vanilla extract to taste
1 tsp Biochavan herbal supplement (optional)
1 banana, sliced
1 tbsp aloe vera juice

Drain the almonds and discard the water. Place the almonds in a blender, add the remaining ingredients and blend until smooth. Take as a morning protein supplement and digestive aid.

NUTRITIONAL FACTS per serving
Calories 424 | Total fat 6.8g | Saturated fat 2.8g | Carbohydrates 61.3g | Protein 29.8g

NUTTY FRENCH TOAST

~ SERVES 4 ~

70g almonds or cashew nuts, whole or pieces
2 tbsp sunflower seeds
2 tbsp sesame seeds
2 tbsp flax seeds
1 tsp ground cinnamon
1 tsp ground nutmeg
600ml light soya milk or rice milk
1 tsp vanilla extract
8 slices wholemeal bread
Vegetable oil spray or ghee for frying

Preheat the oven to 120°C/Gas mark ½. Combine the almonds, sunflower, sesame and flax seeds and cinnamon and nutmeg in a food processor; pulse until a coarse meal forms. Slowly add the soya milk and vanilla extract and continue blending until a smooth, thick consistency forms. Pour the mixture into a shallow baking tin or bowl. Soak the bread slices in the mixture for about one minute on each side, allowing the liquid to soak in.

Heat a large skillet or griddle over a medium heat until a sprinkle of water sizzles when it hits the heat. Spray with oil. Add as many bread slices as will fit and cook for 2–4 minutes on each side until the toast is golden brown. Remove the toast from the pan and keep warm while you fry the remainder. Always keep the heat medium, not too hot. Serve with maple syrup and sautéed fruit.

❖ ❖ ❖ ❖

NUTRITIONAL FACTS per 2-slice serving

Calories 360 | Total fat 15.3g | Saturated fat 4g | Carbohydrates 43g | Protein 12.5g

PUMPKIN MUFFINS

~ MAKES 12 MUFFINS ~

Vegetable oil spray for the muffin tin
370g wholemeal pastry flour or spelt flour
110g turbinado sugar
1 tsp ground cinnamon
1 tsp ground nutmeg
2 tsp baking powder
½ tsp bicarbonate of soda
½ tsp salt
45g blanched almonds, sliced
75g raisins or dried cranberries
225ml light soya or rice milk
A few drops vanilla extract, to taste
1 tbsp rapeseed oil
4 tbsp maple syrup
200g pumpkin purée

Preheat the oven to 180°C/Gas mark 4. Spray a 12-hole deep American-style muffin tin with oil and set aside. Combine the flour, sugar, cinnamon, nutmeg, baking powder, bicarbonate of soda and salt in a bowl and use a wire whisk to stir together. Stir in the almonds and raisins. Combine the soya milk, vanilla, oil, maple syrup and pumpkin purée in a separate bowl. Add the dry ingredients to the wet ingredients and combine gently. Spoon the mixture into the muffin tin, filling each hole two-thirds full. Put the tin in the oven and bake for 20–25 minutes until golden brown and a cocktail stick inserted in the centre of each muffin comes out clean.

❖ ❖ ❖ ❖

NUTRITIONAL FACTS per muffin

Calories 200 | Total fat 3.7g | Saturated fat 0.6g | Carbohydrates 37.9g | Protein 3.7g

SEASONAL FRUIT SALAD

~ SERVES 4 ~

125ml orange juice
1 tbsp maple syrup
1 tsp ground nutmeg
1 mango, deseeded and cubed
1 peach, unpeeled
1 pear, unpeeled
1 Granny Smith apple, unpeeled
75g blueberries, thawed if frozen

Combine the orange juice, maple syrup and nutmeg in a large serving bowl. Cube all the fruit into bite-sized pieces and add to the bowl as each is prepared. Gently stir well to combine. Cover and chill until required.

NUTRITIONAL FACTS per 90g serving
Calories 142 | Total fat 0.8g | Saturated fat 0.2g | Carbohydrates 32.4g | Protein 1.1g

STRAWBERRY BANANA YOGURT

~ SERVES 4 ~

1 banana, sliced
150g strawberries, sliced
1 tsp ground cinnamon
½ tsp ground ginger
1 tbsp apple or orange juice
450g low-fat vanilla yogurt
2 tbsp maple syrup or raw organic honey, or to taste

Heat a small frying pan over a medium heat. Add the strawberries and the bananas and cook for 1–2 minutes, gently stirring. Add the cinnamon, ginger and apple juice and continue simmering and stirring for a further 3–4 minutes. Remove the pan from the heat and place the fruit in a bowl, then set aside and allow to cool slightly. Add the maple syrup and the yogurt and mix until well combined. Adjust sweetness according to taste by adding more maple syrup. Serve for breakfast with fruit, granola and hot cereal.

◆ ◆ ◆ ◆

NUTRITIONAL FACTS per 225g serving

Calories 186 │ Total fat 1.8g │ Saturated fat 1.1g │ Carbohydrates 35.7g │ Protein 6.6g

TEMPEH AND POTATO HASH

~ SERVES 4 ~

350g tempeh, cubed and marinated overnight in Simple Marinade for
Tofu and Tempeh (page 52)
300g russet potatoes, scrubbed and cubed
1 tsp ghee or olive oil
90g leeks or onions, chopped
1 tbsp Bragg Liquid Aminos or tamari soy sauce
1 red or green pepper, deseeded and chopped
½ tsp ground black pepper
1 tsp dried marjoram
1 tsp dried thyme
2 tsp dried sage
½ tsp ground nutmeg
125ml vegetable stock
300g frozen peas

Preheat the oven to 180°C/Gas mark 4. Bake the tempeh in its marinade
for 20–30 minutes, then remove from the oven and set aside. Meanwhile,
bring a large pan of water to the boil. Add the potatoes and blanch for 4
minutes, or until just tender. Drain well and set aside.

Heat the ghee a large skillet over a medium heat. Add the leeks, the
aminos, chopped pepper, black pepper, marjoram, thyme, sage and nutmeg.
Stir in the potatoes and fry, stirring, for 3 or 4 minutes. Add half of the
stock and all the peas. Remove the tempeh from the marinade and add
to the pan with the remaining stock. Allow the mixture to heat through.
Serve with scrambled tofu, or use in a Breakfast Burrito (page 78).

NUTRITIONAL FACTS per 250g serving

Calories 305 | Total fat 6.8g | Saturated fat 1.1g | Carbohydrates 38.4g | Protein 22.6g

TOFU AND POTATO ITALIANO

~ SERVES 4 ~

450g firm or extra-firm silken tofu, ideally low fat, drained, cubed and
marinated 20–30 minutes in Simple Marinade for Tofu and Tempeh
(page 52)
300g potatoes, scrubbed and cut into bite-sized pieces
1 tsp ghee or olive oil
135g leeks or onions, chopped
½ tsp ground black pepper
1 pinch of red chilli flakes
2 tbsp dried mixed herbs
2 tbsp Bragg Liquid Aminos or tamari soy sauce
1 green pepper, deseeded and chopped
360g tomatoes, diced

Preheat the oven to 180°C/Gas mark 4. Bake the tofu in its marinade for
20–30 minutes, then remove from the oven, drain and set aside. Meanwhile,
bring a large pan of water to the boil. Add the potatoes and blanch for 4
minutes, or until just tender. Drain well and set aside. Heat the ghee in a
large skillet over a medium heat. Add the leeks, black pepper, chilli flakes,
mixed herbs, Aminos and chopped pepper and fry, stirring, for 3–4 minutes.
Stir in the potatoes and tomatoes and continue stirring for 3 minutes. Add
the baked tofu cubes and simmer for 2–3 minutes until they are hot. Serve
for breakfast or as a main course, or use in a Breakfast Burrito (page 78).

NUTRITIONAL FACTS per 350g serving

Made using low-fat tofu

Calories 272 | Total fat 7g | Saturated fat 0.3g | Carbohydrates 33.8g | Protein 18.3g

Traditional French Toast

~ SERVES 4 ~

2 eggs, 4 egg whites
125ml low-fat soya milk or rice milk
2 tsp ground cinnamon
½ tsp ground ginger
1 tsp vanilla extract
1 tsp ghee
Vegetable oil spray for the frying pan
8 slices wholegrain bread, each cut in half

Preheat the oven to 120°C/Gas mark ½. Combine the eggs, milk, cinnamon, ginger and vanilla in a shallow baking tin or bowl and whisk for 1 minute with a fork.

Heat a large skillet or griddle over a medium heat until a sprinkle of water sizzles. Spray with oil. Working with one piece of bread at a time, dip the bread in the batter, turn it to the other side, allowing the liquid to soak in. Place the bread on the skillet. Add as many bread slices as will fit and cook for 2–3 minutes on each side until golden brown. Remove the bread from the pan and keep warm while you fry the remainder. Always keep the heat medium, not too hot. Serve with fresh or sautéed fruit and maple syrup.

❖ ❖ ❖ ❖

NUTRITIONAL FACTS per 2-slice serving
Calories 277 | Total fat 8g | Saturated fat 3g | Carbohydrates 39.2g | Protein 11.9g

VEGETABLE TOFU SCRAMBLE

~ SERVES 4 ~

450g firm or extra-firm silken tofu, ideally low fat, drained and
crumbled
1 tsp ghee
45g leeks or onions, chopped
1 tbsp Bragg Liquid Aminos or tamari soy sauce
1 pinch of ground black pepper
1 tsp ground cumin
1 tsp curry powder
½ tsp ground coriander
½ tsp dried dill
¼ tsp ground nutmeg
90g tomatoes, diced
60g courgettes, diced
70g spinach, rinsed
Vegetable stock, as needed
4 tbsp chopped fresh coriander, to serve

Place the crumbled tofu into a bowl and set aside. Heat the ghee in a large
frying pan over a medium heat. Add the leeks, Aminos, pepper, cumin,
curry powder, coriander, dill and nutmeg and stir-fry for 2 minutes. Add
the tomatoes, courgette and spinach and stir-fry for 4–5 minutes until the
vegetables begin to soften. Stir in a little vegetable stock if the mixture
becomes dry. Add the crumbled tofu, stir until it is well combined and
continue to stir-fry until it is hot. Garnish with the coriander. Serve in a
Breakfast Burrito (page 78) or as a main course with salsa and Country
Potatoes (page 87).

NURTITIONAL FACTS per 225g serving
Made using low-fat tofu
Calories 160 | Total fat 6.7g | Saturated fat 0.8g | Carbohydrates 9.5g | Protein 15.2g

VERY BERRY YOGURT

~ SERVES 4 ~

1 tsp ghee
300g frozen berries, or 450g fresh berries, any variety
½ tsp ground cloves
½ tsp ground allspice
2 tbsp maple syrup or raw organic honey, or to taste
450g low-fat vanilla yogurt

Heat the ghee in a small frying pan over a medium heat. Add the berries and simmer for 1–2 minutes, stirring and allowing the frozen berries to thaw. Add the cloves and allspice and continue to simmer for 3–5 minutes until the berries soften. Transfer the berries to a bowl and leave to cool slightly. If the berries have produced too much liquid, spoon them into the bowl using a slotted spoon. Stir in the maple syrup and yogurt. Adjust sweetness according to taste by adding more maple syrup. Serve for breakfast with fruit, granola and hot cereal.

NURTITIONAL FACTS per 175g serving

Calories 173 | Total fat 3g | Saturated fat 1.8g | Carbohydrates 30.4g | Protein 6.3g

WHOLEMEAL CRÊPES, SWEET OR SAVOURY

~ SERVES 4 ~

2 eggs
350ml semi-skimmed milk or light soya milk or rice milk
½ tsp salt
185g wholemeal pastry flour
2 tbsp ghee, melted, or rapeseed oil, plus extra for frying the crêpes
1 tsp nutmeg

Place all the ingredients in a blender and blend until smooth. Pour the batter into a bowl and chill for 30 minutes. When ready to cook, heat a frying pan over a medium–high heat until a sprinkle of water sizzles when it hits the heat. Brush the pan with ghee. Ladle 60ml of batter onto the pan. Using the handle, swirl the batter around into a very thin crêpe and cook until the surface begins to bubble. Turn the crêpe over and continue cooking until golden brown. Remove the crêpe from the pan and continue until all the batter is used, layering the cooked crêpes with greaseproof paper. Stuff the crêpes with sweet or savoury filling. Roll the filling inside the crêpe and then cover with a sauce.

For sweet crêpes: Use sautéed fruit and paneer or ricotta cheese and blueberry syrup.

For savoury crêpes: Use stir-fried vegetables and serve with a creamy sauce flavoured with fresh herbs. Enjoy as a main dish or a breakfast dish.

NUTRITIONAL FACTS per 2 crêpes without a filling

Made using semi-skimmed milk and rapeseed oil

Calories 248 | Total fat 11.1g | Saturated fat 2.2g | Carbohydrates 26.8g |
Protein 10.2g

Main Courses

'To lengthen thy life, lessen thy meals'
– Benjamin Franklin

We have divided up the 30-Day Nutritional Plan to include light meals and main meals. The light meals are meals that are best eaten in the evening before 6 or 7 pm for optimal digestion. Your metabolic activity slows in the evening so you do not need as much fuel to maintain your energy level. Eating lighter at night is particularly beneficial if you are trying to drop a few kilos. You will also tend to sleep better if you have eaten a lighter evening meal.

The main meals are best enjoyed during the midday period. Your digestion is at its peak then, and since you are most active during the day, your fuel requirements are highest then. Most people in the West are in the habit of having their main meal in the evening when there is more time for meal preparation and the family is together. Try gradually eating more at lunchtime and less at dinner and notice how you feel. You and your family can still spend quality time together in the evening – you just don't need to eat as much.

Helpful Pointers:

1. Almost all of the recipes can be prepared for 1 or 2 people by cutting the ingredients in half. Experiment with your favourites.
2. If you are cooking for one, a trip to the salad bar can yield you just the right vegetable combination of broccoli, cauliflower, carrots, celery and peppers for a soup, stir-fry or stew. Look for the freshest produce you can find.
3. Use low-fat fresh silken tofu that is firm or extra firm for the best results, if you can find it.

4. Keep some marinated tofu in the fridge to speed up the process of making a quick stir-fry or sandwich. It also makes a protein-rich snack. See page 52 for the Staple Recipe.

5. Always keep a cup vegetable stock nearby whenever you are cooking. When you are tempted to add additional oil or fat to a dish for extra moisture, get in the habit of adding vegetable stock instead. This will help to reduce extra fat in your diet. We have used only 1 teaspoon of ghee or oil in our dishes serving four. You can increase or decrease as desired.

6. For added variety, you can add some chicken or fish to some of the recipes. Take a look at the Main Course Recipe Index on page 109; we've marked the recipes most suitable for this adaptation with *

7. We have used 450g of tofu or tempeh in these main-course recipes. Package sizes will vary according brand, so use the amount of tofu or tempeh that is available. It does not need to be an exact amount.

8. When menu planning, whether for a day or a week, think about what you may be doing. Will you need some extra food to take for lunch the next day? Will you have a very quick, eat-on-the-run supper before a meeting? Planning ahead will give you time to prepare foods that will be not only good for you and nourishing, but will also help you to resist the temptation to run through a fast-food place or stop by a store or take-away and pick up food that may not be very nourishing.

Try to arrange your planning with the following intention: make lunch, whenever possible, the largest meal of the day and your evening meal the lighter meal of the day.

General Outline for a Day's Main Courses

Main Meal	**Light Meal**
Soup	Soup or stew
Grain	Grain or bread
Dish with protein	Dessert
Steamed or stir-fried vegetable	
Vegetables or stew	
Chutney or sauce	
Dessert	

MAIN COURSE INDEX

Aubergine Cauliflower Curry
Braised Tofu with Mango Tomato Salsa ★
Buddha's Delight Vegetable Stir-fry ★
Cashew Tofu or Tempeh
Curry Filo Tart
Mediterranean Pasta ★
Moroccan Vegetables ★
Rainbow Risotto
Roasted Aubergine and Spinach Pasta ★
Roasted Tofu and Yams
Simple Wholegrain Pizza
Spinach Polenta
Szechwan Baked Egg Rolls
Thai-style Noodles with Tofu or Tempeh
Tofu Burger or Tofu 'Meatballs'
Tofu, Tempeh or Chicken Fajitas ★
Vegetarian Paella
Winter Vegetables and Couscous

★ The asterisk indicates entrees with optional chicken or fish additions

AUBERGINE CAULIFLOWER CURRY

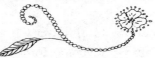

~ SERVES 4 ~

2 tsp ghee or olive oil
1 tbsp Bragg Liquid Aminos or tamari soy sauce
2 tbsp apple juice
1 tbsp curry powder
1 tbsp dried dill
240g aubergine, cut into 2.5cm cubes
330g cauliflower, cut into small florets
90g leeks or onions, chopped
2 tsp finely chopped peeled root ginger
1 tbsp Bragg Liquid Aminos or tamari soy sauce
4 tbsp vegetable stock, plus extra if needed
2 tsp ground cumin
4 tbsp home-made fruit chutney or apricot jam
2 tsp ground coriander
2 tsp garam masala
2 tsp lemon juice
125ml coconut milk
225ml light soya milk with vanilla extract to taste
4 tbsp chopped fresh coriander leaves
Toasted coconut flakes and roasted cashews, to garnish (optional)

Preheat the oven to 180°C/Gas mark 4. Put 1 teaspoon of the ghee, the aminos, apple juice, curry powder and dill in a non-metallic bowl and whisk together. Add the aubergine cubes and toss until well coated. Arrange the cubes in a single layer on a baking tray and roast for 20 minutes. Remove from the oven and set aside.

Meanwhile, bring a large saucepan of water to the boil. Add the cauliflower, return the water to the boil and blanch for 5–6 minutes until just starting to become tender. Drain well and set aside.

Heat the remaining ghee in a large saucepan. Add the leeks, ginger, the aminos, vegetable stock, cumin, chutney and ground coriander. Reduce the heat and simmer for 5 minutes, stirring occasionally. Stir in the lemon juice, coconut milk, soya milk and fresh coriander. Add the aubergine and the cauliflower and continue to simmer over a medium–low heat for a further 4 or 5 minutes. If the mixture gets dry, add extra vegetable stock. Garnish with toasted coconut flakes and roasted cashews, if desired. This is particularly good served over hot rice.

❖ ❖ ❖ ❖

NUTRITIONAL FACTS per 225g

Calories 237 | Total fat 4.1g | Saturated fat 2.2g | Carbohydrates 44g | Protein 6.2g

BRAISED TOFU WITH MANGO TOMATO SALSA

~ SERVES 4 ~

450g firm or extra-firm silken tofu, ideally low fat, drained and cut into 1cm-thick slices, or 4 x 125g salmon fillets, or 4 x 125g boneless, skinless chicken breasts
1 tsp ghee or olive oil
1 recipe quantity Mango Tomato Salsa (recipe follows)

MARINADE

225ml apple juice
4 tbsp lemon juice or rice vinegar
4 tbsp Bragg Liquid Aminos or tamari soy sauce
4 tbsp maple syrup or raw organic honey
1 pinch of red chilli flakes
1 tsp ground cumin
½ tsp ground cardamom
1 tsp grated root ginger, or ½ tsp ground ginger

Put all the marinade ingredients in a non-metallic bowl and stir together. Add the tofu, cover and refrigerate overnight. Or bake in a preheated 180°C/Gas mark 4 oven. If the tofu is baked, leave it to cool completely before using.

The next day, strain the tofu and reserve the marinade. Heat the ghee in a frying pan over a high heat. Add the tofu and fry briefly on each side until golden brown, drizzling 1 tablespoon of the marinade over as it fries. Remove the tofu from the pan and arrange on a serving platter. Drizzle some marinade over and serve with the Mango Tomato Salsa.

If you are using fish or chicken, marinate it overnight first to optimize the flavour, then roast in a preheated oven at 180°C/Gas mark 4 or grill until tender just before serving. Baste the chicken or fish with the marinade during roasting or grilling.

MANGO TOMATO SALSA

~ SERVES 4 ~

1 ripe mango, deseeded and cubed
2 tomatoes, diced
1 Anaheim chilli, roasted and peeled, or 2 tbsp mild canned chillies
45g leeks or onions, chopped
1 tsp ghee or olive oil
2 garlic cloves, very finely chopped, or 1 tsp very finely chopped
peeled root ginger
1 tbsp Bragg Liquid Aminos or tamari soy sauce
1 tbsp lemon juice
4 tbsp chopped fresh coriander
1 tsp cumin, ground
½ tsp ground coriander

Using a pair of tongs, hold the raw chilli over a flame or place under a preheated grill. Carefully turn the chilli constantly, allowing the flame to char the skin of the chilli until it blisters, charring as much of the surface as possible. Seal the hot chilli in a plastic bag, which allows the steam to loosen the skin. When the chilli is cool enough to handle, peel off the skin under cold running water.

Chop the chilli and place it in a small bowl. Add the mango and tomato and set aside. Heat the oil in a small frying pan over a medium heat. Add the leeks and garlic and fry, stirring, until softened and transparent. Stir in the aminos, then add to the mango mixture. Add the remaining ingredients and toss well. Serve spooned over the braised tofu, or use as a side dish or condiment with other main courses.

◆ ◆ ◆ ◆

NUTRITIONAL FACTS per 125g serving

Made with low-fat tofu

Calories 309 | Total fat 8.2g | Saturated fat 0.4g | Carbohydrates 40.7g | Protein 17g

Made with salmon

Calories 343 | Total fat 10.2g | Saturated fat 1.5g | Carbohydrates 35.4g |
Protein 27.6g

Made with chicken breast

Calories 306 | Total fat 4.4g | Saturated fat 0.8g | Carbohydrates 35.4g |
Protein 31.3g

BUDDHA'S DELIGHT VEGETABLE STIR-FRY

Plan on about 225g total of mixed raw vegetables per person before cooking. Choose any of the following vegetables – up to 1.3–1.5kg total – for a stir-fry for four people. Cook the vegetables in the order given.

~ SERVES 4 (SAUCE MAKES ABOUT 450ML) ~

150g carrots
150g cauliflower florets
90g broccoli florets
125g celery
135g asparagus
135g green beans
140g pak choy
140g white or nappa cabbage
210g mung bean sprouts
140g spinach
135g mangetouts
1 tbsp ghee, olive oil, or sesame oil, or 2 tbsp apple juice or vegetable stock
Hot cooked rice or udon noodles, to serve
Sesame seeds and spring onions, sliced, to garnish

BASIC CHINESE SAUCE

1 tbsp sesame oil
2 garlic cloves, crushed, or ½ tsp garlic granules
1 tsp grated peeled root ginger, or 1 tsp ground ginger
¼ tsp red chilli flakes
4 tbsp Bragg Liquid Aminos or tamari soy sauce
3 tbsp rice vinegar
1 tbsp lemon juice
1 tbsp maple syrup
1 tsp mustard powder
350ml vegetable stock
2 tbsp arrowroot, dissolved in 2 tbsp water

To make the Chinese sauce, heat 1 teaspoon sesame oil in a small saucepan over a medium heat. Add the garlic, ginger and chilli flakes, the aminos, vinegar, lemon juice, maple syrup and mustard, stirring together. Add the vegetable stock, stirring, and bring to a rolling boil. Just as the sauce begins to boil, add the remaining 2 teaspoons sesame oil and the dissolved arrowroot, stirring or whisking constantly until the sauce is thickened. Remove the pan from the heat and set aside.

Select your choice of vegetables and cut them into uniform, bite-sized pieces and shred the cabbage and spinach. Place all the vegetables in separate piles or bowls until you are ready to begin stir-frying. Heat the ghee in a wok or large frying pan over a high heat (using apple juice or vegetable stock reduces the fat content). Keep the heat on high and add the vegetables that take the longest to cook first, stirring. Keep adding vegetables and stirring, one kind at a time in the order listed, until all the vegetables are cooking in the wok. Allow the vegetables to cook until they are al dente – still a little crunchy – no more than 5–7 minutes. Pour the sauce into the wok and reheat, if necessary. Serve over rice or udon noodles. Garnish with sesame seeds and spring onions.

BUDDHA'S DELIGHT WITH CHICKEN

Stir-fry 100–125g diced skinless chicken breast per person in 1 teaspoon sesame oil for 4 minutes. Add the Basic Chinese Sauce and continue stir-frying for a further 2 minutes. Remove the chicken and sauce from the wok and set aside. Stir-fry the vegetables as above, then return the chicken and sauce to the wok to reheat and mix together.

NUTRITIONAL FACTS per 300g serving

Made with low-fat tofu, olive oil, vegetables and sauce

Calories 172 | Total fat 7.5g | Saturated fat 1g | Carbohydrates 20g | Protein 6.3g

Per 450g serving

Made with chicken

Calories 360 | Total fat 18g | Saturated fat 4g | Carbohydrates 20g | Protein 29.9g

CASHEW TOFU OR TEMPEH

~ SERVES 4 ~

2 tsp ghee, olive oil or sesame oil, plus extra as needed
225g firm or extra-firm silken tofu or tempeh, ideally low fat, drained if
necessary and cut into 2.5cm triangles, 2.5cm thick
2 tbsp apple juice, plus extra as needed
2 tbsp Bragg Liquid Aminos or tamari soy sauce
90g leeks or onions, chopped
2 garlic cloves, very finely chopped, or ½ tsp garlic granules
1 pinch of red chilli flakes
1 tbsp finely chopped peeled root ginger
1 tsp ground cumin
150g carrots, sliced on the diagonal
1 green pepper, deseeded and chopped
1 red pepper, deseeded and chopped
270g broccoli florets
125ml vegetable stock, plus extra if needed
4 tbsp toasted cashew nuts

Heat 1 teaspoon of the ghee in a large frying pan. Add as many tofu pieces
as will fit without overcrowding the pan and sprinkle both sides with
apple juice and the aminos. Fry until they are browned on both sides, then
remove from the pan and set aside. Continue until all the tofu is fried.
Add more oil (or some vegetable stock) if necessary. Remove the tofu or
tempeh from the heat and set aside.

Heat the remaining teaspoon of ghee in the pan or a large wok over
a high heat. Add the leeks, garlic, red chilli flakes, ginger and cumin, and
stir-fry until the leeks are translucent. Add the carrots and the peppers and
continue to stir-fry for 2 to 3 minutes. Add the broccoli and the vegetable
stock and return the tofu to the pan. Allow the mixture to simmer, adding
more vegetable stock if necessary, until all the ingredients are hot and
tender-crisp. Serve with rice and Lettuce Wraps (page 205).

NUTRITIONAL FACTS per 360g serving

Made with low-fat tofu

Calories 269 | Total fat 11.3g | Saturated fat 3g | Carbohydrates 25.3g | Protein 16.8g

CURRY FILO TARTS

~ SERVES 4 ~

Olive oil spray for the muffin tin and spraying the pastry before baking
2 tsp ghee or olive oil
90g leeks or onions, chopped
1 tbsp Bragg Liquid Aminos or tamari soy sauce
1 pinch of ground black pepper
330g cauliflower, cut into bite-sized pieces
400g carrots, cut into bite-sized pieces
125ml vegetable stock, plus extra if needed
180g broccoli, coarsely chopped
2 tsp curry powder
1 tsp dried dill
2 tsp garam masala
4 sheets wholemeal or white filo pastry, thawed if frozen

Preheat the oven to 180°C/Gas mark 4. Spray 4 holes in a deep American-style muffin pan, or four 225ml custard cups or other ovenproof bowls and set aside. Heat 1 teaspoon of the ghee in a large frying pan over a medium heat. Add the leeks, the aminos and pepper and stir-fry until the leeks are translucent. Increase the heat to high, add the cauliflower and the carrots and stir-fry for 4–5 minutes until the vegetables are cooked but not soft. Add the vegetable stock as needed. Add the broccoli and the spices and continue to stir-fry for a further 4 minutes. Be careful not to over-cook the vegetables. Turn off the heat, cover the pan and set aside.

Lay out the sheets of filo pastry on the work surface and brush with the remaining ghee or olive oil. Fold each sheet in half, then in half again. Line the cups with the filo pastry. Using a slotted spoon, fill the pastry with the vegetable mix, straining off the excess liquid. Bring up the ends of the filo pastry and twist together at the top. Spray lightly with olive oil and bake for 15 minutes, or until golden brown.

NUTRITIONAL FACTS per tart

Calories 227 | Total fat 5.2g | Saturated fat 2.3g | Carbohydrates 37.8g | Protein 7.7g

Mediterranean Pasta

This sauce is also great served over grilled fish or chicken, over rice or as a side dish. Garnish with toasted pine nuts, if you like.

~ SERVES 4 ~

1 tsp ghee or olive oil
90g leeks or onions, chopped
1 tbsp Bragg Liquid Aminos or tamari soy sauce
½ tsp ground black pepper
1 tsp dried thyme
1 tsp dried basil, or 2 tbsp chopped fresh basil
1 tsp dried oregano
135g asparagus, trimmed and cut into 2.5cm pieces
75g fresh or tinned artichoke hearts, rinsed and halved or quartered
100g green beans, cut into 2.5cm pieces
140g watercress or red Swiss chard, torn into small pieces
360g tomatoes, diced
125ml vegetable stock, plus extra if needed
2 tbsp stoned Kalamata olives, chopped
225g fresh pasta, or 175g dried pasta, such as fettuccini, rotelli or penne
Extra virgin olive oil
Balsamic vinegar

Heat 1 teaspoon of the ghee in a large frying pan over a high heat. Add the leeks, the aminos, pepper, thyme, basil and oregano and simmer for 2 minutes, stirring. Stir in the asparagus, artichokes, green beans and stock, cover the pan and continue to simmer for a further 3 or 4 minutes. Add the watercress or Swiss chard, tomatoes and extra stock, if necessary, and continue simmering until the greens are just wilted. Stir in the olives.

Meanwhile, bring a large pan of salted water to the boil. Add the pasta and cook for 2–3 minutes for fresh, or according to the packet instructions for dried, until al dente. Drain well and divide between bowls and top with the vegetable sauce. Drizzle a little extra virgin olive oil and balsamic vinegar over the pasta before adding the sauce to add extra zest.

❖ ❖ ❖ ❖

NUTRITIONAL FACTS per 300g serving

Calculations include sauce and pasta

Calories 269 | Total fat 4g | Saturated fat 0.9g | Carbohydrates 47.8g | Protein 10.3g

MOROCCAN VEGETABLES

~ SERVES 4 ~

2 large carrots, peeled and cut into 0.5cm slices
110g cauliflower, cut into small florets
4 tbsp vegetable stock, plus extra if needed
2 large courgettes, cut in half-moon slices
280g spinach, rinsed and torn into pieces
90g broccoli, cut into florets
2 tbsp pine nuts, toasted
4 tbsp finely chopped fresh dill
40g feta cheese, drained and crumbled (optional)

MOROCCAN CHILLI SAUCE

1 tsp ghee or olive oil
90g leeks or onions, chopped
3 garlic cloves, very finely chopped, or 1 tsp garlic granules
2 tsp dried oregano
1 pinch of ground black pepper
2 tsp curry powder
1 tsp ground allspice
2 tbsp Bragg Liquid Aminos or tamari soy sauce
1 large green pepper, deseeded and finely chopped
100g celery, finely chopped
360g tomato, finely chopped
125ml vegetable stock or tomato juice

To make the sauce, heat the ghee in a large saucepan. Add the leeks, garlic, black pepper, curry powder, allspice and the aminos and stir-fry over a medium heat for 2 or 3 minutes. Add the green pepper, celery and tomatoes and continue to stir-fry for 2 or 3 minutes. Reduce the heat to low, add the stock, cover the pan and leave the sauce to simmer for up to 30 minutes.

Meanwhile, bring a large pan of water to the boil. Add the carrots and the cauliflower, return the water to the boil and blanch for 2 minutes, or lightly steam in a steamer. Drain the vegetables well and set aside. Heat the vegetable stock in the same pan. Add the courgettes and simmer for 2–3 minutes, then add the carrots, cauliflower, spinach and the chilli sauce. Increase the heat and bring just to the boiling point. Add the broccoli and stir, then reduce the heat to low, and simmer for 3–4 minutes. Be careful not to over-cook the broccoli. Garnish with freshly chopped dill, toasted pine nuts and feta cheese. Serve over pasta, couscous, grains or as a side dish.

VARIATION

Simmer four 125g boneless, skinless chicken breasts or four 125g sea bass fillets in the sauce until cooked and tender, and serve with the vegetables on the side.

❖ ❖ ❖ ❖

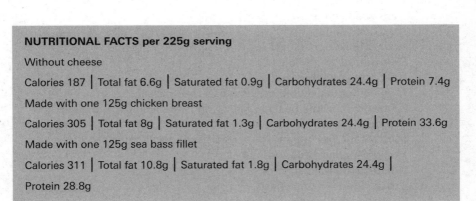

NUTRITIONAL FACTS per 225g serving

Without cheese

Calories 187 | Total fat 6.6g | Saturated fat 0.9g | Carbohydrates 24.4g | Protein 7.4g

Made with one 125g chicken breast

Calories 305 | Total fat 8g | Saturated fat 1.3g | Carbohydrates 24.4g | Protein 33.6g

Made with one 125g sea bass fillet

Calories 311 | Total fat 10.8g | Saturated fat 1.8g | Carbohydrates 24.4g |

Protein 28.8g

RAINBOW RISOTTO

This is a perfect dish for a dinner party

~ SERVES 8 ~

2 tsp ghee or olive oil
135g leeks, shallots or onions, chopped
1.3 litres vegetable stock, hot
1 tbsp Bragg Liquid Aminos or tamari soy sauce
1 tsp balsamic vinegar
1 tsp ground black pepper
1 tsp dried basil
1 tsp dried thyme
1 tsp dried sage
400g Arborio rice, rinsed
130g carrots, thinly sliced
100g celery, thinly sliced
115g courgettes, cut into 0.5cm half-moon slices
200g cooked white beans, or 400g tinned white beans, drained and rinsed
140g rocket, or a mixture of spinach and rocket, coarsely torn
1 tbsp chopped fresh rosemary
1 tbsp chopped fresh mint
2 tbsp shredded fresh basil
Chopped fresh parsley, to garnish

Heat 1 teaspoon of the ghee in a large saucepan. Add the leeks, the aminos, vinegar, black pepper and dried basil, thyme and sage and stir-fry until the leeks are translucent. Add the rice and stir until golden brown or caramelized. Lower the heat. As the rice dries out, begin to add the stock, 225ml at a time, stirring constantly. Allow the rice to absorb the stock each time before adding more. Risotto should have a soft (not mushy) texture with a creamy consistency. Be careful not to over-cook or let the rice dry out. The cooking process will take 20–30 minutes in total. Taste the rice for texture.

Heat the remaining ghee in a frying pan over a medium-high heat. Add the carrots, celery, courgettes and beans and a little of the stock if it necessary to keep the vegetables moist. Stir-fry until the carrots are al dente, or almost tender. Add the rocket and continue to stir-fry until it is wilted. Pour all the vegetables into the pan with the rice, add the fresh herbs and stir to combine. Place the rice in a festive serving dish and garnish with the parsley. Traditionally, a good-quality grated Parmesan or asiago cheese and cream might be added to the dish to achieve a creamier consistency.

❖ ❖ ❖ ❖

NUTRITIONAL FACTS per 300g serving
Calories 328 | Total fat 2.8g | Saturated fat 0.4g | Carbohydrates 55.8g | Protein 19.7g

ROASTED AUBERGINE AND SPINACH PASTA

You can replace the white beans with small pieces of grilled or roasted chicken or fish.

~ SERVES 4 ~

Vegetable oil spray for the baking tray
2 tbsp balsamic vinegar
1 tsp olive oil and 1 tsp ghee or oil
1 tbsp dried basil, plus an extra 2 tsp
1½ tsp ground black pepper
1 aubergine, cut into 0.5cm slices
90g leeks, shallots or onions, very finely chopped
2 garlic cloves, crushed or very finely chopped
1 tbsp Bragg Liquid Aminos or tamari soy sauce
2 tsp dried dill, or 1 tbsp finely chopped fresh dill
425g spinach, rinsed and coarsely chopped or torn
200g cooked white beans, or a 400g tin of white beans, drained and rinsed
4 tbsp vegetable stock (optional)
225g fresh pasta
125ml Pesto Tomato Pasta Sauce (page 250), or 125ml ready-made sauce
40g feta cheese, drained and crumbled, or good-quality Parmesan cheese, grated
2 tbsp finely chopped fresh parsley

Preheat the oven to 180°C/Gas mark 4. Grease a baking tray and set aside. Combine the balsamic vinegar, 1 teaspoon olive oil, 1 tablespoon dried basil and 1 teaspoon of the black pepper in a large bowl and whisk together. Add the aubergine slices and toss until the aubergine is well coated. Lay the aubergine in a single layer in the baking tray and brush on both sides with any remaining oil. Roast for 20 minutes, then set aside and leave to cool. Cut the aubergine into thin strips and set aside.

Heat the remaining ghee in a large frying pan over a medium heat. Add the leeks, garlic, the aminos, remaining black pepper, dill and basil in that order and stir-fry until the leeks are translucent. Add the spinach and continue stir-frying until just wilted, then add the sliced aubergine and white beans. Add the vegetable stock only if necessary to add moisture and continue simmering until all the ingredients are heated through.

Meanwhile, bring a large pan of water to the boil. Add the pasta and cook until it is al dente, or just tender. Drain the pasta and place it in a shallow serving bowl or individual bowls and toss with a little olive oil to prevent sticking. Pour the sauce into the aubergine mixture and heat briefly, then pour the sauce over the hot pasta. Toss together and serve. Garnish with the cheese and the parsley.

NUTRITIONAL FACTS per 300g serving

With cheese

Calories 306 | Total fat 8.1g | Saturated fat 2.4g | Carbohydrates 45.6g | Protein 12.7g

ROASTED TOFU AND YAMS

~ SERVES 4 ~

450g firm or extra-firm silken tofu, ideally low fat, drained and cut into
2.5cm cubes
Vegetable oil spray for the baking tray
1 tsp ghee or olive oil
½ tsp ground black pepper
½ tsp dried oregano
1 tsp dried or fresh dill
1 tsp curry powder
1 tsp garam masala
2 tsp Bragg Liquid Aminos or tamari soy sauce
1 tsp lemon juice
125ml apple juice or vegetable stock
2 large yams or sweet potatoes, peeled and cut into 2.5cm cubes
Finely chopped fresh coriander, to garnish

MARINADE

125ml lemon or orange juice
225ml apple juice
1 tbsp Bragg Liquid Aminos or tamari soy sauce
1 tsp olive oil
1 tsp garam masala

Combine all the ingredients for the marinade in a shallow non-metallic
bowl and whisk together. Add the tofu and leave to marinate, ideally
overnight. (Or, to speed up the process, put the tofu and the marinade into
a shallow baking tin and bake in a preheated oven at 180°C/Gas mark 4
for 20–30 minutes. Remove the pan from the oven and set aside to cool
completely.)

Preheat the oven to 180°C/Gas mark 4. Spray a baking tray with
vegetable oil and set aside. Combine the oil, pepper, oregano, dill, curry
powder, garam masala, the aminos, lemon juice and apple juice in a large
non-metallic bowl and whisk together. Add the yams and toss until well

coated with the marinade. Spread the yams in a single layer on the greased roasting tray and roast for 20–30 minutes until they are soft and golden brown but not mushy. If the tofu has been marinated overnight but not baked yet, add it to the yams and roast for the same time until golden brown. If you have already roasted the marinating tofu, remove the tofu cubes from the marinade with a slotted spoon and add to the baking yams after they have been in the oven 15 minutes. Serve over your favourite grain with some steamed vegetables and sautéed greens. Garnish with some freshly chopped coriander.

❖　❖　❖　❖

NUTRITIONAL FACTS per 360g serving

Made with low-fat tofu

Calories 305 | Total fat 8.2g | Saturated fat 0.5g | Carbohydrates 41.7g | Protein 16.1g

Simple Wholegrain Pizza

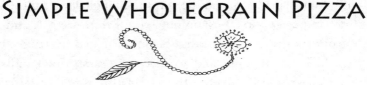

~ Makes two 25 cm pizzas ~

2 tbsp dried yeast
2 tbsp turbinado sugar
450ml water, very warm
280g organic unbleached white plain flour, plus extra for rolling out
370g organic wholemeal pastry flour
1 tsp sea salt
1 tbsp dried basil
1 tbsp olive oil or ghee, plus extra for greasing the bowl and the pizza
tins

Combine the yeast, water and 1 tablespoon of the sugar in a bowl and set aside until the yeast becomes frothy. Meanwhile, sift together the flours and salt, tipping in any bran left in the sieve. Make a well in the centre of the flours.

When the yeast has foamed, add it and the oil to the well. Use your hands to mix the flours and yeast together until a soft dough forms. Knead the dough in the bowl for about 5 minutes, or until it is smooth and elastic. If the mixture is very dry, add up to 125ml more water, tablespoon by tablespoon. Place the dough into a greased bowl, cover and leave to rise in a warm place for 45–60 minutes until doubled in size.

Meanwhile, preheat the oven to 180°C/Gas mark 4 and lightly grease two 25cm tins. When the dough has risen, punch it down to release the air and knead for 4 minutes in the bowl. Divide the dough in half and use a lightly floured rolling pin to roll each half into a 25cm round pizza. Place the pizzas in the greased pizza tins. Top with your favourite toppings (see below), then bake for about 20 minutes, or until browned and crusty.

SAUCES *(amounts given are per pizza)*

2 tbsp Basil and Friends Pesto (page 238)
125ml Roasted Tomato Sauce (page 251)

VEGETABLE CHOICES *(amounts given are per pizza)*

300g roasted vegetables, such as aubergines, carrots, courgettes and red peppers, cut into bite-sized pieces
4 sliced tomatoes with 2 tbsp shredded fresh basil
3 diced courgettes stir-fried with ½ diced roasted red pepper
225g sliced mushrooms stir-fried with 90g chopped leeks
200g cooked spinach, squeezed dry

CHEESE AND EXTRAS

Feta or paneer cheese, 40–75g per pizza, drained, if necessary
Black olives, stoned
Soya 'pepperoni'
Artichoke hearts

NUTRITIONAL FACTS per slice (1/8 pizza)

Plain pizza, without topping

Calories 134 | Total fat 1.1g | Saturated fat 0.5g | Carbohydrates 20.9g | Protein 3.1g

SPINACH POLENTA

~ SERVES 4 ~

Olive oil for brushing the ovenproof dish
675–800ml water or vegetable stock
175g coarse polenta
½ tsp salt
1 tbsp dried basil
300g frozen or fresh spinach, thawed and drained if necessary

Preheat the oven to 180°C/Gas mark 4. Brush a 20 x 20cm ovenproof dish with olive oil and set aside. Bring 450ml water to the boil in a large saucepan. Add the salt and the basil. Slowly begin to pour in the polenta, using a wire whisk to stir as you pour. Reduce the heat to low and continue to stir while adding the remaining water. Keep stirring until the mixture begins to thicken. Use more water for a smooth creamy texture; use less for a more solid finished dish. Stir in the spinach. Pour the polenta mixture into the ovenproof dish. The polenta will begin to solidify. Bake the polenta for 20 minutes, or until heated through. Serve with Roasted Tomato Sauce (page 251) or Ratatouille (page 191).

❖ ❖ ❖ ❖

NUTRITIONAL FACTS per slice

Calories 172 | Total fat 1.9g | Saturated fat 0.2g | Carbohydrates 28g | Protein 10.8g

SZECHWAN BAKED EGG ROLLS

~ MAKES 8 ROLLS (2 PER SERVING) ~

Vegetable oil spray and fine cornmeal for the baking sheet
1 tsp ghee or olive oil
1 tsp sesame oil
130g carrots, finely diced
2 tsp very finely chopped peeled root ginger
1 tsp ground coriander
1 tsp Chinese five-spice powder
45g leeks or spring onions, very finely chopped
110g cabbage, shredded
½ red pepper, deseeded and diced
55g mung bean sprouts, chopped
175g firm or extra-firm silken tofu, ideally low fat, marinated (page 52), drained and diced
8 egg roll wrappers, thawed if frozen
1 egg, beaten
1 tbsp sesame seeds

Preheat the oven to 220°C/Gas mark 7. Lightly grease a baking sheet and sprinkle it with cornmeal, then set aside. Heat the ghee in a wok or large frying pan over a high heat. Add the carrots, ginger, coriander, five-spice powder and leeks and stir-fry for 2–3 minutes until the leeks are translucent. Add the cabbage, pepper and sprouts and continue stir-frying for a further 2 minutes. Add the tofu and simmer for 2 minutes, then remove the pan from the heat and drain any excess liquid from the pan. Lay the egg wrappers on the work surface. Using a slotted spoon, place 4 tablespoons of the mixture into the centre of each wrapper. Fold the wrapper over the filling, by tucking in the sides and then rolling over. Place the egg rolls on the prepared baking sheet. Brush each egg roll with the egg wash and sprinkle with sesame seeds. Bake for 15–20 minutes until golden brown. Serve with rice and a stir-fry or with Thai-style Noodles (page 135).

NUTRITIONAL FACTS per 2 egg rolls

For egg rolls only without sauce, made with low-fat tofu

Calories 186 | Total fat 5.5g | Saturated fat 1.1g | Carbohydrates 25.1g | Protein 9.1g

THAI-STYLE NOODLES WITH TOFU OR TEMPEH

~ SERVES 4 ~

1 recipe quantity Simple Marinade for Tofu or Tempeh (page 52),
marinated overnight, or 300g diced skinless chicken breast
225g Pad Thai, soba or rice noodles
1 tsp ghee, sesame oil or olive oil
45g leeks, onions or spring onions, chopped
1 pinch of red chilli flakes
1 tsp ground coriander
2 tbsp finely chopped peeled root ginger
2 garlic cloves, crushed or very finely chopped (optional)
2 tbsp vegetable stock
2 tbsp sliced almonds, toasted
4 tbsp chopped spring onions
210g mung beans sprouts, rinsed
4 tbsp chopped fresh coriander

THAI STIR-FRY SAUCE

125ml vegetable stock
4 tbsp rice vinegar
2 tbsp apple juice
2 tsp lemon juice
1 tsp miso paste
1 tsp paprika
1 tsp Chinese five-spice powder
1 tbsp maple syrup
2 tbsp Bragg Liquid Aminos or tamari soy sauce
2 tbsp shredded fresh basil

Remove the tofu or tempeh from the marinade and cut into 2.5cm strips,
then set aside.

Combine all the ingredients for the sauce, except the basil, in a blender and blend until smooth. Stir in the basil and set aside.

Cook or soak the noodles according to the packet instructions. Rinse, place in a large bowl and sprinkle with sesame oil to keep the noodles from sticking.

Heat the ghee in a wok or large frying pan. Add the leeks, chilli flakes, coriander, ginger and garlic and stir-fry for 2 minutes, adding the stock after 1 minute. Add the tofu or tempeh, cover, reduce the heat and simmer for 3–4 minutes. Add the almonds, spring onions, mung bean sprouts and coriander and continue simmering for a further 3–4 minutes until everything is hot. Add the stir-fry sauce and simmer for 2–3 minutes, then pour the mixture over the noodles and toss until well combined. Serve with steamed vegetables.

NUTRITIONAL FACTS per 300g

Made using low-fat tofu

Calories 414 | Total fat 9g | Saturated fat 0.5g | Carbohydrates 64.3g | Protein 18.9g

Made using chicken

Calories 469 | Total fat 7.8g | Saturated fat 1.6g | Carbohydrates 59g | Protein 40.8g

TOFU BURGERS OR TOFU 'MEATBALLS'

~ SERVES 4 (MAKES 8 BURGERS OR 24 MEATBALLS) ~

Vegetable oil spray for the baking tray
3–4 slices dry bread
450g firm or extra-firm silken tofu, ideally low fat, drained and crumbled
1 tsp ghee or olive oil, plus extra for frying the burgers or meatballs
90g leeks or onions
½ tsp ground black pepper
40g mixed almonds, pine nuts and sunflower seeds
115g courgettes, grated
110g carrots, grated
1 tsp dried basil
1 tsp dried oregano
1 tsp dried thyme
1 tsp very finely chopped garlic
1 tbsp Bragg Liquid Aminos or tamari soy sauce

Preheat the oven to 180°C/Gas mark 4. Lightly spray a baking tray and set aside. Place the bread in a food processor and pulse until breadcrumbs form. Remove from the food processor and set aside. Heat the ghee in a small frying pan. Add the leeks and pepper and stir-fry for 2–3 minutes until the leeks are translucent, then remove from the pan and allow to cool. Place the cool tofu, mixed nuts and seeds, courgette, carrot and leeks in the food processor and pulse a few times. Add the basil, oregano, thyme, garlic and the aminos and continue to pulse to a smooth consistency. The mixture should be thick, yet firm. Divide the mixture into 8 equal portions and roll into balls. Flatten the balls into burgers and pat the breadcrumbs on each side. Heat some ghee in a frying pan. Add the burgers and fry to brown on both sides. Place the burgers on the baking tray and bake for 15 minutes, or until firm. Serve with Leek Sauce (page 246) or in a wholemeal hamburger bun with all the traditional trimmings.

You can also this recipe to make 'meatballs' for serving in tomato sauce with pasta, or as an alternative to ground meat in tacos and casseroles. Change the spices according to the use.

❖ ❖ ❖ ❖

NUTRITIONAL FACTS per serving (2 burgers or 4 meatballs)

Made with low-fat tofu

Calories 261 | Total fat 10.4g | Saturated fat 0.7g | Carbohydrates 24.1g |

Protein 17.5g

TOFU OR TEMPEH FAJITAS

~ SERVES 4 ~

450g firm or extra-firm silken tofu, ideally low fat, or tempeh, drained if necessary, cut into 0.5cm slabs

1 tsp ghee or olive oil
2 tbsp Bragg Liquid Aminos or tamari soy sauce
1 tsp ground black pepper
90g leeks, thinly sliced into long strips
1 red pepper, deseeded and cut into long strips
115g yellow courgette, cut into thin strips
115g green courgette, cut into thin strips
90g broccoli, cut into small florets
225ml vegetable stock
360g tomatoes, diced
2 tsp ground cumin
1 tsp chilli pepper
1 tsp dried oregano
30g coriander, chopped

MARINADE

2 tbsp chopped fresh coriander, plus extra, to garnish
125ml lime, lemon or orange juice
225ml apple juice
2 tsp dried oregano
1 tbsp ground cumin
4 tbsp Bragg Liquid Aminos or tamari soy sauce
1 pinch of ground black pepper
1 pinch of red chilli flakes
3 garlic cloves, crushed

Combine the fresh coriander, lime juice, apple juice, oregano, cumin, the aminos, black pepper, chilli flakes and garlic and whisk together. Add the tofu and toss until well coated in the marinade. Cover and marinate overnight in the fridge. The next day, bake in a preheated oven at 180°C/

Gas mark 4 for 20–30 minutes. Or bake immediately, without marinating. In either case, remove the tofu from the oven and set aside, and turn the oven to a low setting.

Heat the ghee in a large frying pan over a medium-high heat. Remove the tofu from the marinade and brown on both sides. Remove the pan from the heat and return the tofu strips to the marinade, then keep warm in the oven. Add the aminos, 1 teaspoon black pepper and leeks to the pan and stir-fry for 2–3 minutes until the leeks are translucent. Add the remaining ingredients, except the coriander, one at a time and continue to stir-fry until the vegetables are cooked. Be careful not to over-cook the broccoli. Remove the tofu from the oven and strain off the marinade. Add the tofu to the pan, then sprinkle with the coriander to garnish. Serve with corn or flour tortillas, Spanish Pilaf (page 222) or Mexican Rice (page 223), and Mandarin Tomato Salsa (page 247).

VARIATION: CHICKEN FAJITAS

Chicken can also be used in this recipe: marinate four 125g chicken breasts overnight. Just before you are ready to start cooking, cut the chicken into thin strips and use to replace the tofu in the above recipe.

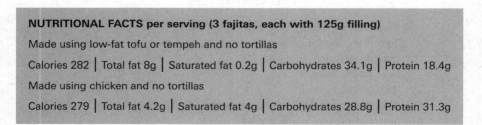

NUTRITIONAL FACTS per serving (3 fajitas, each with 125g filling)

Made using low-fat tofu or tempeh and no tortillas

Calories 282 | Total fat 8g | Saturated fat 0.2g | Carbohydrates 34.1g | Protein 18.4g

Made using chicken and no tortillas

Calories 279 | Total fat 4.2g | Saturated fat 4g | Carbohydrates 28.8g | Protein 31.3g

Vegetarian Paella

A festive party dish.

~ SERVES 12 ~

400g basmati rice
950ml–1 litre water or vegetable stock, plus extra if needed
2 tsp ground cardamom
1 pinch of saffron threads
1 cinnamon stick
1 tbsp ground cumin
1 tsp ground coriander
1 tsp turmeric
1 tsp dried dill
1 tsp ground allspice
½ tsp ground cloves
1 tsp ghee or olive oil
90g leeks, shallots or onions, chopped
1 tsp ground black pepper
1 tbsp Bragg Liquid Aminos or tamari soy sauce
1 roasted red pepper, deseeded and chopped
1 green pepper, deseeded and chopped
230g courgettes, cut into half-moon slices
200g marinated artichoke hearts, drained and quartered
300g tinned chickpeas, drained and rinsed
180g broccoli florets
450g spinach, rinsed, torn into small pieces, thawed if frozen
225g asparagus, trimmed and cut into bite-sized pieces
1 small bunch fresh parsley, finely chopped
55g spring onions, finely chopped
75g Kalamata olives, stoned, whole or chopped
180g tomatoes, chopped
125g pine nuts, toasted

Combine the rice, water, 1 teaspoon cardamom, saffron and cinnamon stick into a stockpot with a tight-fitting lid. Cover and cook the rice for 20–30 minutes until tender. Meanwhile, preheat the oven to 200°C/Gas mark 6. After the rice has cooked, remove the cinnamon stick and fluff the rice with a fork. Place the rice into a stainless-steel bowl or large ovenproof dish.

Combine the cumin, coriander, remaining cardamom, turmeric, allspice and cloves in a small bowl. Sprinkle the spices into the hot rice and toss gently to combine. Cover with foil and place in the oven.

Heat the ghee in a large frying pan over a medium-high heat. Add the leeks, black pepper and the aminos and stir-fry for 2–3 minutes until the leeks are translucent. Add the red and green peppers, courgettes and artichoke hearts and simmer over a low heat for 3–4 minutes. Add the chickpeas and 60ml of the stock and bring to the boil. Add the broccoli and the spinach, immediately remove the pan from the heat, cover and set aside.

In a separate frying pan, heat the remaining stock, add the asparagus and simmer for 4–5 minutes until it turns light green. Strain the remaining liquid out of the pan.

Remove the rice from the oven. Drain any liquid from the vegetable mixture. Combine the vegetables with the rice and toss gently to incorporate all the ingredients. Place the rice and vegetable mixture into a festive serving dish and garnish with the asparagus, parsley, spring onions, olives, tomatoes and the pine nuts. Keep warm in a low oven until ready to serve.

❖ ❖ ❖ ❖

NUTRITIONAL FACTS per 225g serving

Calories 348 | Total fat 10.4g | Saturated fat 1.6g | Carbohydrates 51.7g | Protein 11.8g

WINTER VEGETABLES WITH COUSCOUS

~ SERVES 4 ~

2 carrots, cut into 1cm slices
1 sweet potato, cut into 1cm cubes
1 small acorn squash, peeled and cut into 1cm pieces
90g Brussels sprouts or green beans, cut in half
1 tsp ghee or olive oil
1 tsp brown mustard seeds (seeds may pop from the pan during cooking)
1 tsp cumin seeds
90g leeks or onions, chopped
2 tbsp Bragg Liquid Aminos or tamari soy sauce
1 tsp ground coriander
½ tsp turmeric
½ tsp ground coriander
1 tsp ground ginger
125ml vegetable stock, plus extra if needed
200g chickpeas, cooked, or one 400g tin, drained and rinsed
225ml coconut milk or light soya milk
175g couscous, soaked
2 tbsp currants, to garnish
2 tbsp pine nuts, toasted, to garnish
2 tbsp coconut flakes, toasted, to garnish
2 tbsp chopped fresh coriander, to garnish

Bring a large saucepan of water to the boil. Add the carrots, sweet potato, acorn squash and Brussels sprouts, return the water to the boil and blanch for 4–5 minutes. Drain the vegetables and set aside. Heat the oil in the same pan. Add the mustard and cumin seeds and fry briefly until they pop. Add the leeks, the aminos, coriander, turmeric, cardamom and ginger and a little of the stock if the mixture begins to dry. Simmer for 3–4 minutes, stirring. Stir in the blanched vegetables and add more vegetable stock, if necessary. Cover and cook for 5–7 minutes, stirring frequently to incorporate the spices, until the vegetables are tender, but not over-cooked. Add the chickpeas and coconut milk, stir and continue to simmer until they are hot. Serve over couscous. Garnish with currants, toasted pine nuts, toasted coconut flakes and coriander.

NUTRITIONAL FACTS per 225g serving

Calories 352 | Total fat 14.6g | Saturated fat 3.8g | Carbohydrates 43.9g | Protein 11g

SOUPS

'Of soup and love, the first is best'
— SPANISH PROVERB

The base of a good soup is the stock. Make a tasty vegetable stock (page 45) and keep it in your refrigerator. The second most important item is the stockpot or saucepan. You need good stainless-steel – 18- to 20-gauge steel – with a 6–9-litre capacity, and a good long spoon to go with it. A large pan will allow room for movement and is perfect to use for making your vegetable stock. A smaller, 4-litre pan will also come in handy for small batches of soup, and will also be good for cooking rice and other grains. Be sure to have tight-fitting lids for all your pans.

Helpful Pointers:

1. Be creative. Make simple soups by trying different vegetables and mixing and matching spices. A general rule about spices is that you can always add more but it's difficult to disguise the taste of too much spice. Start simple, and then go from there.
2. Use Bragg Liquid Aminos or tamari soy sauce to help create a rich savoury flavour. Use a good stock, the aminos, leeks or onions, spices and a dash of pepper to make just about any vegetable taste great in a soup.
3. Soup makes the perfect light supper after a long day. Learn to make several simple soups in just 20 minutes. See the Staple Recipes chapter (page 35) for recipes and ideas about simple soups.
4. One of the most useful tools for blending soups is an immersion blender. It makes blending soups easy and washing up is a snap! Using a slow-cooker is also an easy and carefree way to make soup,

especially those containing beans. If you are adding dried beans, for the best results always soak dried beans overnight in water first, which will make them easier to digest. Drain and rinse the beans and place them into the slow-cooker. Add enough vegetable stock or water to the cooker to cover the beans by at least 5–7.5cm. The uncooked beans will absorb a lot of liquid as they cook. To enhance the flavour, briefly fry some vegetables, such as leeks, celery and carrots, with spices before adding them. Once all the ingredients are combined in the cooker, place the setting on 'low' and cook for 4–6 hours, or according to the manufacturer's instructions, until the beans and the vegetables are tender. Keep in mind, however, that a soup with vegetables only – without meat or beans – will only take 2–4 hours to cook in a slow-cooker. So, with that in mind, don't leave a vegetable soup in slow-cooker to cook for 8 hours while you are at work for the day.

5. Time Saver: pre-cook dried beans in a slow-cooker the day before or earlier during the day you plan to make your soup. Also keep a supply of beans in tins or jars on hand to speed up the soup-making process.

SOUP INDEX

Asian Clear Broth ★
Butternut Squash Soup
Courgette Tofu Bisque
Cuban Black Bean and Sweet Potato Soup ★
Italian Vegetable Soup
Nutty Broccoli Soup
Potato Leek Soup
Rosemary White Bean Soup
Spinach and Lentil Soup
Spinach Soup
Summertime Tomato Basil Soup
Sweet Potato Ginger Soup
Tomato Florentine Soup
Tortilla Soup with Avocado and Coriander ★
Vegetable Barley Soup ★
Vegetable Hot-and-Sour Soup ★
Very Simple Pumpkin Soup

★The asterisk indicates soups with an optional chicken or fish addition.

ASIAN CLEAR BROTH

~ SERVES 4 ~

Olive oil spray for the baking tray
2 tsp ghee or olive oil
2 tbsp Bragg Liquid Aminos or tamari soy sauce
1 pinch of red chilli flakes
½ tsp ground cumin
1½ tsp ground coriander
2 tbsp lemon, apple or orange juice
360g firm or extra-firm silken tofu, ideally low fat, drained and cut into small cubes
1 tbsp finely chopped peeled root ginger
45g leeks or onions, chopped
½ tsp ground black pepper
50g celery, sliced diagonally
130g carrots, thinly sliced, julienne style
40g red cabbage, thinly sliced
125g pak choy, thinly sliced
1 tsp Chinese five-spice powder
900ml vegetable stock
55g sunflower sprouts, to garnish
55g mung bean sprouts, to garnish
4 tbsp chopped spring onions, to garnish

Preheat the oven to 180°C/Gas mark 4. Spray a baking tray with olive oil spray and set aside. Combine 1 teaspoon of the oil, 1 tablespoon of the aminos, chilli flakes, cumin, coriander and juice in a bowl. Add the tofu cubes and toss to combine. Place the tofu in a single layer on the baking tray and bake for 30 minutes, or until golden brown. Remove the tofu from the tray and set aside.

Heat the remaining ghee in a stockpot or large saucepan. Add the leeks, ginger, pepper, coriander and remaining aminos and stir-fry for 2–3 minutes until the leeks are translucent. Add the remaining vegetables and continue stir-frying for a further 3–4 minutes. Add the Chinese five-spice powder and stir-fry 2 minutes. Add the vegetable stock and bring just to the boil. Reduce the heat, add the tofu cubes and simmer for 5 minutes. Ladle into individual bowls and garnish with the sprouts and the spring onions. Add cooked shrimp or chicken pieces to the soup as an additional garnish.

❖ ❖ ❖ ❖

NUTRITIONAL FACTS per 350ml serving

Made with low-fat tofu

Calories 158 | Total fat 6.5g | Saturated fat 0.4g | Carbohydrates 11.6g | Protein 13.3g

BUTTERNUT SQUASH SOUP

~ SERVES 4 ~

1 tsp ghee or olive oil
45g leeks or onions, chopped
½ tsp ground black pepper
1 tsp Bragg Liquid Aminos or tamari soy sauce
560g butternut squash, peeled and cut into 1cm cubes
1 tsp curry powder
1 pinch of garam masala
Up to 1.25 litres vegetable stock
125ml vanilla soya milk or rice milk
Freshly grated nutmeg, to garnish

Heat the ghee in a stockpot or large saucepan. Add the leeks, the pepper and the aminos and stir-fry for 2–3 minutes until the leeks are translucent. Add the squash, curry powder and garam masala and continue stir-frying to allow the squash to brown in the spices. Add just enough vegetable stock to cover the squash and bring to the boil. Reduce the heat to medium and simmer until the squash becomes soft. Purée the soup to a smooth consistency with an immersion blender or in a food processor or blender. Add the soya milk to create a creamy consistency. Garnish with a sprinkle of nutmeg.

❖　❖　❖　❖

NUTRITIONAL FACTS per 350ml serving
Calories123 | Total fat 2.9g | Saturated fat 1.1g | Carbohydrates 20g | Protein 4.3g

COURGETTE TOFU BISQUE

~ SERVES 4 ~

1 tsp ghee or olive oil
90g leeks or onions, chopped
1 pinch of red chilli flakes
2 tbsp Bragg Liquid Aminos or tamari soy sauce
½ tsp ground pepper
1 tsp dried tarragon
1 tsp dried dill
¼ tsp ground nutmeg
1 tsp dried marjoram
½ tsp dried thyme
500g courgettes, cut into half-moon slices
900ml vegetable stock, plus extra, if needed
175g firm or extra-firm silken tofu, ideally low fat, drained and cubed
1 tbsp fresh lemon juice

Heat the ghee in a stockpot or large saucepan. Add the leeks, chilli flakes, the aminos, pepper, tarragon, dill, nutmeg, marjoram and thyme and stir-fry for 4–5 minutes until the leeks are translucent. Add the courgettes and continue stir-frying until well coated in the herbs and spices. Add enough vegetable stock to cover the courgette mixture and bring to the boil. Reduce the heat and simmer for 5 minutes, or until the courgettes are tender. Be careful not to over-cook. Use an immersion blender, food processor or blender to purée the tofu with just enough stock to make a smooth consistency. Stir the tofu purée into the courgettes and purée the soup until a smooth, creamy texture is achieved. Reheat, if necessary, and add the lemon juice just before serving.

NUTRITIONAL FACTS per 300ml serving

Made with low-fat tofu

Calories 142 | Total fat 3.5g | Saturated fat 1g | Carbohydrates 17.9g | Protein 9.8g

CUBAN BLACK BEAN AND SWEET POTATO SOUP

~ SERVES 4 ~

400g dried black beans, sorted, rinsed and soaked overnight in water to cover
2 bay leaves
1 tsp ghee or olive oil
90g leeks or onions, chopped
100g celery, chopped
1 tsp ground black pepper
2 tbsp Bragg Liquid Aminos or tamari soy sauce
1 pinch of red chilli flakes
1 tsp ground cinnamon
1 tsp dried oregano
2 tsp ground cumin
300g sweet potato, peeled and cut into 1cm cubes
130g carrots, cubed
180g tomatoes, chopped or diced
900ml vegetable stock, plus extra if needed
140g greens, such as spinach, red chard or kale, rinsed and coarsely torn
30g coriander, chopped
150–300g boneless, skinless cooked chicken, diced (optional)

Drain the soaked beans and place in a stockpot or large saucepan. Add enough water to come 7.5cm above the beans, then add the bay leaves and bring to the boil. Reduce the heat and allow the beans simmer for 1 to 1½ hours until softened. Drain and rinse the beans, reserving 225ml of the cooking liquid, and set aside. Discard the bay leaves.

Heat the ghee in the same pan. Add the leeks, celery, pepper and the aminos and stir-fry for 2–3 minutes. Add the chilli flakes, cinnamon, oregano, cumin, sweet potatoes and carrots and continue stir-frying for a further 5 minutes, allowing the mixture to brown. Add the black beans and the tomatoes and simmer for 2–3 minutes, stirring, and then add enough vegetable stock and reserved liquid from the beans to cover the contents of the pan. Allow the soup to simmer until the sweet potatoes are soft, then add the greens and stir until they have wilted. Leave the soup chunky or purée to a smooth texture. Garnish with coriander just before serving.

Grilled or smoked chicken makes a flavourful addition to this soup. If you want to include it, add it with the beans and tomatoes.

NUTRITIONAL FACTS per 350ml serving

Calories 294 | Total fat 2.6g | Saturated fat 0.1g | Carbohydrates 53.7g | Protein 14g

With 260g chicken

Calories 471 | Total fat 6.6g | Saturated fat 2.1g | Carbohydrates 53.7g | Protein 49.4g

ITALIAN VEGETABLE SOUP

~ SERVES 4 ~

200g dried white beans, sorted, rinsed and soaked overnight in water
to cover
4 bay leaves
1 tsp ghee or olive oil
45g leeks, shallots or onions, chopped
1 tbsp Bragg Liquid Aminos or tamari soy sauce
½ tsp ground black pepper
1 tsp dried basil
1 tsp dried marjoram
1 tsp dried dill
1 tsp dried oregano
130g carrots, diced
100g celery, sliced
110g small cauliflower florets
125g courgette, cut into half-moon slices
70g mixed greens, such as spinach, kale and Swiss chard, rinsed and
coarsely torn
Up to 1.1 litres vegetable stock
2 tbsp tomato purée
1 tbsp thinly shredded fresh basil, to garnish
1 tbsp finely chopped fresh parsley, to garnish

Drain the soaked beans and place in a stockpot or large saucepan. Add
enough water to come 5cm above the beans, then add 2 of the bay leaves
and bring to the boil. Allow the beans to cook for 1 to 1½ hours until
softened. Replenish the water as needed to maintain a rolling boil. Drain
and rinse the beans and set aside.

Heat the ghee in the same pan. Add the leeks, the aminos, pepper, basil,
marjoram, dill and oregano and stir-fry for 3–4 minutes. Add the carrots,
celery, cauliflower and 125ml of the vegetable stock if the mixture begins
to dry out and continue stir-frying for a further 3–4 minutes. Add the
white beans and courgette, stirring to coat them with the herbs and spices.
Add the greens and simmer for 3 minutes, and then add the vegetable

stock to just cover the mixture. Add the remaining 2 bay leaves and bring the soup to the boil. Reduce the heat and simmer for 10 minutes. Stir in the tomato paste and simmer for a further 10 minutes. Ladle the soup into bowls and garnish with fresh basil and parsley.

NUTRITIONAL FACTS per 300ml serving

Calories 268 | Total fat 2.1g | Saturated fat 0.4g | Carbohydrates 46.3g | Protein 15.9g

NUTTY BROCCOLI SOUP

~ SERVES 4 ~

1 large head broccoli, cut into florets with the stalk peeled and chopped
70g blanched almonds, finely chopped (pulse in the food processor), or 2 tbsp Almond Butter (page 90) for a richer taste
1 tsp ghee or olive oil
90g leeks or onions, chopped
2 tsp Bragg Liquid Aminos or tamari soy sauce
1 tsp dried thyme
1 tsp dried marjoram
1 tsp ground nutmeg
1 tsp dried dill
½ tsp ground black pepper
900ml vegetable stock, plus extra if needed
2 tsp lemon juice
2 tbsp finely chopped fresh parsley, to garnish

Heat the ghee in a stockpot or large saucepan. Add the leeks, the aminos, thyme, marjoram, nutmeg, dill and pepper and stir-fry for 2–3 minutes until the leeks are translucent. Add the broccoli and almonds and stir-fry with the herbs and spices for a few minutes. Add the stock and almond butter, if using, and bring to the boil. Reduce heat and simmer the soup until the broccoli is almost soft. Be careful not to over-cook the broccoli. Allow the soup to cool for 10 minutes, then purée with an immersion blender or in a food processor or blender. Reheat and add the lemon juice. Ladle the soup into bowls and garnish with the parsley.

Use different vegetables in this soup recipe, such as carrots, cauliflower, potato and squash. Each makes a delicious soup combination.

NUTRITIONAL FACTS per 350ml serving

Made with finely chopped almonds, not almond butter

Calories 187 | Total fat 8.9g | Saturated fat 1.5g | Carbohydrates 18.6g | Protein 8.1g

POTATO LEEK SOUP

~ SERVES 4 ~

6 potatoes, peeled or unpeeled, cubed
1 tsp ghee or olive oil
180–270g leeks or shallots, chopped
1 tsp Bragg Liquid Aminos or tamari soy sauce
½ tsp ground black pepper
1 tbsp tarragon
2 tsp dried thyme
1 tsp salt
1.1 litres vegetable stock, plus extra if needed
Freshly grated nutmeg, to garnish
2 tbsp chopped fresh parsley, to garnish

Place the cubed potatoes in a bowl of cold water and aside until needed. Heat the ghee in a stockpot or large saucepan. Add the leeks, the aminos and pepper and stir-fry over a medium-high heat until the leeks until golden brown. Drain the potatoes and add them to the pan with the tarragon, thyme and salt, stirring until the potatoes are well coated with the herbs. Continue stir-frying for 4 minutes, or until the potatoes begin to brown. Pour in enough vegetable stock to cover the potatoes and bring to the boil. Reduce the heat and simmer until the potatoes are tender. Allow the soup to cool for 10 minutes and then purée it using an immersion blender or in a food processor or blender. Garnish with a sprinkle of nutmeg and freshly chopped parsley.

❖ ❖ ❖ ❖

NUTRITIONAL FACTS per 350ml serving

Calories 279 | Total fat 3.4g | Saturated fat 0.3g | Carbohydrates 37.3g | Protein 24.4g

ROSEMARY WHITE BEAN SOUP

~ SERVES 4 ~

200g dried cannellini beans, sorted, rinsed, and soaked overnight in
water to cover
4 sprigs fresh rosemary
2 bay leaves
½ tsp salt
2 tbsp tomato purée
1 tsp ghee or olive oil
3 garlic cloves, crushed
90g leeks, shallots or onions, chopped
½ tsp ground black pepper
1 tbsp Bragg Liquid Aminos or tamari soy sauce
130g carrots, cut into 0.5cm slices
125g courgette, cut into 0.5cm slices
1 tsp dried thyme, 1 tbsp fresh
1 tsp dried dill, or 1 tbsp fresh
125ml vegetable stock, plus extra if needed
2 tbsp chopped fresh parsley or dill, to garnish

Drain the beans, rinse and place them in a stockpot or large saucepan. Add
enough water or vegetable stock to come at least 5cm above the beans,
then add the rosemary, bay leaves and salt and bring to the boil. Reduce
the heat and allow the beans to simmer 1 to 1½ hours, stirring frequently,
until softened. The soup should always have enough liquid in it to allow
the beans to move around, so be prepared to add more water or stock, as
necessary. As the beans cook, foam will appear on top. Skim off the foam
with a spoon and discard. When the beans are softened, do not drain. Stir
the tomato purée into the beans and add enough water so the beans are
covered by 2.5cm. Return to the boil.

Heat the ghee in a saucepan. Add all the remaining ingredients, except
the parsley, and stir-fry for 2–3 minutes until the leeks are translucent. Add
the vegetable mixture to the soup and bring back to the boil. Reduce
the heat and allow the soup to simmer until the carrots are tender and

a smooth consistency is achieved. Remove the bay leaves before serving. Garnish with parsley and serve.

❖   ❖   ❖   ❖

NUTRITIONAL FACTS per 300ml serving

Calories 307 | Total fat 4g | Saturated fat 1.6g | Carbohydrates 53g | Protein 14.7g

SPINACH AND LENTIL SOUP

To make this soup wheat-free, do not add the bulgur.

~ SERVES 4 ~

1 tsp ghee or olive oil
90g leeks or onions, chopped
100g celery, cut into 0.5cm slices
2 garlic cloves, crushed
1 tsp finely chopped peeled root ginger
1 pinch of red chilli flakes
½ tsp ground black pepper
1 tsp chopped fresh rosemary
1 tbsp Bragg Liquid Aminos or tamari soy sauce
130g carrots, diced
70g bulgur wheat
1 tsp ground cumin
½ tsp ground allspice
200g brown lentils, sorted, rinsed and drained
2.3–2.7 litres vegetable stock
2 bay leaves
2 tbsp tomato purée
280g fresh spinach, rinsed and chopped coarsely
4 tbsp chopped fresh parsley, to garnish
180g tomatoes, diced, to garnish

Heat the ghee in a stockpot or large saucepan. Add the leeks, celery, garlic, ginger, chilli flakes, pepper, rosemary, the aminos and carrots and stir-fry for 3 minutes. Add the bulgur, if using, and continue stir-frying until golden brown. Add the cumin and allspice, stirring, then add the lentils, 2.3 litres vegetable stock and the bay leaves and bring to the boil. Reduce the heat and simmer for 30–40 minutes until the lentils are tender. Add more stock as necessary. Add the tomato paste and the spinach and simmer for a further 5 minutes, or until the spinach has wilted. Ladle into soup bowls and garnish with the parsley and tomatoes.

NUTRITIONAL FACTS per 300ml serving

Calories 319 | Total fat 3g | Saturated fat 1g | Carbohydrates 55g | Protein 17.7g

SPINACH SOUP

~ SERVES 4 ~

1 tsp ghee or olive oil
200g celery, cut into 0.5cm slices
90g leeks, shallots or onions, chopped
1 tbsp Bragg Liquid Aminos or tamari soy sauce
½ tsp ground black pepper
1 tbsp tarragon
2 tsp dried thyme
½ tsp ground allspice
1kg fresh spinach, rinsed and coarsely chopped
900ml vegetable stock, plus extra if needed
125ml light soya milk or rice milk
A few drops vanilla extract, to taste
Freshly grated nutmeg, to garnish

Heat the ghee in a stockpot or large saucepan over a medium–high heat. Add the celery, leeks, the aminos, pepper, tarragon, thyme and allspice and stir-fry for 4–5 minutes until the leeks are translucent. Add the spinach by the handful, continuing to stir after each addition, until the spinach is wilted and a light green colour. Don't over-cook it. Add the vegetable stock to just cover the spinach and bring to the boil, and then remove the pan from the heat. Allow the soup cool slightly, then purée with an immersion blender or in a food processor or blender until a smooth, creamy texture is achieved. Add extra stock as necessary to create the desired consistency. Add the soya milk and vanilla just before reheating. Serve the soup in individual bowls, garnished with nutmeg.

NUTRITIONAL FACTS per 350ml serving
Calories 112 | Total fat 2.9g | Saturated fat 1.1g | Carbohydrates 15.2g | Protein 6.3g

SUMMERTIME TOMATO BASIL SOUP

~ SERVES 4 ~

100g dried chickpeas, sorted, rinsed and soaked overnight in water to cover, or use one 400g tin chickpeas, rinsed and drained
2 bay leaves
1 tsp ghee or olive oil
90g leeks, shallots or onions, chopped
1 tbsp Bragg Liquid Aminos or tamari soy sauce
1 tbsp dried mixed herbs
½ tsp ground black pepper
1 tsp dried dill
1 red pepper, deseeded and chopped
125g courgette, cut into half-moon slices
1 large tomato, chopped
450ml vegetable stock
450ml tomato juice
Handful fresh basil leaves, shredded

Drain and rinse the soaked chickpeas and place in a stockpot or large saucepan. Add enough water to come 5cm above the chickpeas, then add the bay leaves and bring to the boil. Reduce the heat to a low rolling boil and cook for 40–50 minutes until the chickpeas are tender. Top up with extra water as necessary. Drain the chickpeas and set aside.

Heat the ghee in the same pan. Add the leeks, the aminos, mixed herbs, black pepper and dill and stir-fry for 3–4 minutes until the leeks are translucent. Add the red pepper and courgette and stir-fry for a further 5 minutes. Add the tomatoes and continue stir-frying for 3–4 minutes, then add the chickpeas and stir for 5 minutes. Add the tomato juice and the vegetable stock and bring to the boil. Reduce the heat, add the basil and simmer for a further 4–5 minutes. Remove the bay leaves before serving.

NUTRITIONAL FACTS per 300ml serving

Calories 257 | Total fat 4.2g | Saturated fat 0.5g | Carbohydrates 37.5g | Protein 17.1g

SWEET POTATO GINGER SOUP

~ SERVES 4 ~

750g sweet potatoes, peeled and cubed
1 tsp ghee or olive oil
1 pinch of red chilli flakes
90g leeks or onions, chopped
1 tbsp finely chopped peeled root ginger, or 1 tsp ground ginger
2 tbsp Bragg Liquid Aminos or tamari soy sauce
1 tsp ground coriander
1 tsp garam masala
2.7 litres vegetable stock
4 tbsp finely chopped fresh coriander, to garnish

Heat the ghee in a stockpot or large saucepan over a medium-high heat. Add the red chilli flakes, leeks, ginger and the aminos and stir-fry for 2–3 minutes until the leeks are translucent. Add the sweet potatoes and continue stir-frying until they are well coated and beginning to brown slightly. Add the ground coriander and the garam masala and stir-fry for a further 2 minutes. Add enough of the vegetables stock to cover the sweet potatoes and bring to the boil. Reduce the heat and simmer until the sweet potatoes are tender. Purée the soup with an immersion blender or in a food processor or blender until a smooth, creamy texture is achieved. Add extra stock, as necessary, to create the desired consistency. Reheat the soup before serving and garnish with the fresh coriander.

NUTRITIONAL FACTS per 350ml serving

Calories 247 | Total fat 2.9g | Saturated fat 0.3g | Carbohydrates 50.5g | Protein 5g

TOMATO FLORENTINE SOUP

~ SERVES 4 ~

4 large tomatoes
½ tsp ground pepper, plus extra for roasting the tomatoes, to taste
1 tsp dried thyme, plus extra for roasting the tomatoes, to taste
Dried rosemary for roasting the tomatoes, to taste
Olive oil spray
300g spinach, rinsed, or 300g frozen spinach, thawed
1 tsp ghee or olive oil
90g leeks or onions, chopped
4 celery stalks, chopped
1 tsp dried tarragon
1 tsp dried basil
1 tsp dried marjoram
½ tsp ground nutmeg
1 tbsp Bragg Liquid Aminos or tamari soy sauce
900ml vegetable stock

Preheat the oven to 180°C/Gas mark 4. Cut off the vine end and make a small 'X' with a knife on the top of the smooth side of each tomato. Place the tomatoes in a shallow baking tin, X side up. Sprinkle generously with pepper, thyme and rosemary, spray lightly with olive oil and roast for 20–30 minutes. Allow the tomatoes to cool, then gently peel off the skins and discard. Place the tomatoes and the juices in a bowl and break up or mash into small pieces with a fork, then set aside.

If you are using thawed spinach, put it in a strainer and press out the excess liquid, then set aside. Heat the ghee in a stockpot or a large saucepan over a medium heat. Add the oil, leeks, celery, pepper, tarragon, thyme, basil, marjoram, nutmeg and the aminos and stir-fry for 3–4 minutes. Add the tomatoes and the spinach and cook for a further 5 minutes. Add enough stock to just cover the tomato mixture and bring to the boil. Reduce the heat and simmer for 5 minutes. Stir in extra stock, if necessary, to create the desired consistency.

NUTRITIONAL FACTS per 350ml serving

Calories 223 | Total fat 4.1g | Saturated fat 0.4g | Carbohydrates 24.8g | Protein 22g

TORTILLA SOUP WITH AVOCADO AND CORIANDER

~ SERVES 4 ~

2 tsp ghee or olive oil
2 corn tortillas, cut each in half, then into long thin strips
90g leeks or red onions, chopped
1 tbsp Bragg Liquid Aminos or tamari soy sauce
1 tsp ground black pepper
1 pinch of red chilli flakes
1 tsp mild chilli powder
1 tbsp ground cumin
1 tsp ground coriander
1 tsp dried marjoram
250g carrots, cut into bite-sized pieces
½ green pepper, deseeded and diced
½ roasted red pepper, deseeded and diced
140g organic sweetcorn kernels, thawed if frozen
900ml vegetable stock
1 avocado, cut into cubes and sprinkled with lemon juice
4 tbsp chopped fresh coriander, with 4 large sprigs to garnish
210g cooked prawns or chopped grilled fish of your choice (optional)

Heat 1 teaspoon of the ghee in a large frying pan over a medium-high heat. Add the tortilla strips in a single layer and fry until they are crisp. Remove from the pan and drain on kitchen paper, then set aside. Continue until all the strips are cooked.

Heat the remaining ghee in a stockpot or large saucepan. Add the leeks, the aminos, black pepper, chilli flakes, chilli powder, cumin, coriander and marjoram and stir-fry for 3–4 minutes until the leeks are translucent. Add the carrots and continue stir-frying for a further 3 minutes. Add the green and red peppers and the sweetcorn, reduce the heat and stir-fry for 4–5 minutes, adding 125ml of the vegetable stock as the mixture becomes dry. Allow the vegetables to cook until the carrots are almost soft. Add the remaining vegetable stock to cover the vegetables and bring to the boil. Reduce the heat and cook for 4–5 minutes, then add the chopped coriander. Divide the avocado between individual bowls. Ladle the soup over the avocado and garnish with the coriander sprigs and the crispy tortilla strips. Serve right away.

As part of the garnish, you can add the cooked prawns or grilled fish to this tasty soup.

NUTRITIONAL FACTS per 225ml serving

Made with vegetables only

Calories 347 | Total fat 14.7g | Saturated fat 1.8g | Carbohydrates 32.6g | Protein 21.1g

Made with 210g cooked prawns

Calories 401 | Total fat 15.3g | Saturated fat 2g | Carbohydrates 32.6g | Protein 33g

Made with 210g sea bass

Calories 426 | Total fat 17.4g | Saturated fat 2.4g | Carbohydrates 32.6g | Protein 34.8g

VEGETABLE BARLEY SOUP

A traditional barley soup is usually made with beef. For added flavour without the additional fat, add 210g diced uncooked skinless chicken to this soup with the leeks and celery, if you wish.

~ SERVES 4 ~

1 tsp ghee or olive oil
1 tsp yellow or brown mustard seeds
1 pinch of red chilli flakes
½ tsp ground black pepper
90g leeks or onions, chopped
100g celery, cut into 0.5cm slices
1 tbsp Bragg Liquid Aminos or tamari soy sauce
100g pearl barley, rinsed and drained
1 tsp ground cumin
1 tsp ground coriander
½ tsp ground allspice
130g carrots, cut into bite-sized pieces
140g floury potato, peeled and diced
1 tsp dried marjoram
2 bay leaves
210g spinach or rocket, or a mix, rinsed and coarsely torn
900ml vegetable stock, plus extra if needed
4 tbsp chopped fresh parsley, to garnish

Heat the ghee in a stockpot or large saucepan over a medium–high heat. Add the mustard seeds and allow them to pop briefly in the hot oil. Add the chilli flakes, pepper, leeks, celery and the aminos and stir-fry for 2–3 minutes until the leeks are translucent. Add the barley and stir until well combined, then add the cumin, coriander and allspice and continue to stir-fry for a further 2–3 minutes until the barley browns slightly. Add the carrots, potatoes and marjoram and continue cooking for 3 minutes, adding some of the stock as the mixture gets dry. When the barley is browned, add the remaining stock and bay leaves and bring to the boil. Reduce the heat to low and allow the soup to simmer until the carrots and potatoes are cooked and the barley is soft. Add the spinach or rocket and more vegetable stock, if necessary, as the barley absorbs the liquid. Garnish with parsley and serve.

NUTRITIONAL FACTS per 300ml

Calories 280 | Total fat 4g | Saturated fat 0.4g | Carbohydrates 38.8g | Protein 22.5g

Made with 210g chicken

Calories 367 | Total fat 5.1g | Saturated fat 0.7g | Carbohydrates 38.8g | Protein 42.1g

VEGETABLE HOT-AND-SOUR SOUP

~ SERVES 4 ~

80g Japanese aubergine, cut into long thin strips
Lemon juice
240g firm or extra-firm silken tofu, ideally low fat, drained
3 tsp Bragg Liquid Aminos or tamari soy sauce,
1 tsp ghee or sesame oil
1 pinch of red chilli flakes
130g carrots, thinly sliced
950ml vegetable stock, plus extra if needed
2 tbsp cider vinegar
1 tbsp arrowroot powder
2 tbsp chopped spring onions, to garnish
150g sunflower sprouts, to garnish
150g mung bean sprouts, to garnish

Place the aubergine in a bowl, sprinkle with lemon juice and cover with water, then set aside. Cut the tofu into thin strips, then place in a bowl and toss with 1 teaspoon of the aminos and set aside. When ready to cook, drain the aubergine.

Heat the remaining 1 teaspoon ghee in a stockpot or large saucepan over a medium heat. Add the chilli flakes and the aubergine and stir-fry for 2–3 minutes. Add the carrots and continue to stir-fry for a further 3–4 minutes until the carrots are almost tender. Add the vegetable stock and bring to the boil, then add the tofu, vinegar and remaining 1 teaspoon aminos and simmer for 5 minutes.

Meanwhile, dissolve the arrowroot in 4 tablespoons cold vegetable stock by stirring with a fork. Drizzle the arrowroot mixture into the soup, stirring constantly. Very quickly, the soup will begin to thicken. Remove the pan from the heat. Ladle the soup into bowls and garnish with the spring onions and sprouts.

A traditional garnish used in hot-and-sour soups is chicken pieces and small prawns. If desired, divide 140g grilled fish, chicken or prawns along with the spring onions and sprouts.

❖ ❖ ❖ ❖

NUTRITIONAL FACTS per 350ml serving

Made with low-fat tofu

Calories 148 | Total fat 4.8g | Saturated fat 0.2g | Carbohydrates 16.1g | Protein 10.1g

Made with 140g grilled sea bass

Calories 221 | Total fat 7.5g | Saturated fat 0.8g | Carbohydrates 16.1g | Protein 23.8g

Made with 140g cooked prawns

Calories 202 | Total fat 5.4g | Saturated fat 0.4g | Carbohydrates 16.1g | Protein 22g

Very Simple Pumpkin Soup

~ SERVES 4 ~

1 large pumpkin, about 1.3kg, cut in half and deseeded, or 675g
tinned pumpkin purée
350ml water
1 tsp ghee or olive oil
90g leeks or onions, chopped
1 tsp Bragg Liquid Aminos or tamari soy sauce
½ tsp ground black pepper
1 tsp ground cinnamon
1 tsp ground cumin
1 tsp curry powder
½ tsp ground cloves
450–675ml vegetable stock
225ml light soya milk
A few drops vanilla extract, to taste
Freshly grated nutmeg, to garnish

Preheat the oven to 180°C/Gas mark 4. If using fresh pumpkin, place the pumpkin halves, face down, in a roasting tin. Pour in the water, cover with foil and bake for 30 minutes, or until a knife inserted into the pumpkin pulls out easily. Set aside the pumpkin to cool, then remove the pumpkin flesh from the rind with a spoon and set aside.

Heat the ghee in a stockpot or large saucepan. Add the leeks, the aminos, pepper, cinnamon, cumin and cloves and stir-fry for 4–5 minutes until the leeks look translucent, adding some of the stock if the mixture begins to dry. Add the pumpkin pulp or purée and continue to stir-fry for a further 3–4 minutes to brown the pumpkin pulp slightly. Pour in enough vegetable stock to cover the pumpkin and bring to the boil. Purée the soup with an immersion blender or in a food processor or blender until smooth, adding the soya milk and vanilla until a creamy texture is achieved. Reheat before serving and garnish with a sprinkle of nutmeg.

NUTRITIONAL FACTS per 300ml

Calories 172 | Total fat 3g | Saturated fat 0.4g | Carbohydrates 23.8g | Protein 12.2g

STEWS

'Small cheer and great welcome makes a merry feast'
– WILLIAM SHAKESPEARE

One of the greatest pleasures at the end of a day is to come home to a meal ready and waiting for you. Especially during the cold months, a warm stew and a piece of good bread make the perfect light meal. Making a stew in a slow-cooker in the morning will ensure that a hearty and healthy meal is available for the whole family later in the day. Stews provide us with an abundance of tastes and textures, all found in a convenient one-pot meal that is hearty, warm, healthy, comforting and very nurturing.

Stews are easily made from a mixture of beans, vegetables, spices and fresh herbs. Traditional stews are 'stewed' with large cuts of meats and vegetables for long periods of time. The modern twist on stew cuisine, however, decreases the stewing time to make a quick and delicious stew in less than 30 minutes if you include already cooked beans. Using either a stockpot on the hob or a slow-cooker, you can create wonderful, hearty stews with a variety of beans, pulses, root vegetables, seasonal vegetables and fresh herbs. Vegetable and bean stews made without meat can be cooked in a slow-cooker in 4 to 6 hours. Stews made with meats such as beef or chicken can take longer, from 6 to 8 hours. Pre-soaking your beans overnight before placing them in the slow-cooker will aid digestion, and the beans will not absorb as much liquid during the cooking process.

If you want to add meat to a stew, always brown the meat first, before adding the beans, vegetables and any other ingredients.

Helpful Pointers

1. Keep marinated tofu or tempeh (page 52) on hand add to a vegetarian stew for added protein.

2. Using tinned beans and other pulses shortens the cooking time of the stew.

3. Use good-quality vegetable stock for the best flavour.

4. It's preferable to use finely chopped or crushed fresh garlic, rather than garlic granules, but freeze-dried granulated is an option. Use ½ teaspoon granulated garlic to replace two or three whole cloves.

5. Use fresh or dried herbs. Generally, use double the amount of fresh herbs as you would use dried herbs. For example, 1½ teaspoons dried basil equals 1 tablespoon finely shredded fresh basil.

6. Be creative. Use what you have in your refrigerator and pantry to create your own stew recipes.

7. Use a slow-cooker for effortless cooking. For the best results, soak the beans overnight. You can place all the ingredients into the slow-cooker, making sure there is at least 7.5cm vegetable stock above the level of the beans. Stir-fry the leeks and herbs and spices together first, and then add the leek mixture to the slow-cooker with the other ingredients. Leave out quick-cooking vegetables, such as spinach, until almost the end of cooking. Cook approximately 6 hours on the low setting and 4 hours on the high setting. Slow-cookers vary in temperature range. Make sure the beans are tender to the touch when you finish cooking.

Using Tinned Beans

Always drain and rinse tinned or bottled beans before using them. The benefit of using ready-cooked beans is that it speeds up the cooking process. When you use them in the slow-cooker, reduce the cooking time to 4 hours on low. When cooking a stew on the hob, the beans should be added along with the heavier vegetables, such as carrots, potatoes and squash. All the recipes include instructions for cooking dried beans. You can use a 400g tin of cooked beans to replace the 200g dried beans specified in recipes. And, if you are using canned beans, the cooking process will take less than 30 minutes.

STEW INDEX

Aubergine and Yam Curry
Black Bean and Yam Stew ★
Cajun Bean and Tempeh Stew ★
Curried Chickpea Stew
French Vegetable Stew
Italian White Bean Stew ★
Mexican Tofu Stew
Ratatouille ★
Roasted Winter Vegetable Stew
Thai Tofu Vegetable Stew
Tofu, Aubergine and Potato Stew
Vegetable and White Bean Chilli ★

★ The asterisk indicates stews with optional chicken or fish additions.

AUBERGINE AND YAM CURRY

~ SERVES 4 ~

1 tbsp olive oil, plus extra for greasing the baking tray
1 tbsp curry powder
1 tbsp garam masala
1 tbsp Bragg Liquid Aminos or tamari soy sauce
4 tbsp vegetable stock or apple juice
1 large aubergine, cut into 2.5cm cubes with the skin on
2 large yams, peeled and cut into 2.5cm cubes

CURRY MASALA SAUCE

1 tsp ghee or olive oil
90g leeks or onions, chopped
4 tbsp finely chopped peeled root ginger
1 tbsp Bragg Liquid Aminos or tamari soy sauce
900ml vegetable stock, plus extra if needed
1 pinch of asafoetida
2 bay leaves
1 tbsp mild chilli powder
1 tbsp ground cumin
1 tbsp ground coriander
1 tbsp garam masala
1 tsp ground cardamom
1 tsp turmeric
725g tomatoes, diced
4 tbsp finely chopped fresh parsley
4 tbsp finely chopped fresh mint
145g currants, raisins or diced ready-to-eat dried apricots
1 tbsp lemon juice

Preheat the oven to 180°C/Gas mark 4. Grease a baking tray with olive oil, the set aside. Combine the olive oil, curry powder, garam masala, the aminos and the stock in a large bowl and whisk together. Add the aubergine and yams and toss gently. Arrange the vegetables in the baking tray in a single layer and roast for 30 minutes. Remove the tray from oven and set aside.

Meanwhile, to make the masala sauce, heat the ghee in a large frying pan over a medium heat. Add the leeks, ginger, the aminos and 1 tablespoon of the stock and stir-fry for 2–3 minutes. Add the asafoetida and the bay leaves and continue stir-frying until the leeks and ginger are tender. Stir in the chilli powder, cumin, coriander, garam masala, cardamom, turmeric, tomatoes and remaining stock. Simmer for 4–5 minutes, then add the roasted aubergine and yams and simmer for a further 3–4 minutes. Stir in the parsley, mint, apricots and lemon juice. Continue to simmer until hot. Remove the bay leaves and serve with rice and cooling yogurt.

❖ ❖ ❖ ❖

NUTRITIONAL FACTS per 135g serving
Calories 424 | Total fat 7.5g | Saturated fat 1.1g | Carbohydrates 73.1g | Protein 15.9g

Black Bean and Yam Stew

~ SERVES 4 ~

200g dried black beans, picked over, rinsed and soaked overnight in water to cover
900ml vegetable stock, plus extra if needed
5 tsp ground cumin
2 bay leaves
1 tsp ghee or olive oil
90g leeks or onions, chopped
½ tsp ground black pepper
1 pinch of red chilli flakes
1 tbsp Bragg Liquid Aminos or tamari soy sauce
300g yams, peeled and cubed
260g carrots, cut into 0.5cm slices
180g tomatoes, diced
225g skinless smoked chicken, cubed (optional)
2 tsp ground cinnamon
2 tsp dried oregano
2 tbsp tomato purée
30g fresh coriander, chopped

Drain and rinse the beans. Combine the beans and enough vegetable stock to cover by 7.5cm in a stockpot or large saucepan and bring to the boil. Add 3 teaspoons of the cumin and the bay leaves, reduce the heat and allow the beans to cook at a low rolling boil for about 1 hour, adding extra stock as needed, or until tender.

Meanwhile, heat the ghee in a frying pan over a medium heat. Add the leeks, chilli flakes and the aminos and stir-fry for 3–4 minutes. Add the yams and carrots and continue stir-frying for 5 minutes. Add the tomatoes, the remaining 2 teaspoons cumin, the cinnamon, oregano, tomato purée and the coriander. Add more vegetable stock to just cover the vegetables if the mixture looks like it is drying.

After the beans have cooked for 30 minutes, add the yam mixture and continue simmering. The stew will be ready to serve when the beans, yams and carrots are tender. Remove the bay leaves just before serving.

For variety, add 225g diced skinless smoked chicken to the stew when you add the tomatoes.

NUTRITIONAL FACTS per 350g serving

Calories 418 | Total fat 4.5g | Saturated fat 1.1g | Carbohydrates 64g | Protein 31.1g

Made with 225g smoked chicken

Calories 551 | Total fat 7.5g | Saturated fat 2g | Carbohydrates 64g | Protein 57.5g

CAJUN BEAN AND TEMPEH STEW

~ SERVES 4 ~

200g dried red kidney beans, or pinto beans, picked over, rinsed and
soaked overnight in water to cover
2 bay leaves
900ml–1.4 litre vegetable stock, plus extra if needed
1 tsp ghee or olive oil
90g leeks, shallots or onions, chopped
1 pinch of red chilli flakes
2 garlic cloves, finely chopped, or ½ tsp garlic granules
100g celery, chopped
1 tbsp Bragg Liquid Aminos or tamari soy sauce
1 green pepper, deseeded and diced
360g tomatoes, diced
350g andouille chicken 'sausage', sliced (optional)
1 tsp turmeric
1 tsp dried thyme
1 tsp dried oregano
1 tsp ground coriander
1 tsp ground cumin
2 tsp paprika
250g marinated tempeh, drained and cubed (page 52)
2 tbsp maple syrup

Drain and rinse the beans. Combine the beans, enough stock to cover by
7.5cm and the bay leaves in a stockpot or large saucepan and bring to the
boil. Reduce the heat and allow the beans to cook at a rolling boil for
about 1 hour, adding extra stock as necessary, or until tender.

Meanwhile, melt the ghee in a frying pan over a medium heat. Add
the leeks, chilli flakes, garlic and celery and stir-fry for 2 minutes. Add
the aminos, green pepper and tomatoes. If you are using the chicken
sausages, add them now. Combine the turmeric, thyme, oregano, coriander,
cumin and paprika. Add the spices all at once to the vegetables, stirring to
incorporate, and continue stir-frying for a further 4–5 minutes.

After the beans have cooked for 30 minutes, add the vegetable mixture to the beans and continue cooking. The stew will be ready to serve when the beans are tender. Add the tempeh cubes and the maple syrup just before serving and reheat gently. Remove the bay leaves before serving.

NUTRITIONAL FACTS per 350g serving

Using tempeh only

Calories 449 | Total fat 9.4g | Saturated fat 1.9g | Carbohydrates 61.9g | Protein 29.6g

CURRIED CHICKPEA STEW

~ SERVES 4 ~

200g dried chickpeas, picked over, rinsed and soaked overnight in
water to cover
900ml–1.4 litres vegetable stock
1 tsp ghee or olive oil
2 tsp cumin seeds
90g leeks or onions, chopped
1 pinch of red chilli flakes
1 tsp ground ginger
2 tsp curry powder
300g sweet potatoes, cubed
220g large cauliflower florets
150g shelled peas, fresh or frozen
225ml light coconut milk
2 tbsp coconut flakes, to garnish
2 tbsp chopped fresh coriander, to garnish

Drain and rinse the chickpeas. Combine the chickpeas and enough stock
to cover by 7.5cm in a stockpot or large saucepan and bring to the boil.
Reduce the heat and allow the beans to cook at a rolling boil for about 1
hour, adding extra stock as needed, or until tender.

Meanwhile, heat the ghee in a frying pan over a medium heat. Add
the cumin seeds and the leeks and stir-fry for 3 minutes. Add the chilli
flakes, ground ginger and the curry powder and stir-fry for 2 minutes. Add
the sweet potatoes and the cauliflower and stir-fry for a further 5 minutes,
making sure the vegetables are well coated in the spices.

After the beans have cooked for 30 minutes, add the vegetable mixture.
Return to the boil, then reduce the heat and simmer until the beans and
the sweet potatoes are tender. Add the peas and the coconut milk and
simmer for a further 3–4 minutes until heated through and frozen peas
are cooked. Serve over basmati rice and garnished with coconut flakes and
coriander.

NUTRITIONAL FACTS per 350g serving

Calories 498 | Total fat 12.6g | Saturated fat 5.1g | Carbohydrates 64.9g | Protein 31.4g

French Vegetable Stew

~ SERVES 4 ~

1 tsp ghee or olive oil
90g leeks or onions, chopped
1 tbsp Bragg Liquid Aminos or tamari soy sauce
½ tsp ground black pepper
1 tsp ground coriander
1 tsp balsamic vinegar
1 tsp dried tarragon
1 tsp dried marjoram
1 tsp dried basil
225ml vegetable stock, plus extra if necessary
1 tbsp wholemeal pastry flour, oat flour or rice flour
260g carrots, cut into 1cm half-moon slices
220g cauliflower florets
180g broccoli florets
150g shelled peas, fresh or frozen
150g French beans, cut into 2.5cm pieces
Finely shredded fresh basil or chopped fresh parsley, to garnish

Heat the ghee in a stockpot or large saucepan over a medium heat. Add the leeks and the black pepper, then add the coriander, balsamic vinegar, tarragon, marjoram and basil and stir-fry for 2 minutes, or until the leeks are beginning to become translucent. Add 2 tablespoons of stock and the flour and whisk to work the flour into the leek mixture. As the flour begins to brown, stir in the remaining stock. Add the carrots and simmer until the carrots are tender. Add the peas, remove the pan from the heat and cover, adding more stock, as necessary to maintain a slightly thickened sauce, then set aside.

Bring a large saucepan of water to the boil. Add the cauliflower, return the water to the boil and blanch for 2 minutes. Use a slotted spoon to transfer the cauliflower to the pan with the carrots, then re-cover the pan. Add the French beans to the water, return it to the boil and blanch for 3 minutes, then transfer to the carrots and cauliflower. Add the broccoli to the water, return it to the boil and blanch for 1 minute. Add it, the peas and the beans to the pan with the other pan, stirring the stew frequently after each addition so the vegetables are well coated. Heat the stew through until the beans and peas are cooked, being careful not to over-cook the broccoli. Garnish with the fresh basil or parsley. Serve over toasted millet or rice pilaf.

❖ ❖ ❖ ❖

NUTRITIONAL FACTS per 375g serving

Calories 145 | Total fat 2.1g | Saturated fat 0.2g | Carbohydrates 24.1g | Protein 7.7g

ITALIAN WHITE BEAN STEW

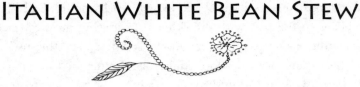

~ SERVES 4 ~

200g dried cannellini beans, picked over, rinsed and soaked overnight
in water to cover
900ml–1.4 litre vegetable stock
1 tsp ghee or olive oil
90g leeks or onions, chopped
1 red or green pepper, deseeded and chopped
1 tsp ground black pepper
1 tbsp dried mixed herbs
1 tsp garlic granules
1 tbsp Bragg Liquid Aminos or tamari soy sauce
260g carrots, cut into 0.5cm slices
125g courgette, cut into half-moons slices
70g spinach, rinsed and coarsely torn
175ml Roasted Tomato Sauce (page 251)
225g chicken 'sausages', finely sliced, or cooked skinless chicken,
chopped
Freshly grated Parmesan cheese, to garnish
Finely chopped fresh parsley, to garnish

Drain and rinse the beans. Combine the beans, enough stock to cover by 7.5cm and bay leaves in a stockpot or large saucepan and bring to the boil. Reduce the heat and allow the beans to cook at a rolling boil for about 1 hour, adding extra stock as needed, or until tender.

Meanwhile, heat the ghee in a frying pan over a medium heat. Add the leeks, red or green pepper, black pepper, ground mixed herbs, garlic and the aminos and stir-fry for 2–3 minutes. Add the carrots and continue to stir-fry for a further 2–3 minutes.

After the beans have cooked for 30 minutes, add the vegetable mixture. Return the liquid to the boil, then reduce the heat and simmer until the beans and carrots are tender. Add extra stock as necessary. When the beans are tender, add the courgettes, spinach and tomato sauce. If you are using sausage or chicken add it now and simmer for a further 5 minutes or until the courgettes are tender. Remove the bay leaves before serving, garnished with freshly grated Parmesan cheese and chopped parsley.

❖ ❖ ❖ ❖

NUTRITIONAL FACTS per 200g

Calories 349 | Total fat 5.2g | Saturated fat 1g | Carbohydrates 59g | Protein 16.8g

Made with 225g cooked chicken breast

Calories 482 | Total fat 8.2g | Saturated fat 1.9g | Carbohydrates 59g | Protein 43.2g

MEXICAN TOFU STEW

~ SERVES 4 ~

Olive oil spray for spraying the baking tray
5 tsp Bragg Liquid Aminos or tamari soy sauce
1 tsp chilli powder
450g firm or extra-firm silken tofu, ideally low fat, drained
2 tsp ghee or olive oil
90g leeks or onions, chopped
1 tsp ground black pepper
1 tsp turmeric
1 tsp ground cumin
2 tsp dried oregano
2 carrots, sliced
100g celery, finely chopped
360g tomatoes, diced
225–450ml vegetable stock
4 tbsp chopped fresh coriander

Preheat the oven to 180°C/Gas mark 4. Spray a baking tray with olive oil spray and set aside. Combine 2 teaspoons of the aminos and 1 teaspoon of the chilli powder in a bowl and whisk together. Add the tofu and gently toss so it is well coated. Arrange the tofu in a single layer on the baking tray and roast for 20 minutes. Remove the baking tray from the oven and set aside.

Heat the ghee in a frying pan over a medium heat. Add the leeks, the remaining 3 teaspoons of the aminos, the pepper, the remaining 1 teaspoon of the chilli powder, the turmeric, cumin and oregano and stir-fry for 3 minutes. Add the carrots, celery and tomatoes and stir-fry for a further 5 minutes. Add the tofu and enough stock to just cover all the ingredients and simmer for 5 minutes, or until the carrots are tender. Stir in the coriander. Serve with Spanish Pilaf (page 222).

NUTRITIONAL FACTS per 300g serving

Made with low-fat tofu

Calories 256 | Total fat 8.1g | Saturated fat 0.2g | Carbohydrates 21g | Protein 24.2g

RATATOUILLE

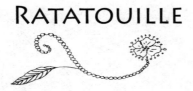

Ratatouille makes a wonderful base for an Italian fish stew. Add 150–300g marinated and grilled fish, such as salmon, halibut or cod, cut into bite-sized pieces.

~ SERVES 4 ~

1 large aubergine, cut into 2.5cm cubes
2 large courgettes, cubed
3 large red and green peppers, deseeded and chopped
1 tsp ghee or olive oil
2 large leeks or onions, chopped
2 tsp dried mixed herbs
1 tsp dried marjoram
1 tsp dried thyme
½ tsp ground black pepper
1 tsp garlic granules
1 tbsp Bragg Liquid Aminos or tamari soy sauce
360g tomatoes, diced
350ml vegetable stock
15g fresh basil leaves, shredded
150–300g chopped marinated grilled salmon, halibut or cod
(optional)

Submerge the aubergine in a bowl of salted water and set aside. Heat the ghee in a stockpot or large saucepan over a medium heat. Add the leeks, mixed herbs, marjoram, thyme, black pepper, garlic and the aminos. Drain the aubergine and add it to the pan along with the courgettes and red and green peppers and stir-fry for 4–5 minutes. Add the stock as the mixture looks like it is drying out. Add the tomatoes and simmer for 20–30 minutes over a low heat. The liquid should just cover the vegetables. If you are adding the seafood, stir it in and warm through for 2–3 minutes. Add the fresh basil just before serving.

NUTRITIONAL FACTS per 225g serving

Calories 215 | Total fat 6.8g | Saturated fat 3.4g | Carbohydrates 27.1g | Protein 11.5g

Made with 225g Atlantic salmon

Calories 370 | Total fat 14g | Saturated fat 4.5g | Carbohydrates 27.1g | Protein 34g

ROASTED WINTER VEGETABLE STEW

Make this hearty stew for guests on a cold winter's day

~ SERVES 6 ~

200g dried cannellini beans, picked over, rinsed and soaked overnight in water to cover
900ml–1.4 litres vegetable stock, plus extra if needed
300g floury or sweet potatoes, cubed
280g butternut squash, peeled and cubed
2 tsp olive oil, plus extra for greasing the baking tray
1 tbsp dried sage
1 tbsp dried thyme
2 tbsp Bragg Liquid Aminos or tamari soy sauce
220g cauliflower florets
90g leeks, shallots or onions, chopped
3 fresh rosemary sprigs, leaves removed from the stalks and chopped
½ tsp ground black pepper
4 tbsp finely shredded fresh basil, to garnish

SAUCE

1 tsp ghee or olive oil
45g leeks, chopped
1 tsp ground black pepper
1 pinch of salt
1 tsp dried thyme
1 tsp dried sage
1 tbsp finely chopped fresh rosemary leaves
2 tbsp vegetable stock
2 tbsp wholemeal or unbleached pastry flour
675–900ml light soya milk or coconut milk

Drain and rinse the beans. Combine the beans and enough stock to cover by 7.5cm in a stockpot or large saucepan and bring to the boil. Reduce the heat and allow the beans to cook at a rolling boil for about 1 hour, adding extra stock as needed, or until tender. When the beans are tender, drain them and set aside.

Preheat the oven to 180°C/Gas mark 4 and grease a baking tray with a little olive oil. Combine 1 teaspoon of the olive oil, the sage, thyme, 1 tablespoon stock and 1 tablespoon of the aminos and whisk together. Add the potatoes and squash to this mixture and toss until well coated. Arrange the vegetables in a single layer on the baking tray and roast for 20–30 minutes. Remove the baking tray from the oven and set aside.

Bring a stockpot or large saucepan of water to the boil. Add the cauliflower, return the water to the boil and blanch for 3 minutes. Drain the cauliflower and set aside.

Return the pan to the hob over a medium heat and heat the remaining 1 teaspoon olive oil. Add the leeks, remaining 1 tablespoon of the aminos, the rosemary, black pepper and the reserved cooked beans and stir-fry for 4–5 minutes. Add 4 tablespoons stock as needed. Stir in the blanched cauliflower and roasted vegetables and stir-fry over a very low heat for a further 3–4 minutes. Remove the pan from the heat, cover and set aside.

Meanwhile, to make the sauce, heat the ghee in a small saucepan. Add the leeks, pepper, salt, thyme, sage and rosemary and stir-fry for 2–3 minutes. Using a whisk, add the stock and flour while stirring frequently to allow the flour to brown. Slowly add the soya milk, whisking continuously, until the sauce has a creamy consistency. Add additional soya milk as the sauce begins to thicken. Add more soya milk if the sauce is too thick. Add the sauce to the stew and garnish with the basil just before serving.

NUTRITIONAL FACTS per 300g serving
Calories 368 | Total fat 7.1g | Saturated fat 2.1g | Carbohydrates 61.3g | Protein 14.5g

THAI TOFU VEGETABLE STEW

~ SERVES 4 ~

450g firm or extra-firm silken tofu, ideally low fat, drained and diced
250g broccoli florets
1 tsp ghee or sesame oil
1 tsp cumin seeds
45g leeks or onion, chopped
2.5cm piece root ginger, peeled and very finely chopped or grated
3 garlic cloves, very finely chopped, or 1 tsp garlic granules
1 jalapeño chilli, whole with the top cut off the stalk
2 tbsp Bragg Liquid Aminos or tamari soy sauce
1 tsp turmeric
125ml apple juice
300g sweet potatoes, peeled and cut into 1cm cubes
1 tsp ground cumin
1 tsp ground coriander
½ tsp ground ginger
400ml light coconut milk or soya milk
225ml vegetable stock
2 tbsp chopped fresh coriander, to garnish
55g beansprouts, to garnish

MARINADE

225ml apple juice
125ml Bragg Liquid Aminos or tamari soy sauce
4 tbsp lemon juice
1 tsp ground cumin
1 tsp ground coriander
1 tsp ground ginger

Preheat the oven to 180°C/Gas mark 4. To make the marinade, combine the apple juice, the aminos, lemon juice, cumin, coriander and ginger in a shallow ovenproof dish and whisk with a fork. Add the tofu and place the dish in the oven to roast for 20–30 minutes. Remove the dish from the oven and set aside.

Meanwhile, bring a stockpot or large saucepan of water to the boil. Add the broccoli, return the water to the boil and blanch for 1 minute. Be careful not to over-cook. Strain the broccoli from the pot and rinse in cold water and set aside. Heat the ghee in the same pan. Add the cumin seeds and stir until they brown lightly. Add the leeks, root ginger, garlic and chilli and stir-fry for 2–3 minutes. Add the aminos, turmeric, 2 tablespoons of apple juice, the sweet potatoes, ground cumin, ground coriander and ground ginger, stirring frequently as the sweet potatoes, leeks and spices begin to brown. Stir-fry for 4–5 minutes until the sweet potatoes look caramelized. Add the coconut milk and the remaining apple juice. Bring to the boil, and then reduce the heat, add the stock and simmer for about 10 minutes, or until the sweet potatoes are soft, but not mushy. Add the broccoli and the tofu cubes. Garnish with the coriander and beansprouts. Remove the chilli before serving.

NUTRITIONAL FACTS per 350g serving

Made with low-fat tofu

Calories 444 | Total fat 15.6g | Saturated fat 6.1g | Carbohydrates 48.6g | Protein 27.5g

TOFU, AUBERGINE AND POTATO STEW

~ SERVES 4 ~

1 tbsp olive oil, plus extra for greasing the baking tray
2 tsp ground allspice
2 tsp ground coriander
1 tsp dried dill
4 tsp Bragg Liquid Aminos or tamari soy sauce
160g aubergine, cut into 2.5cm cubes with the skin left on
3 waxy potatoes, unpeeled and cubed
480g firm or extra-firm silken tofu, ideally low fat, drained and cubed
1 tsp ghee or olive oil
90g leeks or onions, chopped
½ tsp ground black pepper
130g carrots, diced
1 red pepper, deseeded and diced
180g tomato, diced
225–450ml vegetable stock, plus extra, if necessary
15g fresh basil or coriander, chopped

Preheat the oven to 180°C/Gas mark 4. Lightly grease a baking tray with olive oil and set aside. Combine the olive oil, 1 teaspoon of the allspice, the ground coriander, dill and 3 teaspoons of the aminos in a large bowl. Add the aubergines, potatoes and tofu and toss together with your hands until well coated. Arrange the vegetables and tofu in a single layer on the roasting tray and roast for 20–30 minutes. Remove the pan from the oven and set aside.

Meanwhile, heat the ghee in a stockpot or large saucepan over a high heat. Add the leeks, black pepper, the remaining 1 teaspoon aminos and the remaining 1 teaspoon allspice and stir-fry for 2–3 minutes. Add the carrots, red peppers and tomatoes and continue to stir-fry for 5 minutes. Add just enough stock to cover the tomatoes and stir-fry for a further 3–4 minutes until the carrots are tender. Add the roasted aubergine, potatoes and tofu and more stock if necessary. Add the fresh basil or coriander just before serving.

❖　❖　❖　❖

NUTRITIONAL FACTS per 350g serving

Made with low-fat tofu

Calories 318 | Total fat 8.6g | Saturated fat 0.7g | Carbohydrates 40.1g | Protein 19.8g

VEGETABLE AND WHITE BEAN CHILLI

~ SERVES 4 ~

200g dried cannellini beans, picked over, rinsed and soaked overnight in water to cover
900ml–1.4 litres vegetable stock, plus extra if needed
1 tsp ghee or olive oil
90g leeks or onions, chopped
2 tbsp deseeded and chopped canned or freshly roasted Anaheim mild chillies
2 garlic cloves, very finely chopped
1 tbsp chilli powder
1 tsp dried cumin
1 tsp ground coriander
225g skinless smoked chicken or turkey, cubed, or south-western-style chicken 'sausage', or ground turkey or chicken (optional)
130g carrots, cut into 2.5cm pieces
180g tomatoes, chopped
125g courgette, diced
35g spinach, rinsed
150g sweetcorn kernels, fresh or frozen
2 spring onions, chopped, to garnish
4 tbsp chopped fresh coriander, to garnish

Drain and rinse the beans. Combine the beans and enough stock to cover by 7.5cm in a stockpot or large saucepan and bring to the boil. Reduce the heat and allow the beans to cook at a low rolling boil for about 1 hour, adding extra stock as needed, or until tender.

Meanwhile, heat the ghee in a frying pan over a medium heat. Add the leeks, chillies, garlic, chilli powder, cumin and ground coriander. If you are using the ground turkey or chicken, add it now. Stir fry for 3 minutes. Add the carrots and the tomatoes. If you are using the smoked chicken or turkey or the chicken 'sausage', add it now. Allow the stew to simmer for 5–7 minutes until the carrots are tender. Add the courgette during the final 2 minutes. Add the vegetable mixture to the cooking beans when the beans are almost tender. Stir in the spinach and the sweetcorn and continue simmering for 5 minutes, or until the sweetcorn is tender. Serve garnished with spring onions and fresh coriander.

NUTRITIONAL FACTS per 350g serving

Calories 364 | Total fat 4.2g | Saturated fat 0.5g | Carbohydrates 53.2g | Protein 28g

Made using 225g smoked turkey breast

Calories 445 | Total fat 5.1g | Saturated fat 0.8g | Carbohydrates 54.6g | Protein 44.8g

Vegetables, Grains and
Quick Light Meals

'The true essentials of a feast are only fun and feed'
– Oliver Wendell Holmes

Side dishes provide a great complement to any meal. They play an important role in rounding out the nutritional value and tastes of a meal. Several side dishes can constitute a meal in themselves. Mix and match several smaller dishes to make a simple, nutritious meal. Be creative.

As a light meal, mix and match a soup or stew with a side dish. For example: try Tortilla Soup with Avocado and Coriander (page 167) along with Spicy Mexican Rice, or try Aubergine and Yam Stew (page 178) with Green Quinoa Pilaf. See more suggestions in the 30-Day Nutritional Plan beginning on page 296. The side dishes can be used in many creative ways. Combine a grain dish, such as Indian Rice on a bed of stir-fried greens with Cucumber Raita, or use Greek Goddess Salad (page 228) as a stuffing for a squash dish. Enjoy!

VEGETABLES, GRAINS AND QUICK LIGHT MEALS INDEX

★ The asterisk indicates Quick Meals with optional chicken or fish additions.

WRAPS

Making a wrap is a great lunch-on-the-run, and a healthy alternative to fast food. Be creative. Use 20–25cm wholemeal or plain tortillas for your wraps. Any leftover salads, stews, grains, sauces, vegetables, or condiments from your daily meals make ideal fillings for wraps. When making a wrap, layer the filling ingredients in the centre of the tortilla and use enough sauce so the wrap will stay rolled up. Roll up the tortilla to enclose the filling, and wrap in cling film or place in a container.

In addition to the wrap recipes that follow, try wrapping up some of the other recipes in this book.

Wrap Suggestions:

Egg-Less Tofu (page 214)
Indian Rice (page 217) and Cucumber Raita (page 241)
Tofu Fajitas (page 139) with Tomato Salsa (page 256)
Spanish Pilaf (page 222) and Cajun Bean Stew (page 182)
Thai Tofu Vegetable Stew (page 195) and Spicy Lime and Red Pepper Sauce (page 254)
Curried Chickpea Stew (page 184) and Indian Rice (page 217)
Curried Potato (page 210) and Cucumber Raita (page 241)

BLACK BEAN AND RICE WRAP

~ SERVES 1 ~

One 20–25cm wholemeal or plain tortilla
125g Black Bean and Yam Stew (page 180)
4 tbsp cooked rice
2 tbsp tomato salsa
4 tbsp sprouts
2 tbsp grated carrot
1 lettuce leaf

Place the stew in the middle of the tortilla. Add the rice, salsa, sprouts, carrots and lettuce leaf. Roll up tightly into a 5–7.5cm-wide wrap.

NUTRITIONAL FACTS per wrap

Calories 444 | Total fat 6.6g | Saturated fat 2.3g | Carbohydrates 82.7g | Protein 13.5g

LETTUCE WRAP

~ SERVES 4 (2 WRAPS PER SERVING) ~

8 large webb lettuce leaves, rinsed and dried
225g Hummus (page 243)
125g marinated firm or extra-firm silken tofu (page 52), ideally low fat, drained and cut into long, thin strips
130g carrots, very thinly sliced like matchsticks
100g sunflower sprouts

Lay all the lettuce leaves flat on the work surface. Spread the hummus in the centre of each leaf. Lay the tofu strips, carrot sticks and sunflower sprouts on top of the hummus, leaving some sprouts to hang about 2.5cm over the edge of the tortilla. Fold the bottom of the lettuce over the filling and gently roll up from one side to the other to enclose all the ingredients. Serve with Nutty Dipping Sauce (page 248) and Spicy Lime and Red Pepper Dipping Sauce (page 254) as a first course.

NUTRITIONAL FACTS per 2 wraps

Made with low-fat tofu and served with 2 sauces

Calories 331 | Total fat 14.6g | Saturated fat 2.1g | Carbohydrates 37.5g | Protein 12g

MARINATED TOFU THAI WRAP WITH NUTTY DIPPING SAUCE

~ SERVES 1 ~

60g marinated firm or extra-firm silken tofu (page 52), ideally low fat,
drained and thinly sliced
One 20–25cm wholemeal or plain tortilla
1 tbsp Nutty Dipping Sauce (page 248)
1 tbsp grated carrot
1 tbsp shredded red cabbage
1 tbsp grated courgette
1 tbsp chopped fresh coriander
4 tbsp sprouts
1 leaf red-leaf or cos lettuce

Place the tofu strips in the centre of the tortilla, and spread about 1 tablespoon of the sauce over them. Top with carrot, cabbage, courgette, coriander, sprouts and lettuce leaf. Drizzle some additional sauce over the vegetables. Roll up tightly into a 5–7.5cm–wide wrap.

CHICKEN OR FISH VARIATION

Replace the tofu with 75g sliced grilled skinless chicken or fish, add sauce and roll up as instructed above.

NUTRITIONAL FACTS per wrap

Made with low-fat tofu

Calories 395 | Total fat 15.8g | Saturated fat 2.3g | Carbohydrates 43.4g | Protein 19.4g

VEGETABLE HUMMUS WRAP

~ SERVES 1 ~

One 20–25cm wholemeal or plain tortilla
2 tbsp Hummus (page 243)
3 tbsp grated carrot
3 tbsp grated courgette
4 tbsp sprouts
1 leaf red-leaf or cos lettuce

Spread the hummus in the centre and to the edge of the tortilla, then add the grated carrot, courgette, sprouts and lettuce mix. Add any additional vegetable, grain, sauce or condiment you like. Roll up tightly into a 5–7.5cm-wide wrap.

VARIATION: CHICKEN OR TURKEY WRAP

Place 75g sliced cooked skinless chicken or turkey breast on top of the hummus and roll up as instructed above.

NUTRITIONAL FACTS per wrap

Calculations for the vegetarian wrap

Calories 320 | Total fat 7.6g | Saturated fat 1.5g | Carbohydrates 51.3g | Protein 11.5g

CAULIFLOWER AND BRAISED TOMATO SAUCE

~ SERVES 4 ~

1 large cauliflower, cut into florets
1 tsp ghee or olive oil
1 tsp mustard seeds
1 tsp ground cumin seeds
90g leeks, onions or shallots, chopped
2.5cm piece root ginger, very finely chopped
1 small jalapeño chilli, stem removed and deseeded but left whole
1 tbsp ground coriander
½ tsp turmeric
1 tbsp Bragg Liquid Aminos or tamari soy sauce
3 tomatoes, diced
350ml vegetable stock, plus extra if needed
1 tbsp tomato purée
2 tsp garam masala

Bring a large saucepan of water to the boil. Add the cauliflower, return the water to the boil and blanch for 5 minutes. Drain the cauliflower and set aside. Heat the ghee in a large frying pan over a medium heat. Add the mustard seeds and cumin seeds and stir until they begin to pop. Add the leeks, ginger and chilli and stir-fry for 2–3 minutes until the leeks are translucent. Add the coriander, turmeric and the aminos and continue to stir-fry for a further 2 minutes. Add the tomatoes and simmer for 5 minutes, or until they begin to breakdown. Stir in the stock and tomato purée and simmer for a further 3–4 minutes until the sauce begins to thicken. Add extra stock if necessary to maintain a smooth texture. Add the cauliflower and the garam masala and continue simmering to heat through. Remove the chilli before serving.

NUTRITIONAL FACTS per 225ml serving

Calories 116 | Total fat 2.8g | Saturated fat 1.1g | Carbohydrates 16.6g | Protein 6.2g

CHINESE FIVE-SPICE GARDEN PILAF

~ SERVES 4 ~

300g organic basmati rice, rinsed in a strainer
450ml water or vegetable stock
1 tsp Bragg Liquid Aminos or tamari soy sauce
1 cinnamon stick
75g fresh or frozen shelled peas
55g carrots, grated
75g sweetcorn kernels, fresh or frozen
1 tsp Chinese five-spice powder
1 tsp ground ginger
2 tbsp finely chopped fresh coriander, to garnish

Combine the stock, the aminos, cinnamon and rice in saucepan with a tight-fitting lid and bring to the boil. Reduce the heat to the lowest possible heat (use a heat diffuser if you have one) and keep it there and allow the rice to simmer for 20 minutes, or until it smells really good. Resist lifting the lid, as the rice cooks best without interruption.

Meanwhile, combine the peas, carrots and sweetcorn in a bowl. Add the five-spice powder and ginger and use a fork to stir together. When the rice has cooked for 20 minutes, remove the lid and fluff with a fork. Re-cover the pan and let the rice rest for 5 minutes. Using your fork, add the rice to the vegetable mixture and combine well. Garnish with the coriander. Serve with a stir-fry.

❖ ❖ ❖ ❖

NUTRITIONAL FACTS per 175g serving
Calories 225 | Total fat 1g | Saturated fat 0.1g | Carbohydrates 49.1g | Protein 5.1g

Curried Potatoes

~ SERVES 4 ~

4 floury potatoes, peeled, cubed and soaked in water to cover
1 tsp ghee or olive oil
1 tsp cumin seeds
1 tsp brown mustard seeds
1 tsp fenugreek seeds
90g leeks or onions, chopped
2 tsp very finely chopped peeled root ginger
4 tbsp fruit chutney or apricot jam
½ tsp turmeric
1 tbsp Bragg Liquid Aminos or tamari soy sauce
1 pinch of cayenne pepper
2 tsp ground coriander
225ml vegetable stock, plus extra if needed
2 tsp lemon juice
225ml light coconut milk
225ml light soya milk
150g frozen peas
4 tbsp finely chopped fresh coriander

Bring a large saucepan of water to the boil. Add the potatoes, return the water to the boil and blanch for 5 minutes, or until just about soft. Drain the potatoes and set aside. Heat the ghee in the same pan. Add the cumin seeds, mustard seeds and fenugreek seeds and stir until the seeds pop. Add the leeks and the ginger and stir-fry for 2 minutes. Stir in the fruit chutney and continue to stir-frying for a further 1–2 minutes. Add the turmeric, the aminos, cayenne, ground coriander and stock and simmer for 3–4 minutes. Add the potatoes and stir coat well with the mixture. Add the lemon juice, coconut milk, soya milk, peas and fresh coriander and bring to the boil, stirring frequently. Reduce the heat and simmer over a low heat for a further 3–4 minutes until the frozen peas are cooked. Be careful not to over-cook this dish.

NUTRITIONAL FACTS per 150g serving

Calories 399 | Total fat 11.2g | Saturated fat 6.1g | Carbohydrates 64.4g | Protein 10.3g

DILLED ASPARAGUS

~ SERVES 4 ~

125ml vegetable stock
½ tsp ground black pepper
1 tsp dried dill
1 tbsp Bragg Liquid Aminos or tamari soy sauce
450g asparagus, 2.5cm cut from the base of each stalk and discarded
1 tsp balsamic vinegar
Chopped fresh dill, to garnish

Combine the stock, pepper, dill and the aminos in a large frying pan with a tight-fitting lid. Arrange the asparagus flat in the pan – the liquid should barely cover the asparagus. Cover the pan and bring to the boil. Reduce to medium and allow the asparagus to simmer for 5 minutes, moving the stalks around occasionally for even cooking, or until tender. Remove the pan from the heat, sprinkle the vinegar over the asparagus, re-cover the pan and set aside to rest for up to 10 minutes. Garnish with fresh dill.

NUTRITIONAL FACTS per serving (6 to 8 spears)
Calories 49 | Total fat 0.4g | Saturated fat 0.1g | Carbohydrates 6.1g | Protein 5.2g

DILLED LEMON COURGETTES

~ SERVES 4 ~

1 tsp olive oil
4 large courgettes, cut into 0.5cm slices
2 tbsp lemon juice
2 tsp spicy stone-ground mustard, such as Dijon
2 tbsp vegetable stock
1 pinch of ground black pepper
1 tbsp dried dill

Heat the oil in a large frying pan over a medium heat. Add the courgettes and fry, gently stirring, for 3–4 minutes. Add the lemon juice and mustard and continue frying for a further 2 minutes, then add the stock, pepper and dill and continue cooking for 4–5 minutes until the courgettes are browned.

NUTRITIONAL FACTS per 125g serving

Calories 42 | Total fat 1.3g | Saturated fat 0.2g | Carbohydrates 5.3g | Protein 2.3g

Egg-less Tofu Salad or Sandwich

~ SERVES 4 ~

450g firm or extra-firm silken tofu, ideally low fat, drained
4 tbsp chopped spring onions
2 tbsp chopped fresh coriander
2 tbsp chopped parsley
2 celery stalks, chopped
4 tbsp grated carrots
1 tsp Bragg Liquid Aminos or tamari soy sauce
1 pinch of ground black pepper
½ tsp turmeric
1 tsp dried dill
1 tsp curry powder
2 tbsp Dijon mustard
4 tbsp natural yogurt or soya mayonnaise

Crumble the tofu into a bowl. Add the spring onions, coriander, parsley, celery, carrots and the aminos. Use your fingers to mix together until the mixture is well combined. Combine the pepper, turmeric, dill, curry powder, mustard and yogurt, then use a fork to combine it with the tofu mixture until a smooth consistency is achieved. Serve on a bed of field greens or as a filling for a sandwich between two slices of your home-made Simple Great Wholegrain Bread (page 50), or use in a wrap.

❖ ❖ ❖ ❖

NUTRITIONAL FACTS per 125g serving

Salad only, doesn't include bread; made with low-fat tofu

Calories 149 | Total fat 5.5g | Saturated fat 0.2g | Carbohydrates 9.7g | Protein 15.1g

GREEN QUINOA PILAF

~ SERVES 4 ~

600ml vegetable stock or water, plus extra if needed
240g quinoa, rinsed
1 tsp ghee or olive oil
1 pinch of red chilli flakes
½ tsp ground black pepper
90g leeks or onions, chopped
1 tsp ground cumin
1 tbsp Bragg Liquid Aminos or tamari soy sauce
2 courgettes, cut into half-moon slices
1 yellow courgette, cut into half-moon slices
2 handfuls mixed cooking greens, such as Swiss chard, spinach and
mustard greens, rinsed and coarsely torn
3 tbsp finely chopped fresh coriander
1 tsp dried oregano
1 tsp paprika or chilli powder
1 large tomato, diced

Bring the stock to the boil in a large saucepan with a tight-fitting lid. Meanwhile, toast the quinoa in a large, dry skillet, stirring frequently, for about 2 minutes, or until golden brown. When the stock is boiling, add the quinoa, reduce the heat and simmer for 15–20 minutes until the liquid is absorbed. Place the quinoa into a bowl and fluff with a fork, then set aside to cool.

Heat the ghee in a frying pan over a medium heat. Add the chilli flakes, pepper, leeks, cumin and the aminos and stir-fry until the leeks are browned. Add a little stock if the mixture begins to dry. Add the green and yellow courgettes and continue stir-frying for 3–4 minutes. Stir in the greens and continue to stir-fry until they are just wilted. Remove the pan from the heat and drain off any excess liquid, then set aside. Add the coriander, oregano, paprika and tomato to the quinoa. Toss together until well combined. This dish can be a hot side dish or a wonderful cold salad on a bed of greens.

NUTRITIONAL FACTS per 175g serving

Calories 287 | Total fat 5.8g | Saturated fat 0.9g | Carbohydrates 40.6g | Protein 18.1g

INDIAN RICE

~ SERVES 4 ~

300g organic basmati rice, rinsed in a strainer
675ml vegetable stock or water
1 cinnamon stick
3 green cardamom pods
1 tsp ghee or olive oil
90g leeks or onion, chopped
1 green pepper, deseeded and diced
½ tsp turmeric
1 tsp garam masala
1 tsp ground coriander
55g carrots, grated
4 tbsp finely chopped roasted pepper, freshly roasted or canned, drained
2 tbsp sultanas
4 tbsp finely chopped fresh coriander

Combine the stock, cinnamon stick, cardamom pods and rice in a saucepan with a tight-fitting lid and bring to the boil. Reduce the heat to the lowest possible heat (use a heat diffuser if you have one) and allow the rice to simmer for 20–25 minutes. Resist lifting the lid, as the rice cooks best without interruption. When the rice has cooked, remove the lid and fluff with a fork. Re-cover the pan and let the rice rest for 5 minutes.

Meanwhile, heat the ghee in a frying pan over a medium heat. Add the leeks and green pepper and stir-fry for 2 minutes. Add the turmeric, garam masala and ground coriander and continue stir-frying for 2 minutes. Remove the pan from the heat and set aside to cool, then combine these ingredients with the rice.

Combine the carrots, red pepper, sultanas and fresh coriander in a bowl. Using a spoon, stir in the rice mixture. Remove the cardamom pods and cinnamon stick just before serving. This can be served as a hot side dish or a cold salad on a bed of greens.

NUTRITIONAL FACTS per 200g serving

Calories 343 | Total fat 2.8g | Saturated fat 1g | Carbohydrates 72.4g | Protein 7g

NUTTY SPINACH GREENS

~ SERVES 4 ~

1 tsp ghee or olive oil
90g leeks or onions, chopped
1 tsp Bragg Liquid Aminos or tamari soy sauce
½ tsp cumin seeds
½ tsp ground black pepper
300g spinach, rinsed and coarsely torn
4 tbsp vegetable stock
2 tbsp apple juice
4 tbsp sliced almonds, toasted, to garnish

Heat the ghee in frying pan over a medium heat. Add the leeks, the aminos, cumin and black pepper and stir-fry for 2–3 minutes until the leeks are translucent. Add the spinach, stirring, until it is just wilted but keeping its vibrant green colour. Add the vegetable stock as the spinach starts to dry out. Finish off the spinach by adding the apple juice and allowing it to simmer for 1 minute, incorporating the flavours. Sprinkle with the almonds just before serving.

❖ ❖ ❖ ❖

NUTRITIONAL FACTS per 180g
Calories 80 | Total fat 4.6g | Saturated fat 1.1g | Carbohydrates 6.1g | Protein 3.4g

OAT GROAT PILAF WITH SPINACH

~ SERVES 4 ~

200g oat or buckwheat groats
450ml vegetable stock or water
1 tsp ghee or olive oil
90g leeks or onions, chopped
1 tsp Bragg Liquid Aminos or tamari soy sauce, plus extra if needed
125g spinach, rinsed and coarsely torn
4 tbsp apple juice
2 tbsp lemon juice
1 tsp dried dill
½ tsp ground black pepper
½ tsp garam masala
30g parsley, finely grated

Combine the oats and stock in a saucepan and bring to the boil. Reduce the heat to a simmer until the groats are tender and most of the water is absorbed. Don't cover and do stir frequently to make sure they don't stick. Rinse the groats with cold water, put in a bowl and leave to cool

Heat the ghee in a saucepan over a medium heat. Add the leeks and the aminos and stir-fry for 2–3 minutes until the leeks are translucent. Add the spinach to the pan and continue stir-frying until it is just wilted. Remove the pan from the heat and set aside.

Combine the apple juice, lemon juice, dill, pepper and garam masala and whisk together. Pour over the groats and add the spinach and parsley and toss gently until combined. Taste for saltiness; you may need to add a little more aminos.

NUTRITIONAL FACTS per 100g

Calories 218 | Total fat 3.1g | Saturated fat 1g | Carbohydrates 40.6g | Protein 7g

SAVOURY SWISS CHARD

~ SERVES 4 ~

1 tsp ghee or olive oil
¼ tsp brown mustard seeds
1 pinch of ground black pepper
45g leeks or onions, chopped
1 tsp Bragg Liquid Aminos or tamari soy sauce, plus extra if needed
280g red or green Swiss chard, rinsed and torn
1 tsp balsamic vinegar
1 tsp garam masala

Heat the oil in a large frying pan. Add the mustard seeds and pepper and fry just until you hear a pop. Add the leeks, the aminos and the chard and stir-fry, until the chard begins to look slightly limp, but still maintains a vibrant colour. Add the balsamic vinegar and garam masala and allow to simmer for a further 2 minutes before serving. Add a little more aminos if the chard tastes too bitter.

NUTRITIONAL FACTS per 175g serving
Calories 42 | Total fat 1.5g | Saturated fat 0.9g | Carbohydrates 5.1g | Protein 1.9g

SPANISH PILAF

~ SERVES 4 ~

200g organic basmati rice, rinsed in a strainer
85g quinoa, rinsed in the same strainer with the rice
675ml vegetable stock or water, plus an extra 2 tbsp
1 tsp ghee or olive oil
45g leeks or onions, chopped
½ tsp ground black pepper
1 tsp Bragg Liquid Aminos or tamari soy sauce
1 tsp paprika
1 tsp chilli powder
1 tsp ground cinnamon
1 tsp ground cumin
75g sweetcorn kernels, fresh or frozen
75g shelled peas, fresh or frozen

Combine the stock, rice and quinoa in a saucepan with a tight-fitting lid and bring to the boil. Reduce the heat to the lowest possible heat (use a heat diffuser if you have one) and keep it there. Allow the grains to simmer for 20–25 minutes. Resist lifting the lid, as the grains will cook best without interruption. Fluff with a fork and set aside, covered.

Meanwhile, heat the ghee in a large frying pan. Add the leeks, pepper and the aminos and stir-fry until the leeks brown slightly. Add the paprika, chilli powder, cinnamon, cumin and the remaining 2 tablespoons vegetable stock when the mixture looks dry. Add the sweetcorn and the peas and continue to stir-fry for 2 minutes. Add the rice and quinoa and combine well.

NUTRITIONAL FACTS per 200g serving

Calories 360 | Total fat 3.4g | Saturated fat 0.1g | Carbohydrates 62.5g | Protein 9.1g

SPICY MEXICAN RICE

~ SERVES 4 ~

300g organic basmati rice, rinsed in a strainer
675g vegetable stock or water, plus extra if necessary
1 tsp ghee or olive oil
45g leeks or onions, chopped
1 tbsp Bragg Liquid Aminos or tamari soy sauce
½ green pepper, deseeded and diced
200g cooked black beans, rinsed if tinned
75g sweetcorn kernels, fresh or frozen
½ tsp ground black pepper
1 tsp dried oregano
1 tsp dried cumin
1 tsp dried coriander
1 pinch of cayenne
1 tsp chilli powder
4 tbsp finely chopped coriander, to garnish
90g tomatoes, freshly diced, to garnish

Combine the stock and rice in a saucepan and bring to the boil. Reduce the heat to the lowest possible heat (use a heat diffuser, if you have one) and keep it there and allow to simmer for 20–25 minutes. Resist lifting the lid, as the rice cooks better without interruption. Fluff with a fork and set aside, covered.

Heat the ghee in a frying pan over a medium heat. Add the leeks, the aminos, green pepper, beans and the sweetcorn and stir-fry for 3 minutes. Combine the black pepper, oregano, cumin, coriander, cayenne and chilli powder with a fork. Add the spice mix to the pan and continue to stir-fry for a further minute. Be prepared to add some stock as necessary if the mixture dries out. Using a rubber spatula, transfer the vegetable mixture into a bowl, add the rice to it and combine well. Garnish with the fresh coriander and the tomatoes.

NUTRITIONAL FACTS per 200g serving
Calories 485 | Total fat 4.5g | Saturated fat 1.3g | Carbohydrates 86.7g | Protein 24.6g

TUSCANY BULGUR PILAF

~ SERVES 4 ~

200g bulgur wheat (cracked wheat)
350ml vegetable stock or water, plus extra if needed
1 tsp ghee or olive oil
45g leeks or onions, chopped
4 tbsp finely chopped roasted and deseeded red peppers, drained if
tinned or bottled
125g courgette, diced
200g cooked or tinned cannellini beans, rinsed if necessary
180g tomatoes, freshly diced
30g flat-leaf parsley, freshly chopped
2 tbsp finely shredded fresh basil
2 tbsp finely chopped fresh mint
2 tbsp sliced stoned kalamata olives

DRESSING

2 tbsp lemon juice
1 tbsp apple juice
1 tbsp Bragg Liquid Aminos or tamari soy sauce
1 tsp dried dill
½ tsp ground black pepper
½ tsp salt
2 garlic cloves, crushed, or ½ tsp garlic granules
2 tsp olive oil

Bring 350ml of the vegetable stock to the boil in a small saucepan with a
tight-fitting lid. Add the bulgur, stir with a fork, remove the pan from the
heat and allow the bulgur to soak for 15 minutes. Fluff with a fork and
place into a large, flat mixing bowl, allowing the bulgur cool down.

Meanwhile, heat the ghee in a frying pan over a medium heat. Add
the leeks and stir-fry quickly. Add the red pepper and the courgette and
stir-fry for a further 2 minutes. Add the beans and continue stir-frying for

2 minutes, adding the remaining stock as the mixture begins to dry out. Remove the pan from the heat and allow the vegetables to cool. Place the tomatoes, parsley, basil, mint and olives in the bowl with the cooled bulgur. Add the stir-fried vegetables and combine gently. In a separate bowl, to make the dressing, combine the lemon juice, apple juice, the aminos, dill, salt, pepper and the garlic, whisking together. Continue to whisk together as you slowly add the olive oil. Pour the dressing over the bulgur wheat and vegetable mixture. This pilaf can be served hot with a main course or used as a stuffing for vegetables, such as artichokes and courgettes and other squash. It also makes a cold salad.

❖　❖　❖　❖

NUTRITIONAL FACTS per 200g serving
Calories 304 | Total fat 6g | Saturated fat 1.3g | Carbohydrates 49.8g | Protein 12.6g

Salad Greens

Always keep some salad greens on hand in your refrigerator. Spinach, mixed greens, cos and webb lettuce are good choices. A cold salad as a side dish can be as simple as tossing some olive oil and a splash of balsamic vinaigrette on a mixture of mixed greens.

Grilled chicken or fish can be added to any salad for additional taste and protein. Slice the chicken or fish into long thin pieces and arrange on top of the salad just before serving. Here are two of our favourite salads.

GARDEN SALAD

~ SERVES 1 ~

3 cos lettuce leaves, rinsed and torn
2 tbsp grated carrot
2 tbsp grated courgette
2 tomato wedges
55g sprouts, such as alfalfa or sunflower
2 cucumber slices
1 tsp sunflower seeds, toasted
1 tsp olive oil
1½ tsp balsamic vinegar

NUTRITIONAL FACTS per serving

For salad only, without chicken or fish

Calories 92 | Total fat 6.4g | Saturated fat 0.8g | Carbohydrates 6.4g | Protein 2.3g

GREEK GODDESS SALAD

~ SERVES 4 ~

175g couscous
2 tbsp pine nuts, toasted
55g carrots, grated
½ red pepper, deseeded and chopped
3 celery stalks, chopped
30g parsley, chopped
4 tbsp kalamata olives, stoned and cut in half

DRESSING

2 tbsp lemon juice
2 tbsp Bragg Liquid Aminos or tamari soy sauce
1 tsp dried oregano
½ tsp ground black pepper
½ tsp salt
1 tbsp dried basil
4 tbsp olive oil

Bring 350ml to the boil in a small saucepan. Remove the pan from the heat, add the couscous and stir with a fork. Re-cover the pan and set aside for 7 minutes, by which time the couscous will have absorbed the water. Fluff the couscous with a fork and transfer it to a large bowl. Add the pine nuts, carrots, red pepper, celery, parsley and olives and toss together.

To make the dressing, combine the lemon juice, the aminos, oregano, black pepper, salt and basil in a bowl and whisk together with a wire whisk. As you whisk, slowly drizzle the olive oil into the bowl. Pour the dressing over the salad and toss together until well incorporated. Serve on a bed of lettuce or in a wrap.

If you like, garnish the salad with 150–300g grilled chicken or fish for added protein. Slice or cube the chicken or fish and toss in with the other ingredients.

NUTRITIONAL FACTS per 175g serving

For salad and dressing only

Calories 262 | Total fat 6.1g | Saturated fat 0.9g | Carbohydrates 42.8g | Protein 9.5g

Organic Mixed Greens – A Mixture of Different Lettuces

~ SERVES 1 ~

2 cos or webb leaves, rinsed and coarsely torn
6 rocket leaves, rinsed and coarsely torn
30g spinach, torn
Small handful watercress leaves
2 cherry tomatoes
1 tsp walnuts, roasted
2 slices cooked beetroot, peeled
1 tsp olive oil
1½ tsp balsamic vinegar

❖ ❖ ❖ ❖

NUTRITIONAL FACTS per serving

Calories 88 | Total fat 6.2g | Saturated fat 0.7g | Carbohydrates 5.5g | Protein 2.4g

Sauces, Condiments and Finishing Touches

'A good meal ought to begin with hunger'
— French Proverb

Sauces, dressings, chutneys, condiments and salsas bring the components of a meal together. A touch of sauce in a sandwich adds moistness and flavour. A salsa on top of tofu adds a Latin flare. Greens tossed with a dressing create a delicious salad. Condiments provide flavour, colour, spiciness, texture, excitement and richness to any meal.

Be creative. Experiment with different tastes, colours and textures. Tofu alone is bland and boring, but serve it with a savoury sauce or a spicy chutney and it assumes a completely new personality. You will notice that some of the recipes make enough for eight servings. This is because most of the condiments can last in the refrigerator for four to five days and will provide a variety of tastes in different meals.

SAUCES AND CONDIMENTS INDEX

APPLE LEEK CHUTNEY

~ SERVES 8 ~

375g apples, unpeeled and chopped
2 tsp lemon juice
1 tsp ghee or olive oil
2 tsp very finely chopped peeled root ginger
4 cloves
2 cinnamon sticks
½ tsp black mustard seeds
½ tsp fenugreek seeds
90g leeks, onions or shallots, chopped
1 pinch of chilli powder
1 pinch of salt
1 tsp ground coriander
1 tsp ground cinnamon
½ tsp ground ginger
2 tbsp cider vinegar
350g frozen apple juice concentrate, plus extra if needed
2 tbsp turbinado sugar or maple syrup
4 tbsp currants or raisins

Put the apples in a small bowl of water with 1 teaspoon of the lemon juice and set aside. Heat the ghee in a frying pan over a medium heat. Add the root ginger, cloves, cinnamon sticks, mustard seeds and fenugreek seeds and stir-fry for 1 minute. Add the leeks and stir-fry for 2–3 minutes. Drain the apples and add them to the pan along with the chilli powder, salt, coriander, cinnamon and ground ginger and stir-fry for a further 4–5 minutes until the apples soften. Add the vinegar, apple juice concentrate and the remaining teaspoon of lemon juice. Bring to a boil, and then reduce the heat to low and simmer for up to 1 hour. Add the currants and sugar or maple syrup about halfway into the cooking process. Continue to add the apple juice as the liquid gets absorbed. The chutney should have a thick consistency. Remove the cinnamon sticks and cloves and serve warm or chilled.

NUTRITIONAL FACTS per 125g serving

Calories 170 | Total fat 1.3g | Saturated fat 0.5g | Carbohydrates 38.3g | Protein 0.9g

APRICOT SALSA

~ SERVES 4 ~

45g leeks, onions, or spring onions, finely chopped
1 tsp ghee or olive oil (optional)
320g fresh or ready-to-eat dried apricots, diced
180g tomato, freshly chopped
½ tsp garam masala
2 tbsp chopped fresh mint, chopped
1 tsp dried or fresh mint, chopped
½ tsp ground cardamom
1 tsp lemon juice
1 tsp Bragg Liquid Aminos or tamari soy sauce

If you're using leeks or onion, heat the ghee in a frying pan over a medium heat and stir-fry them for 2–3 minutes until translucent; spring onions will not need to be stir-fried. Combine the apricots, tomatoes and stir-fried leeks or onions or spring onions in a non-metallic bowl. Add the garam masala, mint, dill, cardamom, lemon juice and the aminos. Toss gently, then taste for seasonings.

NUTRITIONAL FACTS per 125g

Calories 64 | Total fat 0.5g | Saturated fat 0g | Carbohydrates 12.8g | Protein 2g

AUBERGINE TAPENADE

~ SERVES 8 ~

1 aubergine, cut into 2.5cm cubes
1 tbsp olive oil, plus extra for the baking tray
2 tsp balsamic vinegar
1 tbsp dried basil
1 tsp dried sage
1 tsp ground black pepper
60g kalamata olives
125g bottled artichokes hearts, drained and rinsed
4 tbsp chopped canned or freshly roasted red peppers
1 tbsp lemon juice
1 tbsp apple juice or vegetable stock
2 tbsp drained capers
15g fresh parsley, finely chopped

Preheat the oven to 180°C/Gas mark 4 and lightly grease a baking tray and set aside. Combine the olive oil, balsamic vinegar, basil, sage and black pepper into a large bowl and whisk together. Add the aubergine cubes and toss. Arrange the aubergine cubes on the baking tray and roast for 30 minutes. Remove the pan from the oven and leave to cool.

Place the cool aubergine in a food processor. Add the olives, artichoke hearts and red pepper and pulse into a coarse mixture. Add the lemon juice and the apple juice, remove from food processor and transfer to a bowl. Stir in the capers and parsley. Use the tapenade as a condiment, a sandwich spread or as a pizza topping.

NUTRITIONAL FACTS per 4 tablespoons
Calories 70 | Total fat 4.8g | Saturated fat 0.2g | Carbohydrates 5.6g | Protein 1g

BASIC ASIAN-STYLE COOKERY SAUCE

~ MAKES ABOUT 125ML ~

1 tsp sesame oil
2 tbsp Bragg Liquid Aminos or tamari soy sauce
2 tbsp maple syrup
2 tbsp rice vinegar
1 tbsp balsamic vinegar
1 pinch of red chilli flakes
½ tsp Chinese five-spice powder
1 tsp ground ginger
1 tsp ground coriander

Combine all the ingredients in a bowl and whisk together. Use as a marinade or as a stir-fry sauce.

❖ ❖ ❖ ❖

NUTRITIONAL FACTS per 2 tablespoons
Calories 62 | Total fat 1.2g | Saturated fat 0.2g | Carbohydrates 12g | Protein 1g

BASIL AND FRIENDS PESTO

~ MAKES 16 30G SERVINGS ~

1 cup shelled walnut halves or pieces
60g fresh basil
20g fresh rocked
35g spinach, rinsed
2 tbsp lemon juice
2 tsp Bragg Liquid Aminos or tamari soy sauce
2 tsp olive oil
2 tsp apple juice

Preheat the oven to 180°C/Gas mark 4. Place the walnuts on a baking sheet and roast for 20 minutes. Remove from the oven and set aside to cool. Combine the basil, rocket and spinach in a food processor and pulse to combine. Add the walnuts, lemon juice and the aminos and continue to pulse into a smooth consistency. Slowly drizzle in the olive oil with the motor running and blend until the pesto is very smooth.

NUTRITIONAL FACTS per 30g serving (2 tbsp)

Calories 65 | Total fat 5.3g | Saturated fat 0.5g | Carbohydrates 2.4g | Protein 1.8g

CORIANDER MINT SAUCE

~ SERVES 4 ~

35g fresh coriander
50g fresh mint
1 tbsp lemon juice
½ tsp ground cardamom
1 tbsp Bragg Liquid Aminos or tamari soy sauce
1 tbsp apple juice or vegetable stock, plus extra if necessary

Combine the coriander, mint and lemon juice and pulse to combine. Add the cardamom, the aminos and vegetable stock and blend, adding more vegetable stock if necessary, to create a smooth sauce. Serve with spicy foods to cool down the meal. You can add 175g silken tofu for a creamy texture.

❖ ❖ ❖ ❖

NUTRITIONAL FACTS per 4 tablespoon serving

Without tofu

Calories 20 | Total fat 0.2g | Saturated fat 0g | Carbohydrates 3.2g | Protein 1.2g

CORIANDER PECAN SAUCE

~ SERVES 4 ~

175g firm or extra-firm silken tofu, ideally low fat, drained
½ bunch fresh coriander
4 tbsp pecan nuts
1 tbsp lemon juice
2 tbsp vegetable stock
1 garlic clove, or ½ tsp garlic granules
1 tsp ground cumin
1 tbsp Bragg Liquid Aminos or tamari soy sauce
1 pinch of ground black pepper

Place the pecans in a dry frying pan and toast over a high heat until they become golden brown. Immediately transfer them to a blender or food processor. Add the tofu, coriander and lemon juice and blend or pulse until the tofu begins to break down. Add the vegetable stock, garlic, cumin and the aminos and continue to blend until smooth. Add the black pepper and blend until well incorporated. Serve on steamed vegetables, as a sandwich spread or thin with 4 tablespoons apple juice and 4 tablespoons rice vinegar for a salad dressing.

NUTRITIONAL FACTS per 4 tablespoon serving

Made with low-fat tofu

Calories 80 | Total fat 5.4g | Saturated fat 0.4g | Carbohydrates 3.2g | Protein 4.8g

CUCUMBER RAITA

~ SERVES 4 ~

3 small cucumbers, peeled and seeded
2 tbsp lemon juice
1 tsp ground cumin
½ tsp dried dill
1 pinch of salt
2 tsp chopped fresh coriander
225g low-fat plain yogurt

Combine the cucumbers, lemon juice, cumin, dill, salt and coriander and toss gently. Add the yogurt and combine with a fork. Serve as a condiment with curry or as a dressing for salads or wraps.

NUTRITIONAL FACTS per 5 tablespoons

Calories 59 | Total fat 1.1g | Saturated fat 0.6g | Carbohydrates 8g | Protein 3.9g

HOME-MADE CHILLI SAUCE

~ SERVES 8 ~

1 tsp ghee or olive oil
45g leeks or onions, chopped
½ tsp celery seeds
1 tsp ground black pepper
4 cloves
4 large tomatoes, chopped
4 celery sticks, diced
1 large pepper, deseeded and chopped
4 tbsp rice vinegar or cider vinegar
4 tbsp vegetable stock
55g turbinado sugar
½ tsp salt
1½ tsp mustard powder
1 tsp ground allspice
½ tsp ground ginger
½ tsp ground cinnamon
½ tsp ground nutmeg

Heat the ghee in a saucepan over a medium heat. Add the leeks, celery seeds, black pepper and cloves and stir-fry for 1 minute. Add the tomatoes, celery and the bell peppers and continue stir-frying for 1–2 minutes. Add the vinegar and the stock and simmer for 2 minutes, then stir in the sugar and the salt. Combine the mustard powder, allspice, ginger, cinnamon and nutmeg, then add to the sauce. Allow the sauce to simmer over a low heat for up to 30 minutes. Purée into a smooth sauce using an immersion blender or in a food processor. Set aside to cool completely, then store in the fridge in a glass jar with a tight-fitting lid. Use as the base for soups, marinades and sauces. Use as a sauce in chicken and fish preparations.

NUTRITIONAL FACTS per 4 tablespoons

Calories 87.5 | Total fat 1.4g | Saturated fat 0.5g | Carbohydrates 16.6g | Protein 2g

HUMMUS

~ SERVES 8 ~

200g dried chickpeas, picked over, rinsed and soaked overnight in water to cover, or one 400g can chickpeas, drained and rinsed
2 tbsp tahini
4 tbsp chopped fresh parsley
1 large spring onion, chopped, or 1 tbsp chopped leek
2 tsp very finely chopped garlic, or 1 tsp garlic granules
1 tsp of ground cumin
1 pinch of cayenne pepper
1 tsp dried dill
2 tbsp lemon juice, plus extra if needed
2 tsp Bragg Liquid Aminos or tamari soy sauce, plus extra if needed

If using dried chickpeas, drain and rinse them. Put them in a large saucepan of water and bring to the boil and boil for 1 hour, skimming the surface as necessary, or until tender. Drain the chickpeas and set aside.

Place the cooled or canned chickpeas in a food processor. Add the tahini, parsley, onions, cumin, cayenne and dill and pulse the ingredients together. Slowly add the lemon juice and the aminos and continue to pulse until a smooth consistency is achieved. Add more liquid or spices as necessary.

❖ ❖ ❖ ❖

NUTRITIONAL FACTS per 4 tablespoons
Calories 125 | Total fat 3.6g | Saturated fat 0.5g | Carbohydrates 17.2g | Protein 5.9g

KIM CHI CHUTNEY

~ SERVES 4 ~

1 tsp sesame oil
90g leeks or onions, cut into large pieces
2 tbsp peeled and very finely chopped root ginger
1 tbsp Bragg Liquid Aminos or tamari soy sauce
1 pinch of red chilli flakes
½ head cabbage, cut into 2.5cm pieces
2 carrots, thinly sliced
1 pepper, deseeded, cut into 2.5cm pieces
4 tbsp rice vinegar
125ml vegetable stock
1 tsp paprika

Heat the ghee in a frying pan over a medium heat. Add the leeks, ginger, the aminos and chilli flakes and stir-fry for 2 minutes. Add the cabbage, carrots and pepper and continue stir-frying for 5 minutes. Add the vinegar, vegetable stock and paprika and allow the mixture to simmer for up to 30 minutes. Set aside to cool completely, then store in the fridge in a glass jar with a tight-fitting lid. Serve as a spicy condiment with Buddha's Delight (page 115), Thai-style Noodles (page 135) or Cashew Tofu and Tempeh (page 117).

❖ ❖ ❖ ❖

NUTRITIONAL FACTS per 225g

Calories 111 | Total fat 1.9g | Saturated fat 0.2g | Carbohydrates 20.9g | Protein 3.2g

KRAZY KETCHUP

~ SERVES 4 ~

1 tsp ghee or olive oil
90g leeks or onions, chopped
1 celery stick, diced
½ tsp ground black pepper
1 tbsp Bragg Liquid Aminos or tamari soy sauce
1 pinch of cayenne pepper (optional – omit if you are making the
ketchup for children)
1 tsp ground coriander
1 tsp dried rosemary
3 tbsp cider vinegar
1 tbsp lemon juice
4 tbsp vegetable stock, plus extra if needed
260g tomato purée
2 tbsp finely chopped fresh coriander
2 tbsp maple syrup

Heat the ghee in a large frying pan over a medium heat. Add the leeks, celery and black pepper and stir-fry for 2–3 minutes until the leeks are translucent. Add the aminos, cayenne, ground coriander and rosemary and stir-fry for 1–2 minutes. Add the vinegar and the lemon juice and simmer for 4 to 5 minutes. Stir in the vegetable stock and the tomato purée and continue to simmer for at least 5 minutes. Add the fresh coriander and maple syrup. If you have too much liquid in the mixture, allow the ketchup to low simmer until the liquid evaporates. Purée with an immersion blender or in a blender into a smooth consistency. If the ketchup is too thick, add extra vegetable stock to thin down before puréeing. Set aside to cool completely, then store in the fridge in a glass jar with a tight-fitting lid. Serve with Country Potatoes (page 87), Masala Potatoes (page 94) and Tempeh and Potato Hash (page 100).

NUTRITIONAL FACTS per 4 tablespoons

Calories 34 | Total fat 0.5g | Saturated fat 0.3g | Carbohydrates 6.3g | Protein 1g

LEEK SAUCE

~ SERVES 4 ~

1 tsp ghee or olive oil
90g leeks, chopped
½ tsp ground black pepper
1 tbsp Bragg Liquid Aminos or tamari soy sauce
1 tsp dried thyme
½ tsp ground cumin
60–125ml vegetable stock

Heat the ghee in a frying pan over a medium heat. Add the leeks, black pepper, the aminos and thyme and stir-fry until the leeks brown well to create the best flavour. Add 60ml of the stock and allow the leeks to simmer for 4–5 minutes until reduced to the desired consistency. You can add some Basic Roux (page 51) to the leek sauce to create a creamy consistency. Serve on Tofu Burgers (page 137) or as a sauce on stir-fried vegetables.

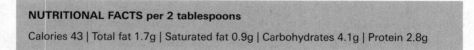

NUTRITIONAL FACTS per 2 tablespoons
Calories 43 | Total fat 1.7g | Saturated fat 0.9g | Carbohydrates 4.1g | Protein 2.8g

MANDARIN TOMATO SALSA

~ SERVES 4 ~

1 tsp ghee
45g leeks, onion or spring onions, chopped
145g mandarin, orange or satsuma segments, deseeded and chopped
360g tomatoes, cubed
1 tbsp mild Anaheim chilli, roasted, peeled, chopped, or 1 tablespoon chopped canned mild green chillies
1 tbsp Bragg Liquid Aminos or tamari or soy sauce
1 tbsp apple juice
1 tbsp lime juice
4 tbsp chopped fresh coriander
1 tsp ground cumin
½ tsp ground coriander

If you're using leeks or onion, heat the ghee in a frying pan over a medium heat and stir-fry them for 2–3 minutes until translucent; spring onions will not need to be stir-fried. Combine the oranges, tomatoes, chillies, spring onions or stir-fried leeks and the aminos in a bowl and stir well. Add the apple juice, lime juice, fresh coriander, cumin and coriander and stir together. Cover and chill for 1 hour before serving.

❖ ❖ ❖ ❖

NUTRITIONAL FACTS per 125g

Calories 66 | Total fat 0.4g | Saturated fat 0g | Carbohydrates 13.6g | Protein 1.8g

NUTTY DIPPING SAUCE

~ SERVES 8 ~

1 tsp ghee or sesame oil
4 garlic cloves, very finely chopped
1 pinch of red chilli flakes
125–225ml vegetable stock
2 tbsp Bragg Liquid Aminos or tamari soy sauce
4 tbsp peanut butter or almond butter
1 tbsp maple syrup
1 tbsp sesame seeds
1 tbsp chopped fresh mint or coriander

Heat the ghee in a frying pan over a medium heat. Add the garlic and chilli flakes and quickly stir-fry. Add 125ml of the stock, the aminos, peanut or almond butter and maple syrup, stirring together, and simmer until hot. Add the sesame seeds and mint and set aside to cool. Purée the ingredients for a smooth texture, and add more stock if necessary to thin the sauce. Serve with Lettuce Wraps (page 205) and Szechwan Baked Egg Rolls (page 133).

NUTRITIONAL FACTS per 2 tablespoons
Made with ghee
Calories 47 | Total fat 3g | Saturated fat 0.5g | Carbohydrates 2.5g | Protein 2.4g

ORANGE PEAR CHUTNEY

~ SERVES 8 ~

Lemon juice
2 pears, unpeeled and cubed
1 orange, peeled and cubed
1 tsp ghee or olive oil
1 tsp brown mustard seed
1 pinch of chilli powder (not cayenne)
45g leeks or onions, chopped
2.5cm piece root ginger, peeled and finely chopped
1 tsp Bragg Liquid Aminos or tamari soy sauce
1 tsp ground coriander
1 tsp ground cinnamon
4 cloves
4 tbsp raisins
4 tbsp cider vinegar
350g apple juice frozen concentrate, undiluted
4 tbsp maple syrup

Put the lemon juice in a bowl and add the pears and orange as they are prepared, and set aside. Heat the ghee in a frying pan over a medium heat. Add the mustard seeds and stir until they pop. Add the chilli powder, leeks, ginger and the aminos and stir-fry for 1–2 minutes. Use a slotted spoon to remove the pears from the water and add them to the pan. Continue stir-frying for 2–3 minutes. Drain the oranges. Add the coriander, cinnamon and the cloves and continue to stir-fry. Add the raisins, orange pieces, vinegar and apple juice. Allow the chutney to simmer over a low heat for up to 1 hour. After 30 minutes, stir in the maple syrup. Serve as a complement to spicy vegetable dishes, Asian dishes and in Wholemeal Crêpes (page 105).

NUTRITIONAL FACTS per 4 tablespoons

Calories 74 | Total fat 0.6g | Saturated fat 0.2g | Carbohydrates 16.7g | Protein 0.4g

PESTO TOMATO PASTA SAUCE

~ SERVES 8 ~

2 tbsp Basil and Friends Pesto (page 238)
180g tomatoes, freshly chopped
2 tbsp balsamic vinegar
125ml vegetable stock
125ml apple juice
4 tbsp olive oil

Combine the pesto, tomatoes and the vinegar in a blender or food processor and blend to combine. Add the apple juice and continue to blend into a smooth consistency. Slowly drizzle the olive oil with the motor running. Serve over your favourite hot or cold pasta dish or steamed vegetables.

NUTRITIONAL FACTS per 4 tablespoons

Made with olive oil

Calories 92 | Total fat 8g | Saturated fat 1g | Carbohydrates 4.1g | Protein 0.7g

ROASTED TOMATO SAUCE

~ MAKES 900ML ~

5 to 6 large tomatoes, roasted
1 tbsp olive oil
5 tsp balsamic vinegar
2 tsp ground black pepper
4 fresh rosemary sprigs, leaves removed from the stalks
1 tbsp dried basil
1 tsp dried thyme
Olive oil spray
1 tsp ghee or olive oil
180g leeks or shallots, chopped
1 pinch of red chilli flakes
1 tbsp Bragg Liquid Aminos or tamari soy sauce
2 tsp balsamic vinegar
4 tbsp finely chopped fresh parsley
15g fresh basil, finely shredded

Preheat the oven to 180°C/Gas mark 4. To roast the tomatoes, cut off the vine end and make a small 'X' with a knife on the top of the smooth side of each tomato. Place the tomatoes in a shallow baking tin, X side up. Sprinkle with 1 teaspoon of the pepper and generously with the thyme and rosemary, spray with olive oil, drizzle with 3 teaspoons of the balsamic vinegar and roast for 20–30 minutes. Allow the tomatoes to cool. Working over bowl, begin to remove and discard the tomato skins. Using your hands, break up the tomatoes, removing the skin as you go. Set aside the bowl of tomato pieces and juice.

Heat the ghee in a large saucepan over a medium heat. Add the leeks, chilli flakes, pepper and the aminos and stir-fry for 2–3 minutes until the leeks are translucent. Add the tomatoes with their juice and the remaining balsamic vinegar. Bring to the boil, then reduce the heat to a low simmer for 1 hour or longer, until the sauce is thickened. Add the parsley and the basil 15 minutes before completion. For a smooth texture, purée with an immersion blender or in a blender or food processor, if desired.

❖ ❖ ❖ ❖

NUTRITIONAL FACTS per 125g serving

Calories 147 | Total fat 5.5g | Saturated fat 1.5g | Carbohydrates 20.8g | Protein 3.6g

RUSSIAN BORSCHT CHUTNEY

~ SERVES 8 ~

1 tsp ghee or olive oil
45g leeks or onions, chopped.
1 pinch of red chilli flakes
1 tsp caraway seeds
1 tsp black mustard seeds
1 tsp ground cinnamon
1 tbsp vegetable stock, plus extra if needed
135g beetroot, peeled and grated
110g carrots, grated
75g red cabbage, cored and thinly sliced
½ red or green bell pepper, deseeded and thinly sliced
125ml rice vinegar

Heat the ghee in a stockpot or large saucepan over a medium heat. Add the leeks, chilli flakes, caraway seeds and mustard seeds and stir-fry until the seeds pop and the leeks are translucent. Add the cinnamon and stock and continue stir-frying for 1 minute. Add the beets, carrots, cabbage and peppers, reduce the heat to a medium allow the mixture to simmer, stirring frequently, for 15–20 minutes. Add additional stock as necessary. Set aside to cool completely, then store in the fridge in a glass jar with a tight-fitting lid. Use as a condiment.

❖ ❖ ❖ ❖

NUTRITIONAL FACTS per 125g

Calories 33 | Total fat 0.5g | Saturated fat 0.2g | Carbohydrates 7g | Protein 0.5g

SPICY LIME AND RED PEPPER DIPPING SAUCE

~ SERVES 4 ~

4 tbsp chopped fresh or canned roasted red pepper, drained if necessary
4 tbsp fresh lime juice
2 tbsp rice vinegar
2 tbsp maple syrup
1 tbsp Bragg Liquid Aminos or tamari soy sauce
1 pinch of salt
1 pinch of cayenne pepper
2 tbsp finely shredded fresh basil

Combine the pepper, lime juice, vinegar, maple syrup, the aminos, salt and cayenne in a blender or food processor and purée until smooth. Add the basil and pulse briefly. Use this sauce as a dipping sauce for Lettuce Wraps (page 205).

❖ ❖ ❖ ❖

NUTRITIONAL FACTS per 2 tablespoons

Calories 54 | Total fat 0g | Saturated fat 0g | Carbohydrates 12.8g | Protein 0.7g

SWEET MIXED FRUIT CHUTNEY

~ SERVES 4 ~

1 tsp ghee
1 cinnamon stick
5 cloves
250g apples or pears, cut into cubes
4 tbsp currants, raisins or dried cranberries
2 tsp ground cinnamon
1 pinch of ground cloves
1 pinch of ground cardamom
1 mango, stoned and cut into cubes
2 tbsp coconut, toasted
350ml frozen apple juice concentrate, undiluted
2 tsp lemon juice
3 tbsp maple syrup

Heat the ghee in a large saucepan over a medium heat. Add the cinnamon stick and cloves and stir for 1 minute. Add the apple, currants, cinnamon, cloves and cardamom and stir-fry for a further 2 minutes. Add the mango, coconut, apple juice concentrate and maple syrup, reduce the heat to low and simmer until the apples are soft and the juice has been absorbed. Use this chutney in Wholemeal Crêpes (page 105), as a complement to a spicy dish or as a simple dessert.

❖ ❖ ❖ ❖

NUTRITIONAL FACTS per 176g

Calories 182 | Total fat 2.5g | Saturated fat 1.5g | Carbohydrates 38.8g | Protein 1g

TOMATO SALSA

~ SERVES 4 ~

1 tsp ghee or olive oil
40g leeks or onions, chopped
360g tomato, diced
4 tbsp finely chopped coriander
1 tsp ground coriander
½ tsp garlic granules
½ tsp ground cumin
½ tsp ground black pepper
1 tbsp lemon juice

Heat the ghee in a frying pan over a medium heat. Add the leeks and stir-fry until translucent, then set aside to cool. Combine the tomatoes, leeks, fresh coriander, ground coriander, garlic granules, cumin, pepper and lemon juice and combine well with a spoon. Cover and chill before serving.

NUTRITIONAL FACTS per 125g

Calories 39 | Total fat 1.6g | Saturated fat 0.9g | Carbohydrates 5.3g | Protein 0.9g

WALNUT YOGURT SAUCE

~ SERVES 4 ~

2 tbsp walnut halves
½ tsp ground nutmeg
225g plain low-fat yogurt
½ tsp salt
1 tbsp apple juice
1 tsp clear honey (optional)

Heat a dry frying pan over a high heat. Add the walnut and toast, stirring, until slightly brown. Remove the pan from the heat and cool off. Transfer the walnuts to a blender and grind into a coarse meal. Add the nutmeg, yogurt, salt and apple juice and blend until smooth. If a sweeter taste is desired, add the honey. Use this sauce with Curry Filo Tarts (page 119).

NUTRITIONAL FACTS per 4 tablespoons

Calories 68 | Total fat 3.2g | Saturated fat 0.8g | Carbohydrates 5.4g | Protein 4.2g

DESSERTS

'A house is beautiful not because of its walls, but because of its cakes'
– OLD RUSSIAN PROVERB

Including desserts in your menu planning is one way of incorporating the 'sweet' taste into each meal. Some of our recipes are wheat-free, dairy-free, egg-free and gluten-free. Some of our recipes are protein-enhanced with tofu and nuts and sweetened with mango purée and apple sauce. Admittedly, some of our recipes cannot be considered low fat, as butter, cream and sugar are used in some of our traditional desserts – we believe that an *occasional* indulgence is good for the body, mind and soul. Balance your decadent desserts with lighter meals.

The quality of ingredients is the most important aspect of good baking. Favour organic dairy products, such as butter, cream and milk. Use organically raised eggs from free-ranging chickens and raw unbleached sugar. Purchase high-quality organic wholemeal pastry flour for your baking, which works well in most applications.

The recipes for Apricot Pecan Cookies, Double Almond Cookies, Linzertorte Cookies and Walnut Chocolate Chip Cookies are all variations on a theme. These power-packed cookies make great midday snacks, and will satisfy your craving for sweets. You can make all of them in less than 30 minutes. The cookie recipes can be made without wheat, by using alternative flour products such as soya, rice, spelt and barley flours. The dough also works well as the base of a baked fruit tart. Press the dough into a tart tin, arrange some fruit, such as apples or apricots, on top and bake for 30–40 minutes. Glaze by brushing the fruit with melted jam. This makes a very simple, healthy and elegant dessert.

The Blueberry Orange Cake recipe can be used in a variety of different ways by following the basic cake recipe and changing the flavouring in the form of the fruit and the spices.

Helpful Pointers:

1. Careful measuring is important in baking.
2. Always blend or combine the ingredients very gently, a technique referred to in baking as folding in. Use a rubber spatula or a large metal spoon.
3. Use a whisk to blend together both wet and dry ingredients. The dry ingredients will sift together well without the use of extra tools.
4. A good assortment of stainless-steel bowls, whisks, spoons and spatulas are excellent hand tools for baking. Our favourite tool is a 30g ice-cream scoop for quickly transferring cookie dough to the baking sheet.

DESSERT INDEX

ALMOND TART

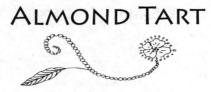

~ SERVES 12 ~

Vegetable oil spray for the tart tin
205g wholemeal pastry flour
4 tbsp ground almonds
4 tbsp turbinado sugar
1 pinch of salt
125g butter, cut into pieces
½ tsp ground nutmeg
1 egg yolk or 2 tsp mango purée
1 tsp vanilla extract
600g fresh or lightly sautéed fruit of your choice, thinly sliced

TOPPING

110g turbinado sugar
1 tsp arrowroot
30g butter, cut into small pieces
160g apricot jam, melted

Preheat the oven to 220°C/Gas mark 7. Spray a 25cm tart tin with vegetable oil spray and set aside. Combine the flour, ground almonds, sugar and the salt in a food processor and pulse together. Add the butter, piece by piece, allowing it to mix with the flour, creating a coarse mixture. Sprinkle in the nutmeg as the processor continues to combine. Add the egg yolk or mango purée and the vanilla and continue to pulse until the mixture looks smooth and begins to form into a ball. Press the pastry into the tin. Create a 1cm lip around the tart tin. Arrange any combination of fresh or sautéed fruit on the pastry in a circular design.

To make the topping, combine the sugar and arrowroot and sprinkle on top. Dot the fruit with the small pieces of butter. Cover with foil and bake for 15 minutes. Reduce the heat to 180°C/Gas mark 4 and bake for a further 30–40 minutes until golden brown. Leave the tart to cool for 10 minutes, then glaze with the jam, using a small pastry brush.

❖ ❖ ❖ ❖

NUTRITIONAL FACTS per 5cm slice

Made using 1 egg, without fruit

Calories 239 | Total fat 11.4g | Saturated fat 6.3g | Carbohydrates 31.6g | Protein 2.3g

APPLE COBBLER

~ SERVES 12 ~

You can decrease the fat in this recipe by using less oil and nuts.

PASTRY CRUST

4 tbsp ghee or canola oil, plus extra for greasing the baking tin
500g wholemeal pastry flour, rice flour or spelt flour
165g turbinado sugar
½ tsp ground nutmeg
175g light soya milk or rice milk
A few drops of vanilla extract, to taste

COBBLER FRUIT FILLING

3 large apples, peeled, cubed and soaked in water with lemon juice
4 tbsp maple syrup
½ tsp ground cinnamon
1 tbsp turbinado sugar
¼ tsp ground cardamom
2 tbsp apple juice
2 tsp arrowroot

COBBLER TOPPING

80g rolled oats
80g wholemeal pastry flour, rice flour or spelt flour
1 tsp ground cinnamon
60g walnut halves, chopped
2 tbsp ghee or 30g butter, melted
2 tbsp turbinado sugar
2 tbsp maple syrup

Preheat the oven to 180°C/Gas mark 4. Grease a 20cm square cake tin with oil and set aside. Combine the flour, sugar and nutmeg in a large bowl and whisk together. Combine the soya milk, vanilla and the canola oil in a separate bowl. Slowly whisk the wet ingredients into the dry ingredients until a soft dough forms. Knead the dough until well combined, then press into the base of the tin. Bake for 10–15 minutes until golden brown. Remove from the oven and set aside. Do not turn off the oven.

To make the filling, drain the apples. Combine the apples, maple syrup, cinnamon, sugar, cardamom, apple juice and arrowroot in a bowl. Spread the apple mixture evenly over the baked crust.

To make the topping, combine the oats, flour, cinnamon, walnuts, ghee, sugar, and maple syrup in a bowl, mixing with a fork or using your hands. Sprinkle the mixture evenly over the apples and cover with foil. Bake for 35–45 minutes until golden brown.

NUTRITIONAL FACTS per 4cm square
Calories 386 | Total fat 11.2g | Saturated fat 1.5g | Carbohydrates 64.7g | Protein 6.8g

Apple Custard Pie

~ SERVES 10 ~

SWEET PIE CRUST

Vegetable oil spray for the springform tin
205g wholemeal pastry flour
110g turbinado sugar
¼ tsp ground cinnamon
1 pinch of salt
125g cold butter, cut into pieces

APPLE PIE FILLING

5 apples, unpeeled, sliced thinly and soaked in water with lemon juice
1 tsp ghee
1 tsp ground cinnamon
1 tsp ground nutmeg
1 tsp ground cardamom
45g coconut flakes
70g currants or raisins
110g turbinado sugar

CUSTARD

3 eggs
125ml cow's milk or cream
1 tsp ground cinnamon
¼ tsp ground cardamom

Preheat the oven to 180°C/Gas mark 4. Spray a 20 or 23cm springform tin with vegetable oil and set aside. Place the flour, sugar and the salt in a food processor and process until combined. With the motor running, drop the butter, piece by piece, into the flour mixture, pulsing until a soft dough forms. Press the dough into the springform tin with a smooth pattern around the edge to about 2.5cm up the side of the tin. Bake for 20–30 minutes until golden brown. Remove tin from the oven and leave the pastry case to cool. Do not turn off the oven.

To make the filling, drain the apples. Heat the ghee in a saucepan. Add the apples, cinnamon, nutmeg and cardamom and sauté for 3–5 minutes. Add the coconut, currants and sugar and simmer for a further 2–3 minutes. Arrange apples slices around the base of the crust-lined tin, then layer in a circular pattern.

To make the custard, whisk together the eggs, milk, cinnamon and cardamom. Pour the custard evenly over the apples. Bake in the oven for 20–30 minutes until golden brown and a wooden cocktail stick inserted in the centre comes out clean. Leave to cool and serve warm or at room temperature.

❖ ❖ ❖ ❖

NUTRITIONAL FACTS per 5cm slice

Calories 336 | Total fat 13.1g | Saturated fat 7.8g | Carbohydrates 49.9g | Protein 4.5g

APRICOT PECAN COOKIES

~ MAKES 24 SMALL COOKIES ~

2 tbsp rapeseed oil, plus extra for greasing the baking sheet
80g rolled oats
100g pecan nuts
30g ready-to-eat dried apricots
165g wholemeal pastry flour, rice flour or spelt flour
½ tsp ground cinnamon
½ tsp salt
4 tbsp maple syrup
120g mango purée, apple sauce or mashed bananas
160g organic apricot jam, melted

Preheat the oven to 180°C/Gas mark 4. Lightly grease a baking sheet with rapeseed oil and set aside. Grind the oats, pecans and apricots together in a food processor into a coarse mixture. Place in a large bowl and stir in the flour, cinnamon and salt. Combine the maple syrup, oil and fruit in a separate bowl and whisk together. Add the wet mixture to the dry mixture and combine with a spatula or place plastic sandwich bags on your hands to mix. Using a 30 or 60g ice-cream scoop or a tablespoon, scoop the dough on to the baking sheet. Make a small indentation with your thumb and spoon in a small amount of apricot jam. Bake for 15–20 minutes until golden brown.

❖ ❖ ❖ ❖

NUTRITIONAL FACTS per cookie

Calories 125 | Total fat 3.7g | Saturated fat 0.4g | Carbohydrates 20.1g | Protein 2.7g

BANANA-COCOA-TOFU FROZEN MOUSSE

~ SERVES 8 ~

4 very ripe bananas, cut into 2.5cm pieces and frozen
350g firm or extra-firm silken tofu, ideally low fat, drained and chopped
2 tbsp organic chocolate sauce, sweetened with natural sugar
2 tbsp maple syrup
1 tsp vanilla extract
1 pinch of ground cloves
Coconut flakes, toasted, to decorate
Sliced almonds, to decorate

Place the bananas in a food processor or blender and pulse until almost smooth. Add the tofu and chocolate syrup and pulse until combined, then add the maple syrup, vanilla and cloves. Continue to run the food processor until the mousse is smooth, without any lumps. Put the mousse in a freezer-proof container and freeze for at least 1 hour. Take out of the freezer 15 minutes before you plan to serve. Scoop into small bowls, decorate with coconut flakes and almonds. Store any unused mousse in the freezer, tightly covered.

❖ ❖ ❖ ❖

NUTRITIONAL FACTS per 125g serving

Made with low-fat tofu

Calories 159 | Total fat 0.9g | Saturated fat 0.2g | Carbohydrates 33.5g | Protein 4.3g

BERRY TOFU SORBET

~ SERVES 8 ~

300g frozen raspberries
300g frozen blackberries or strawberries
350g firm or extra-firm silken tofu, ideally low fat, drained and
chopped
4 tbsp maple syrup, plus extra if needed
1 tsp vanilla extract
1 pinch of ground cloves
Coconut flakes, toasted, to decorate
Sliced almonds, toasted, to decorate

Place the raspberries and blackberries in a food processor or blender and
pulse until almost smooth. Add the tofu and pulse until combined, then
add the maple syrup, vanilla and cloves. Continue to run the food processor
until the mixture is smooth. Taste for sweetness, adding extra maple syrup
if desired. Scoop into small bowls and serve immediately, decorated with
coconut flakes and almonds. Store any unused sorbet in the freezer, tightly
covered.

NUTRITIONAL FACTS per 125g

Made with low-fat tofu

Calories 83 | Total fat 0.6g | Saturated fat 0g | Carbohydrates 15.8g | Protein 3.6g

BLUEBERRY ORANGE CAKE

~ SERVES 16 ~

For a smaller cake, cut the recipe in half and bake in a 20cm square cake tin.

Vegetable oil spray for spraying the Bundt tin
660g wholemeal pastry flour
220g turbinado sugar
3 tsp baking powder
1 tsp bicarbonate of soda
½ tsp salt
2 tsp ground cinnamon
½ tsp ground cloves
1 tsp nutmeg
4 tbsp canola oil
245g mango purée or other fruit purée, apple sauce or mashed banana
225ml orange juice
2 tbsp grated orange rind
1 cup light soya milk or rice milk
A few drops of vanilla extract, to taste
160g maple syrup
300g blueberries, thawed if frozen

Preheat the oven to 180°C/Gas mark 4. Spray a 2.7 litre bundt tin or other baking tin with an equal volume with vegetable oil spray and set aside. Combine the flour, sugar, baking powder, bicarbonate of soda, salt, cinnamon, cloves and nutmeg in a bowl and whisk together. Combine the oil, mango purée or other fruit, orange juice, rind, soya milk, vanilla and maple syrup in a separate large bowl and whisk together. Pour the dry ingredients into the wet ingredients and gently combine with a rubber spatula. Add the blueberries and combine briefly. Pour the mixture into the tin and bake for 30–40 minutes until a wooden cocktail stick comes out clean. Leave the cake to cool, then slice and serve.

NUTRITIONAL FACTS per 2.5cm slice

Calories 252 | Total fat 4g | Saturated fat 0.2g | Carbohydrates 50.4g | Protein 3.6g

VARIATIONS

Add any of these variations to the basic cake mixture:

40g grated coconut, 60g unsweetened cocoa powder and 70g almonds

50g cranberries, 70g almonds and 65g pine nuts

60g unsweetened cocoa powder, 125g chocolate chips and 60g walnut halves

150g blueberries and 145g almonds

110g grated carrots and 70g currants

115g grated courgette and 60g walnut halves

125g raspberries

225g sautéed apples and 70g currants

2 tbsp grated lemon rind, 4 tbsp poppy seeds, 70g almonds

CARDAMOM BUTTER COOKIES

~ MAKES 12 COOKIES ~

Vegetable oil spray for spraying the baking sheet
125g chilled butter, cubed
110g turbinado sugar
245g wholemeal pastry flour
½ tsp salt
½ tsp ground nutmeg
½ tsp ground cardamom
2 tbsp lemon juice

Preheat the oven to 180°C/Gas mark 4. Lightly spray a baking sheet with vegetable oil spray and set aside. Using an electric mixer, beat the butter and the sugar until creamy. Combine the flour, salt, nutmeg and cardamom, then slowly add the flour mixture to the butter mixture, about 70g at a time, and continue beating on a low speed. Slowly add the lemon juice until a stiff dough forms. Using a 30 or 60g ice-cream scoop or a tablespoon, scoop the dough on to the baking sheet, leaving 5cm between cookies. Flatten lightly with the palm of your hand. Bake for 10–15 minutes until light golden brown.

❖ ❖ ❖ ❖

NUTRITIONAL FACTS per cookie
Calories 171 | Total fat 5.9g | Saturated fat 3.8g | Carbohydrates 20.2g | Protein 2.3g

CHOCOLATE TOFU MOUSSE WITH WALNUT COCONUT PRALINE

~ SERVES 6 ~

2 tbsp butter or ghee (or rapeseed oil for a vegan dessert)
2 tbsp apple juice
175g plain chocolate chips
2 tsp vanilla extract
350g firm or extra-firm silken tofu, ideally low fat, drained and chopped
4 tbsp maple syrup
½ recipe quantity Walnut Coconut Praline (recipe follows)

Heat the butter, apple juice and the chocolate chips in a small saucepan, stirring frequently to avoid burning, until all the chips are melted. Remove the pan from the heat and stir into a creamy consistency. Set aside.

Place the tofu, maple syrup and vanilla in a blender or food processor and blend at high speed for 1 minute. Scrape down the sides and continue blending until smooth. Add the chocolate mixture to the tofu mixture and blend again until smooth and well incorporated. Spoon the mousse into small dessert bowls, or refrigerate in a container with a tight-fitting lid until ready to serve. Sprinkle with the praline just before serving.

❖   ❖   ❖   ❖

NUTRITIONAL FACTS per 125g serving

Made with low-fat tofu

Calories 169 | Total fat 8.7g | Saturated fat 5.5g | Carbohydrates 19.1g | Protein 3.9g

WALNUT COCONUT PRALINE

~ MAKES 12 SERVINGS ~

1 tbsp butter or ghee (or canola oil for a vegan option), plus extra to grease the baking sheet
2 tbsp maple syrup
125g walnut halves
4 tbsp coconut flakes

Grease a baking sheet with butter and set aside. Heat the butter and the maple syrup together in a frying pan over a medium-high heat. Add the walnuts and coat well with the syrup mixture. Allow the walnuts to brown slightly, then stir in the coconut and continue to brown in the syrup. When the walnuts and coconut are well coated and golden brown, remove the pan from the heat and spread out the mixture on the baking sheet to cool. When hard, crumble on top of the chocolate mousse, or use as a dessert topping in other recipes. Store the remainder of the praline in a re-sealable plastic bag.

NUTRITIONAL FACTS per 2 tablespoons

Made using butter

Calories 94 | Total fat 7.7g | Saturated fat 1.6g | Carbohydrates 4.7g | Protein 1.5g

COCONUT COOKIES

~ MAKES 24 SMALL COOKIES ~

Vegetable oil spray for spraying the baking sheet
125g butter, softened
165g turbinado sugar
2 tbsp lemon juice
2 eggs
250g wholemeal pastry flour
2 tsp baking powder
½ tsp ground cloves
1 tsp ground nutmeg
180g coconut flakes

Preheat the oven to 180°C/Gas mark 4. Lightly spray a baking sheet with the vegetable oil spray and set aside. Using an electric mixer, beat the butter and the sugar until creamy. Add the lemon juice and the eggs, one at a time. Combine the flour, baking powder, cloves, nutmeg and 90g of the coconut flakes. Slowly add the flour mixture to the butter mixture, about 80g at a time, and continue beating on a low speed until a soft dough forms. Remove the dough from the bowl and knead lightly. Place the remaining coconut in a soup plate. Use a 30g ice-cream scoop to scoop the dough into cookie shapes. Roll each scoop of dough in the coconut, then place on the baking sheet, 5cm apart. Flatten the cookies out slightly with the palm of your hand. Bake for 15–20 minutes until golden brown.

❖ ❖ ❖ ❖

NUTRITIONAL FACTS per cookie
Calories 126 | Total fat 6.3g | Saturated fat 4.3g | Carbohydrates 15.5g | Protein 1.5g

CRANBERRY BLISS BALLS

These make a great quick energy snack.

~ MAKES 20 BALLS ~

135g pine nuts
50g sunflower seeds
145g almonds
300g mixed ready-to-eat dried fruit, such as apricots, blueberries,
cranberries, dates and raisins
2 tbsp maple syrup, plus extra if needed
1 tsp vanilla extract
1 tsp ground nutmeg
45g coconut flakes

Place the pine nuts, sunflower seeds and almonds in a food processor and pulse until coarsely ground. Add the dried fruit and pulse 3 or 4 times, and then add the maple syrup, vanilla and nutmeg. Continue to pulse until the mixture begins to stick together. Taste for sweetness and add more maple syrup if desired. Place the coconut flakes in a soup plate. Roll the nut-and-fruit mixture into 2.5cm balls and roll them in the coconut flakes to coat. Store in an air-tight container.

❖ ❖ ❖ ❖

NUTRITIONAL FACTS per ball

Calories 232 | Total fat 14.4g | Saturated fat 2.3g | Carbohydrates 21.5g | Protein 4.1g

DOUBLE ALMOND COOKIES

~ MAKES 18 SMALL COOKIES ~

2 tbsp rapeseed oil, plus extra for greasing the baking sheet
80g rolled oats
145g almonds
165g wholemeal pastry flour, rice flour or spelt flour
½ tsp ground nutmeg
½ tsp salt
170g maple syrup
125g mango purée, apple sauce or mashed bananas
18 almonds, to decorate

Preheat the oven to 180°C/Gas mark 4. Grease a baking sheet with the oil and set aside. Grind the almonds and oats together in a food processor to make a coarse meal. Put the mixture in a bowl, add the flour, cinnamon and salt and whisk together. Combine the maple syrup, oil and the mango purée or other fruit in a separate large bowl and whisk together. Add the dry mixture into the wet ingredients and combine with a spatula or place plastic sandwich bags on your hands to mix. Use a 30 or 60g ice-cream scoop or a tablespoon to scoop the dough on to the baking sheet. Make a small indentation with your thumb and place a whole almond into the centre of each cookie. Bake for 15–20 minutes or until golden brown.

❖ ❖ ❖ ❖

NUTRITIONAL FACTS per cookie

Calories 140 | Total fat 7.4g | Saturated fat 0.7g | Carbohydrates 15.3g | Protein 3.3g

DOUBLE DELIGHT COOKIES

~ MAKES 24 SMALL COOKIES ~

Vegetable oil spray for the baking sheet
350g plain chocolate chips
125g butter
220g turbinado sugar
2 tsp vanilla extract
1 egg
330g wholemeal pastry flour
½ tsp salt
1 tsp bicarbonate of soda
125g walnut halves or macadamia nuts, chopped coarsely.

Preheat the oven to 180°C/Gas mark 4. Lightly spray a baking sheet and set aside. Melt 175g of the chocolate chips in the top of a double boiler over simmering water or in a small saucepan, stirring often. Set aside and leave to cool slightly. Using an electric mixer, beat the butter and the sugar until fluffy. Add the vanilla and egg and combine briefly, then add the melted chocolate. Combine the flour, salt and the bicarbonate of soda in a separate bowl, then slowly add the flour mixture to the butter mixture and continue beating on a low speed. Once combined, add the nuts and the remaining chocolate chips and stir together. Use a 30g ice-cream scoop or a tablespoon to scoop the dough on to the baking sheet, 5cm apart. Bake for 15–20 minutes or until golden brown.

❖ ❖ ❖ ❖

NUTRITIONAL FACTS per cookie

Calories 203 | Total fat 10.3g | Saturated fat 4.7g | Carbohydrates 24.6g | Protein 2.7g

GINGER COOKIES

~ MAKES 24 COOKIES ~

Vegetable oil spray for spraying the baking sheet
4 tbsp ghee or canola oil
245g apple sauce
175g molasses
220g turbinado sugar
500g wholemeal pastry flour
2 tsp ground ginger
2 tsp ground allspice
1 tsp ground cinnamon
2 tsp bicarbonate of soda
1 tsp salt

Preheat the oven to 180°C/Gas mark 4. Lightly spray a cookie sheet and set aside. Combine the ghee, apple sauce, molasses and 165g of the sugar in a large bowl and whisk together. Combine the flour, ginger, allspice, cinnamon, bicarbonate of soda and salt in a separate bowl and whisk together. Add the dry ingredients to the wet ingredients and mix together until a dough forms. The dough will get thick, so use your hands wrapped in plastic sandwich bags to mix if necessary. Use a 30g ice-cream scoop or a tablespoon to scoop the dough on to the baking sheet, 5cm apart. Sprinkle the remaining sugar over the top of the cookies. Bake for 10–12 minutes.

❖ ❖ ❖ ❖

NUTRITIONAL FACTS per cookie

Calories 149 | Total fat 2.9g | Saturated fat 1.9g | Carbohydrates 28.8g | Protein 1.8g

KABOCHA SQUASH OR PUMPKIN PIE

~ SERVES 8 ~

PASTRY CRUST

125g chilled butter, cut into pieces, plus extra for greasing the pie tin
205g wholemeal pastry flour
1 pinch of salt
1 tbsp cider or distilled white vinegar

PIE FILLING

1 kabocha squash or pumpkin, about 1.3 kg, halved and deseeded
Apple juice
225ml light soya milk, milk or cream
A few drops of vanilla extract, to taste
110g turbinado sugar
2 tbsp maple syrup
2 eggs, or 120g apple sauce or mango purée plus 4 tbsp rapeseed oil
1 tsp ground cinnamon
1 tsp ground ginger
½ tsp ground cloves
1 pinch of salt

Lightly grease a pie tin and set aside. Place the flour and salt in a food processor and pulse to combine. With the motor running, add the butter, one piece at a time, and continue to pulse until the mixture looks like coarse crumbs. Add the vinegar and, with the motor still running, begin to slowly add the water, 1 tablespoon at a time, waiting a moment or two before each addition, until the dough begins to form a ball up in the bowl of the processor. Roll out the pastry into a round that is 2.5cm larger around than your pie tin. Place the dough in the tin, leaving a 1-inch edge around the perimeter of the pie. Create a nice border around the pie tin, trimming off any excess dough. Place the pastry case in the fridge while you make the pumpkin filling.

Preheat the oven to 180°C/Gas mark 4. Place the squash face down in an ovenproof dish with about 1cm apple juice or water, cover with parchment and foil and bake for 45 minutes, or until an inserted knife comes out easily. Remove the squash from the oven and leave until cool enough to handle. Use a large spoon to scoop the flesh into a bowl and discard the skin. Combine 540g pumpkin pulp, the soya milk, vanilla, sugar, maple syrup, eggs, cinnamon, ginger, cloves and salt in a bowl and mix well. Remove your pie case from the fridge and pour the squash mixture up to the rim of the dough. Bake for about 45 minutes, or until the pie is golden brown and a wooden cocktail stick inserted in the centre comes out clean.

NUTRITIONAL FACTS per 6cm slice

Made using eggs and pumpkin

Calories 291 | Total fat 13.4g | Saturated fat 7.7g | Carbohydrates 37.5g | Protein 4.9g

LEMON BIRTHDAY CAKE

~ SERVES 12 TO 16 ~

Vegetable oil spray for spraying the cake tin
280g unbleached organic plain white flour, plus extra for dusting the cake tin
370g wholemeal pastry flour
2 tsp baking powder
2 tsp bicarbonate of soda
1 tsp ground cinnamon
1 tsp ground nutmeg
2 tsp salt
2 tsp grated lemon rind
2½ tbsp rapeseed oil
510g maple syrup
375ml light soya milk
125ml lemon juice (juice of about 6 lemons)
150ml apple juice
2 tsp vanilla extract
2 tsp lemon extract

Preheat the oven to 180°C/Gas mark 4. Spray two round 20cm or one 32.5 x 22.5cm cake tin with oil, then lightly dust with flour, shake off any excess and set aside. Sift both flours, the baking powder, bicarbonate of soda, salt, cinnamon, nutmeg and lemon rind into a bowl, tipping in any bran left in the sieve. Combine the oil, maple syrup, soya milk, lemon juice, apple juice and vanilla and lemon extracts in a separate large bowl. Add the dry ingredients to the wet ingredients and mix together. Avoid over-mixing. Pour the batter into the baking tin and bake for 30–40 minutes or until the cake looks lightly browned, springs back when touched and a wooden cocktail stick inserted in the centre come out clean. Cool on a wire rack for 5 minutes then remove from the tin.

Serve the cake with fresh berries or sprinkle over Walnut Coconut Praline (page 275) or a simple Fruit Syrup made with raspberries (page 48).

NUTRITIONAL FACTS per 5 x 5cm slice

Calories 288 | Total fat 6.1g | Saturated fat 0.5g | Carbohydrates 54.2g | Protein 4.1g

LEMON POPPY SEED CAKE

~ SERVES 8 ~

Vegetable oil spray for spraying the baking tin
375g wholemeal pastry flour
1½ tsp baking powder
1 tsp bicarbonate of soda
½ tsp salt
4 tbsp poppy seeds
1 tbsp grated lemon rind
4 tbsp rapeseed oil
220g turbinado sugar
4 tbsp apple sauce or mango purée
4 tbsp lemon juice
1 tsp vanilla extract
1 tsp lemon extract
225g low-fat vanilla or lemon yogurt

Preheat the oven to 180°C/Gas mark 4. Spray a 20cm cake tin with vegetable oil spray, then lightly dust with flour, shake off any excess and set aside. Combine the flour, baking powder, bicarbonate of soda, salt, poppy seeds and lemon rind in a large bowl. Combine the oil, sugar, apple sauce, lemon juice and the vanilla and lemon extracts in a food processor or blender and pulse until just combined. Pour the wet ingredients into the dry ingredients and mix together with a rubber spatula. Gently fold in the yogurt until just blended. Be careful not to over-mix. Pour the batter into the prepared tin and bake for 30–45 minutes, or until golden brown and a wooden cocktail stick comes out clean. Leave to cool on a wire rack before serving.

◈　◈　◈　◈

NUTRITIONAL FACTS per 5cm slice

Calories 199 | Total fat 5.1g | Saturated fat 0.5g | Carbohydrates 34.5g | Protein 3.6g

LINZERTORTE COOKIES

~ MAKES 24 COOKIES ~

2 tbsp rapeseed oil, plus extra for greasing the baking sheet
90g rolled oats or rolled barley oats
145g almonds
165g wholemeal pastry flour, rice flour or spelt flour
170g maple syrup
120g mango purée or apple sauce
½ tsp ground cinnamon
½ tsp salt
320g organic raspberry jam

Preheat the oven to 180°C/Gas mark 4. Lightly grease a baking sheet with rapeseed oil and set aside. Grind the oats and almonds together in a food processor until coarsely ground. Put them in a bowl, add the flour, cinnamon and salt. Combine the maple syrup, oil and the mango purée in a separate large bowl and whisk together. Add the dry ingredients into the wet ingredients and combine with a spatula or place plastic sandwich bags on your hands to mix. Use a 30g ice-cream scoop or a tablespoon to scoop the dough on to the baking sheet, 5cm apart. Make a small indentation with your thumb and spoon in a small amount of raspberry jam. Bake for 15–20 minutes until golden brown.

❖ ❖ ❖ ❖

NUTRITIONAL FACTS per cookie
Calories 125 | Total fat 3.7g | Saturated fat 0.4g | Carbohydrates 20.1g | Protein 2.7g

MOTHER EARTH'S APPLE PIE

~ SERVES 8 ~

Vegetable oil spray for spraying the pie tin and rolling out the pastry
500g wholemeal pastry flour
1 pinch of salt
125g chilled butter, cut into pieces
1 tbsp cider vinegar
4–6 tbsp ice-cold water (add ice cubes)

FILLING

1 tsp ghee
5 large green apples, unpeeled, thinly sliced and soaked in water with lemon juice
1 tbsp apple juice
1 tsp ground cinnamon
½ tsp ground nutmeg
110g turbinado sugar
2 tsp arrowroot
2 tbsp maple syrup
1 tbsp chilled butter, cut into pieces
1 tbsp milk or soya milk
1 tbsp caster sugar
1 tsp ground cinnamon

Lightly spray a pie tin with oil and set aside. Place the flour and salt in a food processor and pulse to combine. With the machine running, begin to add the butter, one piece at a time and continue to pulse until the mixture looks like a coarse meal. Add the vinegar. With the motor still running, begin to slowly add the water, 1 tablespoon at a time and waiting a moment or two before each addition, until the dough begins to form a ball in the bowl of the food processor. Remove from the bowl and divide the dough in half. Wrap one half in cling film and place in the refrigerator. Roll out the other half of the pastry on a lightly sprayed work surface into a round 2.5cm larger all around than your pie tin. Place the dough into the pie tin, leaving a 2.5cm edge around the perimeter of the tin. Place the pie case in the fridge while you make the filling.

Preheat the oven to 220°C/Gas mark 7.

Drain the apples. Heat the ghee in a large frying pan over a medium heat. Add the apples, apple juice, cinnamon, nutmeg and sugar and stir for 3–5 minutes until the apples are well coated with the spices. Add the arrowroot and the maple syrup and continue stirring for a further 2 minutes. Remove the pan from the heat and set aside.

Remove the pastry case and the remaining pastry from the fridge. Roll out the remaining pastry into a round larger than the piecrust. Arrange the apples in the pastry crust, mounting them in the centre. Dot the apples with the pieces of butter. Place the other piece of pastry on top of the apples. Using your fingers, press the dough into the apples. Trim the pastry to match the bottom layer and press together. To create a finished look, pinch the pastry along the edge by placing the dough between your pointer finger on one hand and your thumb and pointer finger on the other hand. Vent the pie by making small diagonal slashes in the top crust. Bake the pie for 10 minutes, then reduce the heat to 180°C/Gas mark 4 and bake for a further 40 minutes. Brush the pie with milk just as it comes out of the oven. Mix the sugar and cinnamon together and sprinkle on top of the pie. Leave the pie to stand for 20–30 minutes before serving.

❖ ❖ ❖ ❖

NUTRITIONAL FACTS per 7.5cm slice
Calories 343 | Total fat 13.8g | Saturated fat 8.6g | Carbohydrates 34.3g | Protein 2.7g

OATMEAL POWER COOKIES

When you need a high-energy snack, try one of these.

~ MAKES 24 COOKIES ~

Vegetable oil spray for spraying the baking sheet
165g wholemeal pastry flour or spelt flour
80g rolled oats
150g ready-to-eat dried fruit, such as apricots, blueberries, cranberries
or dates, chopped, or fresh apples, chopped
150g raisins or currants
90g coconut flakes
½ tsp bicarbonate of soda
1 tsp ground cinnamon
1 tsp ground allspice
120g mango purée
135g turbinado sugar
170g maple syrup
1 tsp vanilla extract

Preheat the oven to 180°C/Gas mark 4. Lightly spray a baking sheet with the vegetable oil spray and set aside. Combine the flour, oats, mixed dried fruit, raisins, coconut, bicarbonate of soda, cinnamon and allspice in a bowl and whisk together. Combine the mango purée, sugar, maple syrup and the vanilla extract in a separate large bowl and whisk together. Pour the dry ingredients into the wet ingredients and using a rubber spatula or plastic sandwich bags on your hands mix together until a dough forms. Use a 30g ice-cream scoop to scoop the dough on to the baking sheet, 5cm apart. Bake for 15 minutes, or until golden brown.

❖ ❖ ❖ ❖

NUTRITIONAL FACTS per cookie
Calories 145 | Total fat 1.5g | Saturated fat 1g | Carbohydrates 30.9g | Protein 2g

PEANUT BUTTER COOKIES

~ MAKES 18 COOKIES ~

Vegetable oil spray for spraying the baking sheet
4 tbsp ghee or rapeseed oil
135g turbinado sugar
4 tbsp apple sauce
4 tbsp maple syrup
130g peanut butter or almond butter
125ml light soya milk or rice milk
1 tsp vanilla extract
290g wholemeal pastry flour
1 tsp bicarbonate of soda
½ tsp baking powder
½ tsp salt

Preheat the oven to 180°C/Gas mark 4. Lightly spray a baking sheet with vegetable oil and set aside. Beat the ghee and sugar together until creamy with an electric mixer or in a food processor. Add the apple sauce, maple syrup, peanut butter, soya milk and vanilla and combine until smooth. Combine the flour, bicarbonate of soda, baking powder and salt and whisk together. Add the dry ingredients to the wet ingredients, mixing by hand until smooth. Use a 30g ice-cream scoop or a tablespoon to scoop the dough on to the baking sheet. Flatten each cookie slightly with a fork, then press the fork in the opposite direction, to create a criss-cross pattern. Bake the cookies for 12–15 minutes until golden brown. Leave to cool on a rack before eating.

❖ ❖ ❖ ❖

NUTRITIONAL FACTS per cookie
Calories 136 | Total fat 7.2g | Saturated fat 2.8g | Carbohydrates 14.3g | Protein 3.5g

TRADITIONAL AWESOME BROWNIES

~ MAKES 12 SERVINGS ~

125g chilled butter, cut into cubes, plus extra for greasing the baking tin
110g turbinado sugar
120g apple sauce
1 tsp vanilla extract
125ml semi-skimmed cow's milk or light soya milk
2 eggs
250g wholemeal pastry flour
½ tsp salt
75g unsweetened cocoa powder
1 tsp baking powder
60g walnuts halves, macadamia nuts or almonds, chopped and toasted
75g plain chocolate chips

Preheat the oven to 180°C/Gas mark 4. Grease a 20cm square baking tin with butter and set aside. Beat the butter, sugar and apple sauce with an electric mixer until creamy. Add the vanilla and milk, then add the eggs, one at a time, mixing between each addition. Mix altogether only briefly after the addition of the last egg. Combine the flour, salt, cocoa powder and baking powder in a separate bowl and whisk together. Turn the mixer on low and slowly add the flour mixture, about 70g at a time. Scrape down the side of the mixing bowl to incorporate all the ingredients. Be careful not to over-mix. Add the nuts and chocolate chips and mix again, very briefly. Pour the mixture into the baking tin and bake for 30 minutes, or until a wooden cocktail stick inserted in the centre comes out clean. Leave the brownies to cool before eating. Warning: these brownies are really good, so control yourself and only eat a little piece at a time.

NUTRITIONAL FACTS per 5cm brownie

Calories 265 | Total fat 12.4g | Saturated fat 5.8g | Carbohydrates 32.8g | Protein 5.3g

TRADITIONAL CHOCOLATE CHIP COOKIES

~ MAKES 28 COOKIES ~

Vegetable oil spray for spraying the baking sheet
220g turbinado sugar
225g butter, softened
1 tsp vanilla extract
2 eggs
370g wholemeal pastry flour
1½ tsp baking powder
½ tsp salt
350g plain chocolate chips
60g almonds or walnut halves, chopped (optional)

Preheat the oven to 180°C/Gas mark 4. Lightly spray a baking sheet with vegetable oil spray and set aside. Beat the sugar and the butter together until creamy with an electric mixer or in a food processor. Add the vanilla and the eggs, one at a time. Combine the flour, baking powder and salt in a separate large bowl and whisk together. Add the dry ingredients to the butter mixture and fold together. Add the chocolate chips to the dough. Add the almonds or walnuts if desired. Drop the cookie dough on to the baking sheet, using a tablespoon or 30g ice-cream scoop. Bake for 8–10 minutes or until golden brown.

❖ ❖ ❖ ❖

NUTRITIONAL FACTS per cookie

Without nuts

Calories 180 | Total fat 9.3g | Saturated fat 5.7g | Carbohydrates 22.1g | Protein 1.8g

UNBELIEVABLE DOUBLE CHOCOLATE CAKE

~ SERVES 12 ~

165g wholemeal pastry flour
75g unsweetened cocoa powder
2 tsp baking powder
1 tsp bicarbonate of soda
350g firm or extra-firm silken tofu, ideally low fat, drained
4 tbsp ghee or rapeseed oil, plus extra for greasing the baking sheet
185g apple sauce
340g maple syrup
2 tsp vanilla extract
176g plain chocolate chips, ideally non-dairy

Preheat the oven to 180°C/Gas mark 4. Spray a 23cm round or 20cm square baking tin with oil and set aside. Combine the flour, cocoa powder, baking powder and bicarbonate of soda in a large mixing bowl and whisk together. Place the tofu, oil, apple sauce, maple syrup and the vanilla extract in a food processor or blender and blend until smooth. Pour the wet ingredients into the dry ingredients and combine, then gently fold in the chocolate chips. Be careful not to over-mix. Pour the batter into the baking tin and bake for 30–40 minutes until a wooden cocktail stick inserted in the centre comes out clean.

❖ ❖ ❖ ❖

NUTRITIONAL FACTS per 5cm square

Made with low-fat tofu

Calories 286 | Total fat 10.6g | Saturated fat 3.7g | Carbohydrates 42.1g | Protein 5.5g

WALNUT CHOCOLATE CHIP COOKIES

~ MAKES 24 SMALL COOKIES ~

2 tbsp rapeseed oil, plus extra for the baking sheet
80g organic rolled oats
125g walnut halves
165g wholemeal pastry flour, rice flour or spelt flour
½ tsp ground cinnamon
½ tsp salt
170g maple syrup
120g mango purée, apple sauce or mashed bananas
175g plain chocolate chips, ideally non-dairy

Preheat the oven to 180°C/Gas mark 4. Lightly grease a baking sheet with rapeseed oil and set aside. Put the walnuts and oats in a food processor and grind until a coarse mixture forms. Place into a bowl. Add the flour, cinnamon and salt and whisk together. Combine the maple syrup, oil and mango purée in a separate large bowl and whisk together. Add the dry ingredients to the wet ingredients and add the chocolate chips. Combine with a spatula or place plastic sandwich bags on your hands to mix. Use a 30g ice-cream scoop or a tablespoon to scoop the dough on to the baking sheet, 5cm apart. Bake for 15–20 minutes until golden brown.

❖ ❖ ❖ ❖

NUTRITIONAL FACTS per cookie

Calories 148 | Total fat 6.9g | Saturated fat 1.9g | Carbohydrates 17.3g | Protein 3.6g

NUTRITIONAL INFORMATION

The following nutritional information is based upon a projected daily intake of about 2,200 calories. If you are a moderately active person, this diet would stabilize your weight at about 9st 12lb (62.6kg).

You can calculate your ideal daily calorie intake by multiplying your desired weight in pounds by 16. There are 14 pounds in a stone, so if, for example, your desired weight is 8st 8lb (54.4kg; 120lbs), your daily caloric intake should be 1,920.

If your desired weight is 11st 6lb (72.5kg; 160lbs), your daily intake should be 2,560 calories (160 x 16 = 2,560).

Adjust your serving size to reflect your caloric needs. If you want to sustain your weight of 8st 12lb (56.2kg; 124lbs) with an intake of 1,980 calories daily, you will need to reduce your serving size by 10 per cent. If you want to sustain your weight of 10st 11lb (68.5kg; 151lbs) with a daily intake of 2,420 calories, you should increase your serving size by 10 per cent.

Remember that listening to your body's cues of hunger and satiety is more important than counting calories. Honouring the wisdom of your body is the most direct path to health and renewal of body and soul.

Per serving: target Percent of daily calories	2250	50–60g 20–24%	<20g 5–9%	325–375g 59–68%	90–100g 16–18%
Day 1	calories	total fat	sat fat	carbs	protein
Breakfast					
Morning Bliss Shake	424	6.8	2.8	61.3	29.8
Breakfast Bar	339	11.4	3	50.9	8.2
totals	763	18.2	5.8	112.2	38
Main					
Tomato Florentine Soup	223	4.1	0.4	24.8	22
Rainbow Risotto	328	2.8	0.4	55.8	19.7
Nutty Spinach Greens	80	4.6	1.1	6.1	3.4
Almond Tart	239	11.4	6.3	31.6	2.3
totals	870	22.9	8.2	118.3	47.4
Light					
Vegetable Hummus Wrap	320	7.6	1.5	51.3	11.5
Ginger Cookies	149	2.9	1.9	28.8	1.8
totals	469	10.5	3.4	80.1	13.3
Daily Totals	2102	51.6	17.4	310.6	98.7
Percent of Calories		% fat	% sat fat	% carbs	% protein
Daily Totals		22%	7%	59%	19%

Day 2	calories	total fat	sat fat	carbs	protein
Breakfast					
Vegetable Tofu Scramble	160	6.7	0.8	9.5	15.2
Coriander Mint Sauce	20	0.2	0	3.2	1.2
Apple Raisin Muffin	234	5	0.5	42	4.9
totals	414	11.9	1.3	54.7	21.3
Main					
Tofu Fajitas	282	8	0.2	34.1	18.4
Mandarin Tomato Salsa	66	0.4	0	13.6	1.8
Spanish Pilaf	360	3.4	0.1	62.5	9.1
Stir-fried Carrrots and Cauliflowers	68	1.5	0.9	10.7	2.7
Apple Custard Pie	336	13.1	7.8	49.9	4.5
totals	1112	26.4	9	170.8	36.5
Light					
Italian White Bean Stew	349	5.2	1	59	16.8
Oatmeal Power Cookie	145	1.5	1	30.9	2
totals	494	6.7	2	89.9	18.8
Daily Totals	2020	45	12.3	315.4	76.6
Percent of Calories		% fat	% sat fat	% carbs	% protein
Daily Totals		20%	5%	62%	15%

Per serving: target Percent of daily calories	2250	50–60g 20–24%	<20g 5–9%	325–375g 59–68%	90–100g 16–18%
Day 3	calories	total fat	sat fat	carbs	protein
Breakfast					
Rolled Oats Hot Cereal	208	3.3	1	37.3	7.5
Blueberry and Banana Syrup	123	1.9	1.1	25.9	0.8
Courgette Pecan Bread	269	10.1	1.1	39	5.5
totals	600	15.3	3.2	102.2	13.8
Main					
Spinach Soup	112	2.9	1.1	15.2	6.3
Vegetable Paella	348	10.4	1.6	51.7	11.8
Aubergine Tapenade	70	4.8	0.2	5.6	1
Dilled Asparagus	49	0.4	0.1	6.1	5.2
Sautéed Strawberries	167	3.3	1.9	33.2	1.3
totals	746	21.8	4.9	111.8	25.6
Light					
Vegetable and White Bean Chilli	364	4.2	0.5	53.2	28
Simple Great Wholegrain Bread	156	1.4	0.3	30.4	5.8
Peanut Butter Cookie	136	7.2	2.8	14.3	3.5
total	656	12.8	3.6	97.9	37.3
Daily Totals	2002	49.9	11.7	311.9	76.7
Percent of Calories		% fat	% sat fat	% carbs	% protein
Daily Totals		22%	5%	62%	15%
Day 4	calories	total fat	sat fat	carbs	protein
Breakfast					
Coffee Bliss Shake	194	1	0.6	44.2	2.1
Nutty French Toast	360	15.3	4	43	12.5
Sautéed Apples	99	1.4	0.8	21.1	0.3
totals	653	17.7	5.4	108.3	14.9
Main					
Summertime Tomato Basil Soup	257	4.2	0.5	37.5	17.1
Spinach Polenta	172	1.9	0.2	28	10.8
Ratatouille	215	6.8	3.4	27.1	11.5
Savoury Swiss Chard	32	1.3	0.2	3.7	1.4
Walnut Chocolate Chip Cookie	148	6.9	1.9	17.3	3.6
total	824	21.1	6.2	113.6	44.4
Light					
Egg-less Tofu Salad or Sandwich	301	7.7	0.6	37.9	20.1
Lemon Poppy Seed Cake	199	5.1	0.5	34.5	3.6
totals	500	12.8	1.1	72.4	23.7
Daily Totals	1977	51.6	12.7	294.3	83
Percent of Calories		% fat	% sat fat	% carbs	% protein
Daily Totals		23%	6%	60%	17%

Per serving: target Percent of daily calories	2250	50–60g 20–24%	<20g 5–9%	325–375g 59–68%	90–100g 16–18%
Day 5	calories	total fat	sat fat	carbs	protein
Breakfast					
Chai Bliss shake	289	1.2	0.7	43.6	26
Chopra Granola	353	15.6	4.4	43.8	9.8
Fresh Blueberries and	80	0.4	0.1	18.4	0.8
totals	722	17.2	5.2	105.8	36.6
Main					
Vegetable Hot-and-Sour Soup	148	4.8	0.2	16.1	
Buddha's Delight Vegetable Stir-fry	172	7.5	1	20	6.3
Steamed Rice	171	0.3	0.1	38.7	3.2
Kim Chi Chutney	111	1.9	0.2	20.9	3.2
Unbelievable Double Chocolate Cake	286	10.6	3.7	42.1	5.5
totals	888	25.1	5.2	137.8	28.3
Light					
Roasted Tofu and Yams	305	8.2	0.5	41.7	16.1
Garden Salad with Coriander Pecan Sauce	126	7.3	0.6	8.1	7.1
Sautéed Apricots	178	3.2	1.9	35.4	2
totals	609	18.7	3	85.2	25.2
Daily Totals	2219	61	13.4	328.8	90.1
Percent of Calories		% fat	% sat fat	% carbs	% protein
Daily Totals		25%	7%	59%	16%
Day 6	calories	total fat	sat fat	carbs	protein
Breakfast					
Broccoli Tofu Scramble	181	6.9	0.2	13.9	15.9
Mandarin Tomato Salsa	66	0.4	0	13.6	1.8
Simple Great Wholegrain Bread with Almond Butter	231	5.1	1	31.6	7
totals	478	12.4	1.2	59.1	24.7
Main					
Potato Leek Soup	279	3.4	0.3	37.3	24.4
French Vegetable Stew	145	2.1	0.2	24.1	7.7
Toasted Millet	187	2.1	0.4	36.4	5.5
Steamed Carrots and Green Beans	80	0.4	0.1	18.4	0.8
Linzertorte Cookie	125	3.7	0.4	20.1	2.7
totals	816	11.7	1.4	136.3	41.1
Light					
Split Pea Dahl	262	2.6	1.4	43.9	16
Indian Rice	343	2.8	1	72.4	7
Apple Leek Chutney	170	1.3	0.5	38.3	0.9
Cardamom Butter Cookie	171	5.9	3.8	20.2	2.3
totals	946	12.6	6.7	174.8	26.2
Daily Totals	2240	36.7	9.3	370.2	92
Percent of Calories		% fat	% sat fat	% carbs	% protein
Daily Totals		15%	4%	66%	16%

Per serving: target Percent of daily calories	2250	50–60g 20–24%	<20g 5–9%	325–375g 59–68%	90–100g 16–18%
Day 7	calories	total fat	sat fat	carbs	protein
Breakfast					
Almond Bliss Shake	487	12.4	3.3	61.1	32.9
Apples and Rice Hot Cereal	382	6.8	2	71.9	8.2
totals	869	19.2	5.3	133	41.1
Main					
Italian Vegetable Soup	268	2.1	0.4	46.3	15.9
Curry Filo Tarts	227	5.2	2.3	37.8	7.7
Walnut Yogurt Sauce	68	3.2	0.8	5.4	4.2
Roasted Sweet Potatoes	164	1.7	1	34.2	3.1
Berry Tofu Sorbet	83	0.6	0	15.8	3.6
totals	810	12.8	4.5	139.5	34.5
Light					
Marinated Tofu Thai Wrap with Nutty Dipping Sauce	395	15.8	2.3	43.4	19.4
Cranberry Bliss Ball	232	14.4	2.3	21.5	4.1
totals	627	30.2	4.6	64.9	23.5
Daily Totals	2306	62.2	14.4	337.4	99.1
Percent of Calories		% fat	% sat fat	% carbs	% protein
Daily Totals		24%	6%	59%	17%
Day 8	calories	total fat	sat fat	carbs	protein
Breakfast					
Mango Yogurt	178	1.5	0.8	36.4	5
Tempeh and Potato Hash	305	6.8	1.1	38.4	22.6
Orange Pear Chutney	74	0.6	0.2	16.7	0.4
totals	557	8.9	2.1	91.5	28
Main					
Butternut Squash Soup	123	2.9	1.1	20	4.3
Aubergine and Yam Curry	424	7.5	1.1	73.1	15.9
Curried Potatoes	399	11.2	6.1	64.4	10.3
Cucumber Raita	59	1.1	0.6	8	3.9
Sautéed Apples and Blackberries	99	1.4	0.8	21.1	0.3
totals	1104	24.1	9.7	186.6	34.7
Light					
Asian Clear Broth	158	6.5	0.4	11.6	13.3
Thai Tofu Vegetable Stew	444	15.6	6.1	48.6	27.5
Coconut Cookie	126	6.3	4.3	15.5	1.5
totals	728	28.4	10.8	75.7	42.3
Daily Totals	2389	61.4	22.6	353.8	105
Percent of Calories		% fat	% sat fat	% carbs	% protein
Daily Totals		23%	9%	59%	18%

Per serving: target Percent of daily calories	2250	50–60g 20–24%	<20g 5–9%	325–375g 59–68%	90–100g 16–18%
Day 9	calories	total fat	sat fat	carbs	protein
Breakfast					
Chopra Granola	353	15.6	4.4	43.8	9.8
Very Berry Yogurt	173	3	1.8	30.4	6.3
totals	526	18.6	6.2	74.2	16.1
Main					
Italian Vegetable Soup	268	2.1	0.4	46.3	15.9
Fresh Spinach Pasta	104	0.4	0.1	21.2	3.8
Tofu 'Meatballs' with Roasted Tomato Sauce	408	15.9	2.2	44.9	21.1
Stir-fried Rocket and Roasted Aubergine	63	3	1.8	6.2	2.9
Lemon Birthday Cake	288	6.1	0.5	54.2	4.1
totals	1131	27.5	5	172.8	47.8
Light					
Potato Leek Soup	279	3.4	0.3	37.3	24.4
Poached Peaches and Blueberries	147	2.9	1.9	29.3	0.9
totals	426	6.3	2.2	66.6	25.3
Daily Totals	2083	52.4	13.4	313.6	89.2
Percent of Calories		% fat	% sat fat	% carbs	% protein
Daily Totals		23%	6%	60%	17%
Day 10	calories	total fat	sat fat	carbs	protein
Breakfast					
Mango Bliss Shake	281	4.1	2.6	47.5	13.4
Vegetable Tofu Scramble	160	6.7	0.8	9.5	15.2
Russian Borscht Chutney	33	0.5	0.2	7	0.5
Cinnamon Roll	149	3.9	1.5	24.8	3.6
totals	623	15.2	5.1	88.8	32.7
Main					
Vegetable Barley Soup	280	4	0.4	38.8	22.5
Tofu Burger with Leek Sauce	304	12.1	1.6	28.2	20.3
Steamed Broccoli	32	0.3	0	4.6	2.6
Berry Tofu Sorbet	83	0.6	0	15.8	3.6
totals	699	17	2	87.4	49
Light					
Roasted Tofu and Yams	305	8.2	0.5	41.7	16.1
Steamed Asparagus	39	0.3	0.1	6.1	3.1
Blueberry Lemon Cake	252	4	0.2	50.4	3.6
totals	596	12.5	0.8	98.2	22.8
Daily Totals	1918	44.7	7.9	274.4	104.5
Percent of Calories		% fat	% sat fat	% carbs	% protein
Daily Totals		21%	4%	57%	22%

Per serving: target Percent of daily calories	2250	50–60g 20–24%	<20g 5–9%	325–375g 59–68%	90–100g 16–18%
Day 11	calories	total fat	sat fat	carbs	protein
Breakfast					
Tofu and Potato Italiano	272	7	0.3	33.8	18.3
Home-made Chilli Sauce	87.5	1.4	0.5	16.6	2
Courgette Pecan Bread	269	10.1	1.1	39	5.5
totals	628.5	18.5	1.9	89.4	25.8
Main					
Red Lentil Dahl	262	2.6	1.4	43.9	16
Aubergine Cauliflower Curry	237	4.1	2.2	44	6.2
Steamed Green Beans	52	0.3	0.1	9.9	2.4
Orange Pear Chutney	74	0.6	0.2	16.7	0.4
Sautéed Pears with Cardamom	175	3.5	1.9	34.9	1.1
totals	800	11.1	5.8	149.4	26.1
Light					
Black Bean and Vegetable Stew	442	4.4	1.1	70.2	30.5
Oat Groat Pilaf with Spinach	218	3.1	1	40.6	7
Apricot Pecan Cookie	125	3.7	0.4	20.1	2.7
totals	785	11.2	2.5	130.9	40.2
Daily Totals	2213.5	40.8	10.2	369.7	92.1
Percent of Calories		% fat	% sat fat	% carbs	% protein
Daily Totals		17%	4%	67%	17%
Day 12	calories	total fat	sat fat	carbs	protein
Breakfast					
Chai Bliss Shake	289	1.2	0.7	43.6	26
Breakfast Burrito	213	8.6	4.3	25.8	8
Whole Apple	56	0.3	0	13	0.2
totals	558	10.1	5	82.4	34.2
Main					
Tortilla Soup with Avocado and Coriander	347	14.7	1.8	32.6	21.1
Braised Tofu with Mango Tomato Salsa	309	8.2	0.4	40.7	17
Stir-fried Sweetcorn, Peppers and Broccoli	108	2.3	1	17.6	4.3
Stir-fried Greens	28	1.4	0.9	2.2	1.5
Banana-Cocoa-Tofu Mousse	159	0.9	0.2	33.5	4.3
totals	951	27.5	4.3	126.6	48.2
Light					
Black Bean and Rice Wrap	444	6.6	2.3	82.7	13.5
Simple Carrot Soup	72	1.5	0.3	11.6	2.9
Traditional Awesome Brownie	265	12.4	5.8	32.8	5.3
totals	781	20.5	8.4	127.1	21.7
Daily Totals	2290	58.1	17.7	336.1	104.1
Percent of Calories		% fat	% sat fat	% carbs	% protein
Daily Totals		23%	7%	59%	18%

Per serving: target Percent of daily calories	2250	50–60g 20–24%	<20g 5–9%	325–375g 59–68%	90–100g 16–18%
Day 13	calories	total fat	sat fat	carbs	protein
Breakfast					
Traditional French Toast	277	8	3	39.2	11.9
Sautéed Apples and Blackberries	198	3.2	1.9	41.2	1
totals	475	11.2	4.9	80.4	12.9
Main					
Vegetable Barley Soup	280	4	0.4	38.8	22.5
Moroccan Vegetables	187	6.6	0.9	24.4	7.4
Dilled Lemon Courgettes	42	1.3	0.2	5.3	2.3
Hummus	125	3.6	0.5	17.2	5.9
Banana-Cocoa-Tofu Mousse	159	0.9	0.2	33.5	4.3
totals	793	16.4	2.2	119.2	42.4
Light					
Roasted Winter Vegetable Stew	368	7.1	2.1	61.3	14.5
Organic Mixed Greens Salad with Olive Oil	88	6.2	0.7	5.5	2.4
Kabocha Squash or Pumpkin Pie	291	13.4	7.7	37.5	4.9
totals	747	26.7	10.5	104.3	21.8
Daily Totals	2015	54.3	17.6	303.9	77.1
Percent of Calories		% fat	% sat fat	% carbs	% protein
Daily Totals		24%	8%	60%	15%
Day 14	calories	total fat	sat fat	carbs	protein
Breakfast					
Masala Potatoes	372	6.2	2.5	67.7	11.2
Apple Leek Chutney	170	1.3	0.5	38.3	0.9
Mango Yogurt	178	1.5	0.8	36.4	5
totals	720	9	3.8	142.4	17.1
Main					
Tomato Florentine Soup	223	4.1	0.4	24.8	22
Mediterranean Pasta	269	4	0.9	47.8	10.3
Savoury Swiss Chard	42	1.5	0.9	5.1	1.9
Steamed Asparagus	39	0.3	0.1	6.1	3.1
Ginger Cookie	149	2.9	1.9	28.8	1.8
totals	722	12.8	4.2	112.6	39.1
Light					
Tofu, Aubergine and Potato Stew	318	8.6	0.7	40.1	19.8
Greek Goddess Salad	262	6.1	0.9	42.8	9.5
Blueberry Orange Cake	252	4	0.2	50.4	3.6
totals	832	18.7	1.8	133.3	32.9
Daily Totals	2274	40.5	9.8	388.3	89.1
Percent of Calories		% fat	% sat fat	% carbs	% protein
Daily Totals		16%	4%	68%	16%

Per serving: target Percent of daily calories	2250	50–60g 20–24%	<20g 5–9%	325–375g 59–68%	90–100g 16–18%
Day 15	calories	total fat	sat fat	carbs	protein
Breakfast					
Broccoli Tofu Scramble	181	6.9	0.2	13.9	15.9
Russian Borscht Chutney	33	0.5	0.2	7	0.5
Blueberry Muffin	138	1.7	0.4	27.6	2.9
totals	352	9.1	0.8	48.5	19.3
Main					
Rosemary White Bean Soup	307	4	1.6	53	14.7
Vegetarian Paella	348	10.4	1.6	51.7	11.8
Stir-fried Green Beans and Almonds	121	6	1.3	12.6	4.5
Raspberry Lemon Cake	246	4.2	0.5	47.4	4.7
totals	1022	24.6	5	164.7	35.7
Light					
Curried Chickpea Stew	498	12.6	5.1	64.9	31.4
Steamed Rice	171	0.3	0.1	38.7	3.2
Ginger Cookie	149	2.9	1.9	28.8	1.8
totals	818	15.8	7.1	132.4	36.4
Daily Totals	2192	49.5	12.9	345.6	91.4
Percent of Calories		% fat	% sat fat	% carbs	% protein
Daily Totals		20%	5%	63%	17%
Day 16	calories	total fat	sat fat	carbs	protein
Breakfast					
Wholemeal Crêpes	248	11.1	2.2	26.8	10.2
Blueberry Banana Syrup	123	1.9	1.1	25.9	0.8
Country Potatoes	180	3.8	0.5	32.5	4
totals	551	16.8	3.8	85.2	15
Main					
Sweet Potato Ginger Soup	247	2.9	0.3	50.5	5
Stir-fried Broccoli and Almonds with Basic Asian-style Sauce	112	3	0.3	17.3	4.1
Szechwan Baked Egg Rolls	186	5.5	1.1	25.1	9.1
Spicy Lime and Red Pepper Sauce	54	0	0	12.8	0.7
Chinese Five-Spice Garden Pilaf	225	1	0.1	49.1	5.1
Sautéed Peaches with Nutmeg	197	2.9	1.9	41.4	1.6
totals	1021	15.3	3.7	196.2	25.6
Light					
Mexican Tofu Stew	256	8.1	0.2	21	24.2
Garden Salad with No Olive Oil	46	1.9	0.2	4.9	2.3
Coriander Pecan Sauce	80	5.4	0.4	3.2	4.8
Peanut Butter Cookie	136	7.2	2.8	14.3	3.5
totals	518	22.6	3.6	43.4	34.8
Daily Totals	2090	53.7	16	300.5	95.3
Percent of Calories		% fat	% sat fat	% carbs	% protein
Daily Totals		23%	7%	58%	18%

Per serving: target Percent of daily calories	2250	50–60g 20–24%	<20g 5–9%	325–375g 59–68%	90–100g 16–18%
Day 17	calories	total fat	sat fat	carbs	protein
Breakfast					
Coffee Bliss Shake	194	1	0.6	44.2	2.1
Hot Quinoa Breakfast Cereal	293	4.4	0.1	54.1	9.4
Pumpkin Muffin	200	3.7	0.6	37.9	3.7
totals	687	9.1	1.3	136.2	15.2
Main					
Nutty Broccoli Soup	187	8.9	1.5	18.6	8.1
Simple Wholegrain Pizza with Basil and Friends Pesto and Courgettes	229	9	1	24	6.8
Savoury Swiss Chard	32	1.3	0.2	3.7	1.4
Baked Spaghetti Squash	43	0.6	0.1	7.8	1.6
Almond Tart	239	11.4	6.3	31.6	2.3
totals	730	31.2	9.1	85.7	20.2
Light					
Thai Tofu Vegetable Stew	444	15.6	6.1	48.6	27.5
Steamed Rice	171	0.3	0.1	38.7	3.2
Oatmeal Power Cookie	145	1.5	1	30.9	2
totals	760	17.4	7.2	118.2	32.7
Daily Totals	2177	57.7	17.6	340.1	68.1
Percent of Calories		% fat	% sat fat	% carbs	% protein
Daily Totals		24%	7%	62%	13%
Day 18	calories	total fat	sat fat	carbs	protein
Breakfast					
Chopra Granola	353	15.6	4.4	43.8	9.8
Apple Breakfast Syrup	124	1.6	0.9	27.1	0.3
Strawberry Banana Yogurt	186	1.8	1.1	35.7	6.6
totals	663	19	6.4	106.6	16.7
Main					
Vegetable Hot-and-Sour Stew	148	4.8	0.2	16.1	10.1
Thai-style Noodles with Tofu	414	9	0.5	64.3	18.9
Nutty Spinach Greens	80	4.6	1.1	6.1	3.4
Kim Chi Chutney	111	1.9	0.2	20.9	3.2
Double Almond Cookie	140	7.4	0.7	15.3	3.3
totals	893	27.7	2.7	122.7	38.9
Light					
Tofu, Aubergine and Potato Stew	318	8.6	0.7	40.1	19.8
Green Quinoa Pilaf	287	5.8	0.9	40.6	18.1
Sautéed Pears with Cardamom	175	3.5	1.9	34.9	1.1
totals	780	17.9	3.5	115.6	39
Daily Totals	2336	64.6	12.6	344.9	94.6
Percent of Calories		% fat	% sat fat	% carbs	% protein
Daily Totals		25%	5%	59%	16%

Per serving: target Percent of daily calories	2250	50–60g 20–24%	<20g 5–9%	325–375g 59–68%	90–100g 16–18%
Day 19	calories	total fat	sat fat	carbs	protein
Breakfast					
Simple Great Wholegrain Bread with Almond Butter	231	5.1	1	31.6	7
Sautéed Peaches and Currants	144	2.9	1.9	28.2	1.6
Very Berry Yogurt	173	3	1.8	30.4	6.3
totals	548	11	4.7	90.2	14.9
Main					
Courgette Tofu Bisque	142	3.5	1	17.9	9.8
Curry Filo Tarts	227	5.2	2.3	37.8	7.7
Cauliflower and Braised Tomato Sauce	116	2.8	1.1	16.6	6.2
Sweet Mixed Fruit Chutney	182	2.5	1.5	38.8	1
Mother Earth's Apple Pie	343	13.8	8.6	34.3	2.7
totals	1010	27.8	14.5	145.4	27.4
Light					
French Lentil Dahl	262	2.6	1.4	43.9	16
Steamed Rice	171	0.3	0.1	38.7	3.2
Steamed Carrots, Broccoli and Courgettes	38	0.3	0	7	1.8
Cranberry Bliss Ball	232	14.4	2.3	21.5	4.1
totals	703	17.6	3.8	111.1	25.1
Daily Totals	2261	56.4	23	346.7	67.4
Percent of Calories		% fat	% sat fat	% carbs	% protein
Daily Totals		22%	9%	61%	12%
Day 20	calories	total fat	sat fat	carbs	protein
Breakfast					
Toasted Millet Hot Cereal	424	4.9	1.3	83	12
Pear Syrup	166	3.2	1.9	34	0.5
totals	590	8.1	3.2	117	12.5
Main					
Spinach Lentil Soup	319	3	1	55	17.7
Winter Vegetables and Couscous	352	14.6	3.8	43.9	11
Courgettes, Tomato, Feta and Fresh Dill	117	4.8	2.9	13	5.3
Walnut Chocolate Chip Cookie	148	6.9	1.9	17.3	3.6
totals	936	29.3	9.6	129.2	37.6
Light					
Curried Potatoes	399	11.2	6.1	64.4	10.3
Cucumber Raita	59	1.1	0.6	8	3.9
Organic Mixed Greens Salad with Olive Oil	88	6.2	0.7	5.5	2.4
Berry Tofu Sorbet	83	0.6	0	15.8	3.6
totals	629	19.1	7.4	93.7	20.2
Daily Totals	2155	56.5	20.2	339.9	70.3
Percent of Calories		% fat	% sat fat	% carbs	% protein
Daily Totals		24%	8%	63%	13%

Per serving: target Percent of daily calories	2250	50–60g 20–24%	<20g 5–9%	325–375g 59–68%	90–100g 16–18%
Day 21	calories	total fat	sat fat	carbs	protein
Breakfast					
Tempeh and Potato Hash	305	6.8	1.1	38.4	22.6
Tomato Salsa	39	1.6	0.9	5.3	0.9
Courgette Pecan Bread	269	10.1	1.1	39	5.5
totals	613	18.5	3.1	82.7	29
Main					
Spinach Soup	112	2.9	1.1	15.2	6.3
Tuscany Bulgur Pilaf with Stuffed Acorn Squash	326	6	1.3	55.1	13
Leek Sauce	43	1.7	0.9	4.1	2.8
Braised Carrots and Fennel	55	1.4	0.9	8.8	1.6
Almond Tart	239	11.4	6.3	31.6	2.3
totals	775	23.4	10.5	114.8	26
Light					
Aubergine and Yam Curry	424	7.5	1.1	73.1	15.9
Greek Goddess Salad	262	6.1	0.9	42.8	9.5
Oatmeal Power Cookie	145	1.5	1	30.9	2
totals	831	15.1	3	146.8	27.4
Daily Totals	2219	57	16.6	344.3	82.4
Percent of Calories		% fat	% sat fat	% carbs	% protein
Daily Totals		23%	7%	62%	15%
Day 22	calories	total fat	sat fat	carbs	protein
Breakfast					
Chai Bliss Shake	289	1.2	0.7	43.6	26
Seasonal Fruit Salad	142	0.8	0.2	32.4	1.1
Strawberry Banana Yogurt	186	1.8	1.1	35.7	6.6
totals	617	3.8	2	111.7	33.7
Main					
Very Simple Pumpkin Soup	172	3	0.4	23.8	12.2
Rainbow Risotto	328	2.8	0.4	55.8	19.7
Stir-fried Spinach	28	1.4	0.9	2	1.7
Steamed Asparagus with Lemon	44	0.3	0.1	7.4	3.2
Unbelievable Double Chocolate Cake	286	10.6	3.7	42.1	5.5
totals	858	18.1	5.5	131.1	42.3
Light					
Asian Clear Broth	158	6.5	0.4	11.6	13.3
Lettuce Wrap with Two Sauces	331	14.6	2.1	37.5	12
Peanut Butter Cookie	136	7.2	2.8	14.3	3.5
totals	625	28.3	5.3	63.4	28.8
Daily Totals	2100	50.2	12.8	306.2	104.8
Percent of Calories		% fat	% sat fat	% carbs	% protein
Daily Totals		22%	5%	58%	20%

Per serving: target Percent of daily calories	2250	50–60g 20–24%	<20g 5–9%	325–375g 59–68%	90–100g 16–18%
Day 23	calories	total fat	sat fat	carbs	protein
Breakfast					
Wholemeal Crêpes	248	11.1	2.2	26.8	10.2
Sweet Mixed Fruit Chutney	182	2.5	1.5	38.8	1
Strawberry Syrup	124	3.1	1.9	23.3	0.7
totals	554	16.7	5.6	88.9	11.9
Main					
Italian Vegetable Soup	268	2.1	0.4	46.3	15.9
Spinach Polenta	172	1.9	0.2	28	10.8
Roasted Tomato Sauce	147	5.5	1.5	20.8	3.6
Garden Salad with Olive Oil	92	6.4	0.8	6.4	2.3
Linzertorte Cookie	125	3.7	0.4	20.1	2.7
totals	804	19.6	3.3	121.6	35.3
Light					
Cajun Beans and Tempeh Stew	449	9.4	1.9	61.9	29.6
Steamed Rice	171	0.3	0.1	38.7	3.2
Steamed Broccoli	32	0.3	0	4.6	2.6
Apple Cinnamon Cake	351	5.5	1.2	71.2	3.9
totals	1003	15.5	3.2	176.4	39.3
Daily Totals	2361	51.8	12.1	386.9	86.5
Percent of Calories		% fat	% sat fat	% carbs	% protein
Daily Totals		20%	5%	66%	15%
Day 24	calories	total fat	sat fat	carbs	protein
Breakfast					
Seasonal Fruit Salad	142	0.8	0.2	32.4	1.1
Apple Maple Yogurt	184	3.1	1.9	33	6.1
totals	326	3.9	2.1	65.4	7.2
Main					
Tortilla Soup with Avocado and Coriander	347	14.7	1.8	32.6	21.1
Mexican Tofu Stew	256	8.1	0.2	21	24.2
Spicy Mexican Rice	485	4.5	1.3	86.7	24.6
Steamed Yellow and Green Courgettes	28	0.3	0	4.8	1.6
Apricot Pecan Cookie	125	3.7	0.4	20.1	2.7
totals	1241	31.3	3.7	165.2	74.2
Light					
Vegetable Hummus Wrap	320	7.6	1.5	51.3	11.5
Apple Cobbler	386	11.2	1.5	64.7	6.8
totals	706	18.8	3	116	18.3
Daily Totals	2273	54	8.8	346.6	99.7
Percent of Calories		% fat	% sat fat	% carbs	% protein
Daily Totals		21%	3%	61%	18%

| Per serving: target | 2250 | 50–60g | <20g | 325–375g | 90–100g |
Percent of daily calories		20–24%	5–9%	59–68%	16–18%
Day 25	calories	total fat	sat fat	carbs	protein
Breakfast					
Cream of Couscous Hot Cereal	289	1.1	0.7	60.4	9.3
Sautéed Apples and Blackberries	149	1.6	0.3	30.8	2.7
totals	438	2.7	1	91.2	12
Main					
Cuban Black Bean and Sweet Potato	294	2.6	0.1	53.7	14
French Vegetable Stew	145	2.1	0.2	24.1	7.7
Oat Groat Pilaf with Spinach	218	3.1	1	40.6	7
Dilled Asparagus	49	0.4	0.1	6.1	5.2
Chocolate Tofu Mousse with Praline	169	8.7	5.5	19.1	3.9
totals	875	16.9	6.9	143.6	37.8
Light					
Spinach Lentil Soup	319	3	1	55	17.7
Cashew Tempeh	269	11.3	3	25.3	16.8
Coconut Cookie	126	6.3	4.3	15.5	1.5
totals	714	20.6	8.3	95.8	36
Daily Totals	2027	40.2	16.2	330.6	85.8
Percent of Calories		% fat	% sat fat	% carbs	% protein
Daily Totals		18%	7%	65%	17%
Day 26	calories	total fat	sat fat	carbs	protein
Breakfast					
Coffee Bliss Shake	194	1	0.6	44.2	2.1
Cardamom Wholemeal Pancakes	333	10.4	5.8	50.7	9.1
Fresh Blueberries and Sliced Bananas	80	0.4	0.1	18.4	0.8
totals	607	11.8	6.5	113.3	12
Main					
Nutty Broccoli Soup	187	8.9	1.5	18.6	8.1
Tuscany Bulgur Pilaf	304	6	1.3	49.8	12.6
Roasted Sweet Potatoes	93	1.5	0.9	18	2
Steamed Yellow and Green Courgettes	28	0.3	0	4.8	1.6
Apple Custard Pie	336	13.1	7.8	49.9	4.5
totals	948	29.8	11.5	141.1	28.8
Light					
Vegetable and White Bean Chilli	364	4.2	0.5	53.2	28
Stir-fried Chilli	28	1.4	0.9	2	1.7
Traditional Chocolate Chip Cookie	180	9.3	5.7	22.1	1.8
totals	572	14.9	7.1	77.3	31.5
Daily Totals	2127	56.5	25.1	331.7	72.3
Percent of Calories		% fat	% sat fat	% carbs	% protein
Daily Totals		24%	11%	62%	14%

Per serving: target Percent of daily calories	2250	50–60g 20–24%	<20g 5–9%	325–375g 59–68%	90–100g 16–18%
Day 27	calories	total fat	sat fat	carbs	protein
Breakfast					
Country Potatoes	180	3.8	0.5	32.5	4
Krazy Ketchup	34	0.5	0.3	6.3	1
Traditional French Toast	277	8	3	39.2	11.9
Strawberry Syrup	124	3.1	1.9	23.3	0.7
totals	615	15.4	5.7	101.3	17.6
Main					
Vegetable Barley Soup	280	4	0.4	38.8	22.5
Simple Wholegrain Pizza with Roasted Tomatos and Spinach	171	2.2	7	27.3	6
Steamed Carrots and Green Beans	55	0.6	0.1	10.8	1.7
Traditional Awesome Brownie	265	12.4	5.8	32.8	5.3
totals	771	19.2	13.3	109.7	35.5
Light					
Butternut Squash Soup	123	2.9	1.1	20	4.3
Egg-less Tofu Salad on Simple Great Wholegrain Bread	461	8.3	0.8	70.5	26.7
Oatmeal Power Cookie	145	1.5	1	30.9	2
totals	729	12.7	2.9	121.4	33
Daily Totals	2115	47.3	21.9	332.4	86.1
Percent of Calories		% fat	% sat fat	% carbs	% protein
Daily Totals		20%	9%	63%	16%
Day 28	calories	total fat	sat fat	carbs	protein
Breakfast					
Morning Bliss Shake	424	6.8	2.8	61.3	29.8
Pumpkin Muffin	200	3.7	0.6	37.9	3.7
totals	624	10.5	3.4	99.2	33.5
Main					
Yellow Split Pea Dahl	262	2.6	1.4	43.9	16
Tofu Burger with Leek Sauce	304	12.1	1.6	28.2	20.3
Steamed Rice	171	0.3	0.1	38.7	3.2
Steamed Broccoli, Carrots and Courgettes	38	0.3	0	7	1.8
Sautéed Strawberries with Cinnamon	114	3.3	1.9	20	1.3
totals	889	18.6	5	137.8	42.6
Light					
Thai Tofu Vegetable Stew	444	15.6	6.1	48.6	27.5
Kabocha Squash or Pumpkin Pie	291	13.4	7.7	37.5	4.9
totals	735	29	13.8	86.1	32.4
Daily Totals	2248	58.1	22.2	323.1	108.5
Percent of Calories		% fat	% sat fat	% carbs	% protein
Daily Totals		23%	9%	57%	19%

Per serving: target Percent of daily calories	2250	50–60g 20–24%	<20g 5–9%	325–375g 59–68%	90–100g 16–18%
Day 29	calories	total fat	sat fat	carbs	protein
Breakfast					
Nutty French Toast	360	15.3	4	43	12.5
Nectarine, Blueberry Breakfast Syrup	145	3.1	1.9	28.5	0.8
totals	505	18.4	5.9	71.5	13.3
Main					
Sweet Potato Ginger Soup	247	2.9	0.3	50.5	5
Buddha's Delight Vegetable Stir-fry with Tofu Cubes	172	7.5	1	20	6.3
Chinese Five-Spice Garden Pilaf	225	1	0.1	49.1	5.5
Lemon Birthday Cake	288	6.1	0.5	54.2	4.1
totals	932	17.5	1.9	173.8	20.9
Light					
Roasted Aubergine and Spinach Pasta with Beans	306	8.1	2.4	45.6	12.7
Organic Mixed Greens Salad with Olive Oil	88	6.2	0.7	5.5	2.4
Sautéed Mango and Blueberries	223	3.5	2.1	45.9	2.1
totals	617	17.8	5.2	97	17.2
Daily Totals	2054	53.7	13	342.3	51.4
Percent of Calories		% fat	% sat fat	% carbs	% protein
Daily Totals		24%	6%	67%	10%
Day 30	calories	total fat	sat fat	carbs	protein
Breakfast					
Polenta Hot Cereal	221	2.3	0.8	45.4	4.7
Apple Breakfast Syrup	124	1.6	0.9	27.1	0.3
Cinnamon Roll	149	3.9	1.5	24.8	3.6
totals	494	7.8	3.2	97.3	8.6
Main					
Summertime Tomato Basil Soup	257	4.2	0.5	37.5	17.1
Mediterranean Pasta	269	4	0.9	47.8	10.3
Roasted Butternut Squash Rings	47	1.4	0.9	7	1.7
Braised Fennel, Beans and Almonds	65	1.4	0.9	6.2	
Poached Peaches with Blueberry Sauce	147	2.9	1.9	29.3	0.9
totals	785	13.9	5.1	127.8	35.9
Light					
Very Simple Pumpkin Soup	172	3	0.4	23.8	12.2
Marinated Tofu Thai Wrap with Nutty Dipping Sauce	395	15.8	2.3	43.4	19.4
Double Delight Cookies	203	10.3	4.7	24.6	2.7
totals	770	29.1	7.4	91.8	34.3
Daily Totals	2049	50.8	15.7	316.9	78.8
Percent of Calories		% fat	% sat fat	% carbs	% protein
Daily Totals		22%	7%	62%	15%

INDEX